# The Survivor

## Scruffy's War

by Blake Heathcote

Testaments of Honour Publishing

Testaments of Honour Press

# The Survivor: Scruffy's War

by Blake Heathcote

Cover Design: CS Richardson
Editor: Isobel Heathcote

Published in Canada by Testaments of Honour Press
ISBN 978-0-9921227-3-7

If you would like to inquire about use of any of the materials in the book or its
companion website, please seek permission first by contacting us at:
www.ScruffysWar.com.

# TESTAMENTS OF HONOUR

Other Books by Blake Heathcote

TESTAMENTS OF HONOUR
A SOLDIER'S VIEW

About the Author

Blake Heathcote was born and raised in Toronto, the son
and grandson of Canadian veterans. Blake's father,
Lieutenant E.B. Heathcote, served in WW 2, and his grandfather,
Major E.T. Heathcote MM ED, served in both wars.

In 1999, Blake founded the Testaments of Honour project,
a non-profit initiative whose objective was, and is, to chronicle
on digital video first-hand accounts of Canadian veterans.
The goal is to provide future generations with a richer,
deeper understanding of Canadian history through use of
first-person testaments – but also, and of equal importance,
to share and celebrate the stories of Canadian veterans
as they, themselves, told them.

In addition to his books, Blake has written 15 plays
and 2 television documentaries.

For Pierre Lalonde

# Contents

# PROLOGUE

November 8th, 1941, was cool but clear, a good day for being in the air. 401 Squadron RAF (previously known as No. 1 RCAF Squadron) was flying sweeps over Normandy. They had suffered through a few bad days in action with too many men shot down or killed, which meant that all but three of the pilots flying were replacements. Flight Leader John "Scruffy" Weir kept glancing back nervously at his wing man, who was new to the squadron and had precious little battle experience. This put John on edge. He and the new man hadn't flown together in combat and so they couldn't anticipate, let alone rely on, how one another would react under fire. That would take time, and there wasn't any.

A minute after their flight breached the French coast, a flight of German Messerschmitts swept down on them out of the sun. John reflexively gripped his control column to take evasive action, then unwisely glanced back to see if his wing man Gardner was in position. In that split second of distraction the enemy planes flipped behind them, and by the time he looked forward again to see where they had disappeared to, it was too late.

The Germans attacked from above and behind at about 26,000 feet, blowing off the wing of John's Spitfire. His instrument panel was raked by machine gun fire and his fuel tank was pierced, spraying gasoline back over him. The cockpit erupted in flames as his plane spun out of control at 300 miles per hour, and it only took him a matter of seconds to yank back the canopy and jump, cracking his head on the plane's tail as he tumbled out.

When he finally landed, he landed hard, blackened and battered, his uniform in tatters, and all but blind from the fire that had engulfed him and gravely burned his face, head, and hands. Dazed and sitting alone in a French farmer's field, he nursed an uneasy sense of where he was and what was likely to happen to him unless he did something, and fast.

Scruffy Weir had arrived at this particular crossroad in his war as though he had been preparing for it all of his life – as perhaps he had.

# Chapter 1

# SCRUFFY

People sometimes ask me how I, a kid who grew up in the sixties, got interested in war stories. The answer is simple: TV and movies – and one classic movie in particular. *The Great Escape* (1963) tells the story of Allied prisoners of war in Stalag Luft III (a German prisoner of war camp in WWII) and how they hatched a plan to dig a 330-foot long tunnel through which over 200 men would crawl to freedom. In the movie, some of the most determined and accomplished POW escape artists in wartime Europe have been transferred from other camps to Stalag Luft III, the Nazis' new "escape proof" compound. The prisoners are an eclectic mixture of Brits, Americans, Poles, and even an Australian or two (although not a Canadian in sight). We know the odds are heavily stacked against them breaking out, let alone making it out of Germany in one piece. But they are so relentlessly inventive, quirky, and risk-taking that you can't help but get onboard. The movie is a rousing celebration of determined and spirited men working together in grim times to fight a well-defined enemy. It's a classic of its kind, especially famous for Steve McQueen's character's dramatic escape attempt riding a hijacked German motorcycle. He tries to vault over two barbed wire fences into Switzerland, which is particularly impressive as Switzerland was more than a hundred miles away from the real camp. But because it's Steve, we hope he might be able to pull it off.

Thirty years later, while interviewing veterans for my book *Testaments of Honour*, I had the opportunity to meet a number of men who'd been in Stalag Luft III during the actual escape. Captivating as *The Great Escape* had been, it had nothing on the stories those men told. I was riveted. And, gradually, I began to understand the extraordinary culture in the camp that made such an escape possible.

One of the ex-POWs showed me a photo from those days that

grabbed my attention. In it, four slightly haggard men stare at the camera with wary expressions. The picture is unremarkable apart from having been taken inside the POW camp at the height of digging the tunnels. He identified the four men and what he thought had become of them. In the lower left sits Wally Floody, the "Tunnel King" of the escape and the official advisor on the 1963 Hollywood film. Henry (Hank) Birkland is next to him, and standing behind are Sam Sangster and John Weir. Wally and John had known one another from Sunday school in Toronto before the war, and both had worked in hard rock mining in Northern Ontario in the late 1930s. When war was declared, they enlisted and both trained as fighter pilots, were then posted to 401 Squadron, and had been shot down within a couple of weeks of one another. The two of them had ended up in the same barracks in Stalag Luft I and again in Stalag Luft III. And at Luft III they'd worked as a team digging great lengths of "Harry," the 330-foot tunnel ultimately used in the famous escape.

The ex-POW told me that Hank Birkland had been one of the 50 escapees who'd been recaptured and then murdered in cold blood by the Gestapo, and Sam had committed suicide under mysterious circumstances back in the '50s. He knew Wally had died in 1989, and now they were all gone except for "Scruffy" – that was John Weir's nickname, he added – and he was pretty sure that John was still around. He thought John might be interesting to talk to if I could track him down. I determined to do just that.

In fact, Scruffy's name seemed to come up again and again as someone I should talk to. The common opinion was that Scruffy had been more involved in the escape than most. He was said to have had some very unusual experiences during the war, but never spoke of them. So even if I were able to track him down, it would be a challenge to get him to open up with me. Nevertheless, I wanted to try.

I wrote to everyone I'd interviewed to see if anyone knew him or how to contact him. An ex-navigator put me in touch with Ian Ormston, who had flown with John on 401 Squadron back in '41. "Ormie" would be the best bet to find him, it appeared. I called Ian and arranged to drive down to his home in southwestern Ontario and interview him.

Fighter pilots are a breed apart. The boys who were streamed into the year-long training period loved to fly, and never seemed to think twice about skidding sideways through the air inside a ton of metal wrapped in fabric and full of gasoline. It's fair to say that instructors looking for the most promising candidates kept their eyes open for enthusiastic, if occasionally incautious, young men who had a sure hand on the controls, and weren't fazed by landing without brakes, with their engines on fire, and bits and pieces of their aircraft falling off in their wake.

Ian Ormston had been one of those young men. He was frail from a recent illness when we met; but his face flushed with anger as he spoke of being transferred out of action in England and returned to Canada in 1943 to serve as an instructor. This was because he'd "pranged" his Spitfire when he brought the severely damaged aircraft back to the base after a mission. As he touched down, the undercarriage gave way and his plane somersaulted along the runway, breaking Ian's back. But that was nothing more than an inconvenience to him. All he wanted to do was to get back up into action, and six months later he was on his feet and raring to go. But no such luck; the "brass" reassigned him to become an instructor at a flight school back in Canada for the rest of the war. And all these years later, it still ticked him off.

After our interview, Ian said he might be seeing John in a month or so at an informal get-together of 401 Squadron pilots that he would be hosting at his place out in the country. He offered to talk to John about the possibility of my interviewing him; but I never heard anything more about it. At least not until my phone rang seven months later.

"This is John Weir, " the caller said. "I hear you want to talk to me." And with that, we arranged to meet at the Royal Canadian Military Institute in Toronto.

With so many veterans speaking highly of him, I was looking forward to what Scruffy might be like and what he might have to say. Hopefully he would give me some new insights into what the Great Escape had been like, or better yet, maybe he would share some of the unique war experiences that others kept suggesting he'd had. This could be good.

But I also had reservations. I'd been told that John's Spitfire had been hit at 26,000 feet. His port wing was blown off and his fuel tank was pierced by machine gun fire. Gasoline sprayed back over him in the cockpit, which then caught fire. He managed to bail out in a matter of seconds, but had been badly burned. I started wondering if extensive

5

burns were why he'd been nicknamed Scruffy. It made me a little uneasy thinking about possibly meeting my first "Guinea Pig." This was the light-hearted nickname coined by airmen who'd been burned and had then received experimental plastic surgery in East Grinstead.[1] I'd seen photos of burn victims from the air force, and some of the injuries were very unnerving.

I scanned the RCMI lounge for John. It was a large room, but there were only a half dozen people in large leather armchairs scattered around the room's perimeter. No one was sitting alone, let alone anyone fitting the description I had of him in my mind's eye. As I stood at a loss wondering what to do next – he hadn't given me a phone number – a trim, energetic man materialized in front of me. This was a very neat trick, as I had been standing in the doorway of the lounge and knew he couldn't have come from behind me. Which meant I must have been looking straight at him but hadn't seen him. A telling experience, as I would come to learn.

And so we went about our interview. Apart from a parchment-like patina to the skin of his eyelids (but then he was 82 at the time, so perhaps that was normal), scarring from his burns seemed minimal given what I'd been told about him being shot down. But I wasn't about to make this a topic of conversation. He was relaxed and full of interesting stories – although none of them were about the war, being shot down, or the escape. As we were leaving, he turned to me and said, "Okay, I'll talk to you." We scheduled a meeting for a week later.

In that interview, John told me many things about the escape and Wally Floody and the war in general. He didn't seem the least bit hesitant discussing anything, nor was there any hint of mystery about anything he talked about. So, clearly the rumours about his interesting experiences had been nothing but rumour. He said as much when I asked him directly about the talk I'd heard. (But still: no burns and no stories? Maybe he wasn't even the guy the others had been thinking of.) As John and I wrapped things up and said our goodbyes on the steps of the RCMI, he shook my hand, then looked at me intently.

"There are things I won't talk about," he said. Even though I hadn't asked the question. What? And with that, he was gone.

Over the next four years, I wrote to him repeatedly, encouraging him – almost imploring him – to share his whole story, particularly

---

1    This was Archibald McIndoe's famous plastic surgery clinic south of London.

the stuff he was disinclined to talk about. I argued that it would be worthwhile to do so, if only to have a lasting record of what clearly had been a remarkable life, and I promised to keep the information private for as long as he wanted. I heard nothing back from him until the end of the fourth year of my attempts to persuade him. He then responded with a short note thanking me for my interest, but reaffirmed that, despite rumours to the contrary, there actually wasn't anything else to tell, other than a few personal experiences (the likes of which we all have and choose to keep to ourselves). And with that, I stopped writing.

About a year later John called me, asking if he could drop by. When he arrived, he asked if we were alone (we were), then carried in a stack of folders and papers, and set them down on the dining room table. He told me that his oldest and dearest friend in the world, Hughie Godefroy, had died some months before (they'd been friends since high school), and that had changed his thinking. He had decided that there were, in fact, people and events that shouldn't be forgotten. And while he said there were still things he couldn't talk about, he wanted to know if I would be willing to work with him trying to organize "...all this", he said, gesturing to the pile of flight logs, diaries, letters, and snapshots. On top of these, he placed a sheet of paper with a handwritten list of names, dates, and places, things he had jotted down to make sure he covered all the main points. At the top of this he had scribbled the word, '*Survivor.*' Before I could ask him what that meant, he said, "I thought we could call it something like that, because that's what I was trained to be."

Then he smiled and said, "And some of it was fun!"

---

Over the following months we met and talked. I transcribed and pored through those journals, logs, and letters, which ended up totalling over 2,000 pages: a running record that began on his first day in the RCAF and went straight through to his repatriation to Canada in the summer of 1945. It's an astonishing chronicle, and unlike anything I'd ever come across. But it was nothing compared to the story that gradually unfolded as we talked over those many months.

In this book I rely a great deal on John's memory – conversations, anecdotes, and remembered emotions. There are bound to be faults in such memories.[2] But with John there were also meticulous journals, flight logs, and notes spanning the six years of war. His observations are occasionally prosaic, but they always convey a strong sense of a young man growing up much too fast because of going to war. His experiences forever changed my understanding of what that war meant to that generation, and what it meant to commit to something bigger and significantly more important than yourself. I'm still a little astonished that Scruffy managed to survive all that he went through.

What's fascinating is how *much* of it was fun.

---

2    Emotions in particular were still very much alive in John. More so than some other veterans I have interviewed over the years, he seemed to be reliving events as he told his stories. His eyes would fill with tears as he talked about young men dying, or he would hoot with laughter as he relived a particularly funny moment.

## Chapter 2

# BORN TO THE CHALLENGE

John Gordon Weir came from a long line of tough, independent Presbyterian Scots. His grandfather, John Weir Senior, was a successful farmer in West Flamborough, Ontario, just outside Hamilton. He was well known in the community as a convivial – and inventive – soul. Having constructed a tunnel between the house and the barn to facilitate feeding the animals in winter, he added a nice touch: a wine cellar, halfway along, and accessible all year round.

John and his wife Helen raised a family of seven children, a typical size for Scottish Canadian families of the time. Scruffy's father, James Gordon, born in 1888, was the youngest of those seven children and – with two older brothers a few inches taller than he – perhaps even the "runt" of the litter. It may have been because of this that he developed the focus and determination that characterized so much of his later life.

In 1890, when Gordon (as he was known) was only two years old, John Weir Senior died in a farm accident, leaving Helen with seven small children and a large estate to manage.[1] It was a heavy burden and a discouraging time. By the beginning of the new century, she had sold the farm and relocated to nearby Hamilton. Over the next few years, the family, once so close, had begun to disperse. Several of Gordon's siblings, now grown, moved to western Canada, and Gordon to Toronto. There, he obtained a BA at the University of Toronto, and later an MBA at Harvard University in Boston, almost certainly with a focus on business. These were major accomplishments for a young man who had attended a one-room schoolhouse in West Flamborough. The

---

1    The "Farm Accident" was what the family subsequently referred to as "dropsy". Weir Senior, somewhat drunk, apparently fell off a wagon while returning one winter's night from a convivial evening spent with friends in a local tavern. The horse returned to the farm, but Weir remained passed out in the icy ditch until the next morning. He died three days later from pneumonia.

1911 Census of Canada shows Helen and her son Gordon still living in Hamilton, with Gordon employed in a broker's office. But he was restless, and by the end of that year had returned to Toronto. A few years later, Helen moved to California.

In 1911, Canada was still recovering from a mild recession, and jobs were hard to find in Toronto. Ever resourceful, Gordon sought what employment he could find, eventually working for a short time as the financial editor of the *Toronto Star*. But when an opportunity arose to work with the A.E. Ames Company as a bond salesman in 1912, he jumped at the chance, beginning in the profession that would be his true calling. A career in bond sales was not just business, it was *big* business – international finance, huge amounts of money, and the opportunity to work with major corporations. Finally, Gordon had found a place where his talents and determination could take him far.

Alfred Ernest Ames had established his investment company in 1889, eventually building one of the most prominent investment houses in Canada. It was while working at A.E. Ames that Gordon met Donald McLeod and Ewart Young, young men who shared his passion for business. In his life-long friendships with McLeod and Young, Gordon may have found the sense of kinship that was missing from his now-fragmented family. Those friendships formed the foundation on which the three men built their successful brokerage firm, McLeod, Young, Weir. A history of ScotiaMcLeod notes that the partnership was founded on "trust, financial expertise and innovation - strengths that have prevailed ever since".[2]

---

Like so many young men of the time, Gordon was quick to enlist when war broke out in Europe. In November 1914, three months after the war began, he appears as a Lieutenant on the rolls of the Argyll and Sutherland Highlanders of Canada, a Scottish Canadian regiment based in Hamilton. By March 1915, he had been mobilized as a part of the Canadian Expeditionary Force, and by Christmas 1915 he was one of the first of the 3,500 Canadian soldiers to land in France.

The war on the Western Front had stalemated into one of attrition,

---

2     History of ScotiaMcLeod: Over 90 Years of financial expertise and innovation. Available online at www.scotiabank.com/ca/en/0,,885,00.html.

with men living in trenches in appalling conditions, often knee deep in water and mud. There were sporadic actions, but little movement on either front. In December, Gordon was a captain with the 4th Canadian Machine Gun Company, where he managed to survive the "Slaughter of the Somme" from July to December 1916. In September of that year, he had been promoted to Major and had been assigned command of the 5th Canadian Machine Gun Company. Early in 1917, four Canadian Divisions moved north from the Somme, and planning began for the Canadian assault on the formidable German fortifications of Vimy Ridge.

On April 9th, 1917 – Easter Monday – Canadian forces, in driving sleet and snow, began their assault, and by 6:00 am they had taken the first line of enemy trenches. The crest of Vimy Ridge was captured by mid-afternoon, and three days later the battle was won. Gordon served with distinction throughout. He was "Mentioned in Dispatches" on June 1st, 1917, and on July 18th was awarded the Military Cross (MC). The official citation reads: "For conspicuous gallantry and devotion to duty. Under heavy fire he supervised the action of eight machine guns, and with great courage led his men forward to best positions in the new line. Throughout he set a splendid example to his men."

Gordon was wounded multiple times during the war, never fully recovering from his injuries. Although it would be some time before he received the news, his older brother John, serving with the 187th Alberta Battalion, was killed in action on Hill 70 near Lens, France, on August 21st, 1917. His brother Norman, who served with the South Alberta (15th) Light Horse Regiment, survived.

In January 1919, Gordon was awarded the Distinguished Service Order (DSO), and following the completion of some officer training courses, he returned to Canada in May of that year. He was officially deactivated from service on June 18th, 1919. More significantly, he returned to Canada a married man.

History has much to say about the young men of the Great War, but very little about its young women. Yet many women served overseas, as ambulance drivers, clerical staff, and as nurses. In 1915, Mary Frederica Taylor (known as Freda), from Strathroy, Ontario, and Edwina Ratcliffe Lordly (known as Ted) from Nova Scotia, enlisted in the Canadian Army Medical Corps for active service overseas with the Canadian Expeditionary Force. Both Freda and Ted were nursing sisters, and on the five-day trip that brought them to England, they struck up an immediate friendship that carried them through the war, and through the rest of their lives. These were two "new women", educated, independent and career-oriented.

Recovering from his wounds in the base hospital in Le Tréport, Normandy, Gordon met the fiercely intelligent and beautiful Freda Taylor. The courtship did not last long, and the two were married on August 15th, 1915, shortly before he returned to the front line.

By the time they returned to Canada in the spring of 1919, Freda was pregnant with their first child, a son, John Gordon. A year later, a second child, Nancy Ferguson Weir, completed the family.

Gordon was a compact farm boy who had made something of himself; the embodiment of over-achievement. He boxed, fenced, was adept at gymnastics, and excelled at skiing. He loved to fish and hunt, and found outlets for his driving personality in such recreation. Freda was extraordinary too, striking off for service on the front line early in the war. She was exceptionally bright and fired by an unshakeable confidence in her own possibilities. Both Freda and Gordon loved animals, which provided common ground for them; and they shared a passionate enthusiasm for most sports, and were the organizing force and principal funders of a national ski association and team. But it was not a happy marriage. Both Gordon and Freda were forceful, strident personalities, and conflict between them was the norm. There is evidence that Freda sought a divorce shortly after the birth of Nancy in 1920; but Gordon was then ascendant in the Canadian and international financial worlds, and he vetoed any discussion of divorce, concerned about impact on his professional reputation.

Once resettled in Canada, Gordon focussed his energies on his professional life. He resumed his financial career with A.E. Ames in 1919. Within months of his return, Gordon began discussions with Donald McLeod and Ewart Young about forming a brokerage enterprise of their own. And on February 1st, 1921, the three men, along with Harry Ratcliffe (another man they had come to know at the firm), resigned from Ames. With a working capital of approximately $23,000, they formed a new company – McLeod Young Weir – whose objective would be to focus on high-grade bond sales, nationally and internationally.

Their prudence during that decade of economic speculation stood them in good stead, and their little firm eventually grew to be a $300 million business.

---

"Believe half of what you see and half of what you hear," Gordon would later tell his son John. "Take action only on what you know to be true, not merely what you want to be true. Then do the work, and do it right, or get out of the way." Gordon was of the opinion that the reason the Scots had created so much of the Modern World was that they were survivors. His service in the Great War had taught him that survival was not a quirk of fate, nor a dividend of politics or religion: it was the product of man's willingness to think for himself.

Gordon determined that, above all else, he would ensure that from the earliest age his son understood the independence of thought necessary to be a survivor. Not an uncommon aspiration for any parent, perhaps. But for Gordon this was not mere wishful thinking: it would form the heart of young John's education. He had seen too many over-indulged young men grow into wastrels and spendthrifts, and wanted better for his young son. John must learn to be prudent, self-reliant, and above all well prepared. You never knew what life would throw at you.

## Chapter 3

# LIVING OFF THE LAND

Toronto in the 1920s was a growing centre of manufacturing and commerce. It had none of the personality and culture of Montreal, but had become a significant economic force in Canada and was beginning to expand its influence internationally.

From the outset, the partners at McLeod Young Weir decreed that the business would be constructed on new footings. First and foremost, they decided there would be no patronage or favouritism bestowed on family.[1] Many business dynasties in North America had existed for generations (as many would for generations more) on the liberal exploitation of nepotism. This would not be the case at McLeod Young Weir.

The second significant innovation was that staff would be given the opportunity to participate in the business as shareholders, making the individuals one of the firm's greatest assets and beneficiaries. Such original thought transformed the investment profession, and helped build the foundations of one of Canada's great investment companies.

McLeod Young Weir brought Gordon into steady contact with the Toronto establishment, and he quickly became a prominent member of Toronto's business and social worlds. They first moved to Summerhill Avenue, then Blythwood, and finally to a house on Forest Hill Road in Forest Hill Village. At that time, Forest Hill was a pleasant rural community in the northern part of a very reserved and proper Toronto. This was a city that had just begun to expand beyond its 19th century margins. A photograph taken in 1925 just a few blocks south of Forest

---

1    While completing his MBA at Harvard, Gordon studied the British banking system, and learned of disasters caused by the ne'er-do-well sons of wealthy fathers. These young men took advantage of comfortable jobs and high salaries to indulge themselves and their friends (at the cost of the enterprise), and to the detriment of the banks that employed them. Gordon swore never to allow the firm to become vulnerable to nepotism in this way.

Hill Road features a dapper Gordon genially posing with a dozen other businessmen alongside a steam shovel in a grassy undeveloped lot, celebrating the groundbreaking for the new Granite Club building on St. Clair Avenue West. A couple of hundred yards to the east on St Clair, the Badminton & Racquet Club had been founded the previous year in a former streetcar barn. Gordon was integral in establishing and expanding both clubs.

Like Forest Hill Village, these new organizations were being developed at a slight remove, both geographically and socially, from the Toronto establishment. That was intentional; in Gordon's mind, these were sporting clubs for workingmen and professionals, not social clubs for the wealthy. Although Gordon was very much a part of Toronto's professional and social communities, these northern, pastoral fringes of the city were precisely what someone like Gordon would appreciate. He valued his rural upbringing and acquiring the fundamental knowledge and values of that 19th century rustic world. As a boy, he'd been taught always to carry his jackknife with him. Growing up on a farm, he and his friends used their jackknives to play games and to carve their initials in fence posts, but primarily they were tools for practical use. Even though the family now lived in the city, each morning Gordon would ask his son John if he had his knife with him before leaving for school. If not, he'd make him go back upstairs to fetch it.

When work permitted, Gordon would head north and spend as much time as possible in the woods, preferably in Algonquin Park. He never wanted the headaches of owning a vacation home, and preferred to rent cottages and lodges close to the hunting and fishing that had always been so much a part of his life. While Freda liked the socially active communities around Georgian Bay, Gordon developed a particular fondness for Algonquin Park and was never happier than when spending his days in the wilderness.

Algonquin Park was designated as a wildlife sanctuary at the end of the 19th century, constraining the logging concerns that had discovered its wealth of timber and set about aggressively harvesting it. How extraordinary, particularly for the time, to set environmental concerns ahead of pure commerce. Gordon shared that conviction: you must not exploit the riches that the natural world offers. You must understand them, and learn to live in balance with them.

Algonquin was a largely uncharted, astonishingly vast, and

uninhabited forest of ancient pine, hemlock, yellow birch, cedar, oak, maple, black ash, and tamarack. For centuries, Aboriginal families had moved through those lands to hunt and fish, but there were no permanent settlements and the Park remained the wilderness it had always been. Gordon took great pleasure in introducing John to the wonders the Park held.

Gordon had come to know an Ojibway fishing guide, Fiji, who lived and worked in Algonquin. Gordon had hired Fiji as a fishing guide for several summers, and had come to rely on him for his exceptional knowledge of the park. Fiji was a taciturn man in his fifties, or so the young John guessed, which could have placed him twenty years either side of that. He stood about five foot five, and was lean but solid, as though he'd been built for walking instead of riding. He neither smoked nor drank, and said nothing when a look or a gesture would suffice. This is not to romanticize him; he was just a solitary soul who came and went as it suited him, and never spoke of himself or his life. He only talked of the day at hand and the place he was in. And this is where John's story really begins.

Freda never came on these trips to Algonquin, and neither did his sister Nancy, which was probably a good thing: it gave John a chance to spend time alone with his father. Preparing for these trips was for him, in itself, a solid lesson in the one of the most basic elements of survival: learning how to pack. Gordon would give John the details of where they were going, when they were leaving, and tell him to bring everything with him that he thought he would need. Then from that point forward, the responsibility was squarely on John's shoulders. Gordon's message was clear: you're responsible for your own stuff. If you didn't pack it, if you didn't bring it, that's your fault. Next time you'll remember.

From an early age, Gordon took John hunting and taught him how to safely handle pistols and rifles. These were skills that Gordon had learned as a boy, and he felt should be a part of the education of any Canadian boy. Using a firearm meant learning both care and use of the gun, and marksmanship was a necessary part of that as well. John was a fast learner. Almost *too* fast. Grouse hunting was one of their most common outings. On one trip, Gordon led the way through the woods, keeping an eye out for signs of activity and places where grouse might seek cover. John silently followed his lead. Gordon spotted a bird a few feet from him. He quietly raised the gun to his shoulder. But before Gordon could pull the trigger, John – who was carrying a short-barreled child-size .22 rifle – took aim and shot the grouse through Gordon's legs, killing it with one shot. Gordon's temper was formidable and he showed it. Recollecting, John said, "Yes, Dad was pretty mad alright…"

Still, hours spent with his father were a rare pleasure that he valued. John was not asked along with Fiji and Gordon on their fishing days, so he was left back at the camp imagining what the adults were seeing during their daily canoe trips. Typically Fiji and Gordon would come back late in the afternoon, usually with fresh fish, and supper would be fixed with hardly a word spoken. Sometimes John would muster up a question about where they had spent the day, or he'd talk about something he'd seen while they were off fishing. These conversational ploys rarely worked. Fiji would just look at him without comment, and his dad would say, "John, not now," and that would be the end of it. He would attach himself to them like a puppy, hovering behind the two men, trying to make sense of what they were doing and what it was they weren't talking about. A couple of times John found Fiji alone and barraged him with questions. Fiji would listen, smile sometimes, but basically he would wait for John's lips to stop moving and whatever had him wound up to wind down.

On one of these trips, when John was about eight, he woke up early one morning, dressed quickly, and decided that this was a day for some exploring. He thought that maybe he could figure out what it was that was so special about the woods. It was pretty cold when he set off, heading in no direction in particular, so he moved fast to get warm. He just kept walking until he lost all sight of their camp. He continued for an hour or so just to make sure that he was really in the forest.

He finally stopped when he realized that there was a pretty good chance he'd actually got himself good and lost. So he sat down on a fallen log, ate some raisins he'd stuffed in his pocket, and looked around. Nothing but the usual stuff: rocks, trees, brush, birds chirping, squirrels, strange sounds of various manner of wildlife scuttling through the undergrowth. He'd heard his Dad talking to friends about how great Algonquin was. John thought it was nice and everything, but when you got right down to it, it wasn't anything but a great big forest.

The sun was up now and things were getting warmer. He'd been walking for a while, and was starting to think it might be time to try to find his way back. That could be a little scary, he thought. Did he remember his knife? Dad would give him a hard time if he got lost in the woods without his jackknife. No, it was there, on a belt he'd made. That was okay then.

"Hello, John."

The quiet voice from behind him made jump. He turned around to see who it was.

Fiji had appeared as if from thin air, and it took John a moment or two before he caught his breath and could say anything.

"Hi." He wanted to say something about how startled he was, but he didn't. Fiji didn't say anything either. He started walking ahead into the woods. After he'd gone a dozen yards or so he stopped and turned around, waiting for John to catch up. John was still rattled, but ran to join him, crackling twigs and leaves as he ran along.

"How'd you sneak up on me?" he said.

Fiji smiled, but said nothing. He indicated that John should stay put, and then walked away from him in a wide arc, circling around through the trees, out of sight, finally coming back to where John stood waiting.

John wasn't sure what he was supposed to be doing, but to him it sure looked like Fiji's feet weren't walking but instead were kind of gliding over the ground. He didn't make a sound. John started to say something, but Fiji held his hand up to be quiet. Then he pointed to his feet. Moving very slowly, he walked on the outer edges of each foot in a slow, rolling heel-to-toe stride, a little bit pigeon-toed, using the front of each foot to gently feel the ground ahead for anything that might snap or crack or pop. There was almost no sound as he did so.

"Woods walking!" John said. Fiji smiled, then said, "Now you."

John didn't have moccasins like Fiji – he really wanted moccasins now – but he did his best to copy Fiji's movements, and after a few tries got pretty good at it. Fiji smiled again, and then started walking deeper into the forest. John followed.

They walked for a long time without a word. Fiji slowed to a stop, then stood listening. John could hear the sound of rushing water. Fiji slowly moved to the foot of a small rise, lay down on the moist ground, flat on his stomach, and crawled to the crest. He indicated to John to do the same. John did, crawling up after him, and peered over the top where he saw a fast flowing stream five feet or so across. He didn't understand why it had been necessary to crawl and what was so special about it anyway. He was trying to think how to ask Fiji without sounding too stupid, but before he made a sound an oily slip of a thing came out of the water and climbed up the clay bank on the other side of the stream. It paused there, listening.

John got very excited, then couldn't think of what those things were called. Not a weasel, but…

"Otter," Fiji said almost soundlessly.

Otter! That was it. He'd seen pictures of them, but this was something else. This slippery creature bent every which way, then threw itself on its belly and slid down the bank into the stream without a ripple. It popped up again with a squeak of delight, which seemed to signal an "All Clear" to others; five others – relatives, John thought – who then took turns sliding down the clay bank, squealing and chirping, then perking up their ears just to make sure the coast was still clear.

While this was going on, John didn't move, completely wrapped up in this circus that seemed to have shown up just for them. The otters played for another few minutes, then disappeared back into the woods. By then Fiji had also slipped away and was moving further along the bank of the stream. John hurried after him, only remembering to "woods walk" when he almost stumbled over Fiji lying on the ground behind the cover of some brush. John lay down beside him, waiting for instruction. Fiji didn't move or speak, so John was silent.

They lay there without a sound for as long as John thought was possible. He was ready to start asking questions again when a fox appeared from the far shore carrying a morsel of moss in its mouth. It walked into the stream, tucked its head down, dipped it underwater, bobbing up as it waded deeper in the water until only its snout and the sprig of moss could be seen. Then it let go of the moss and waded back ashore, and slipped back into the forest. John was baffled and just looked at Fiji.

"She was getting rid of fleas. Fleas hate water and climb on the moss. She'll do it again in two days."

Well that was it, as far as John was concerned. From that point on, he couldn't get enough of this silent, gentle man's walks through the woods and the world they revealed to him. Gordon watched this unconventional friendship evolve between his talkative son – questions pouring out of him like a spring flood – and this Ojibway who came and went without word or reason. Gordon saw an opportunity for John to gain some exceptional first-hand experience.

He proposed that later that summer John – and a couple of friends, if he wanted – go with Fiji into Algonquin for a week and learn how to live off the land. John was enthusiastic and invited his friends Peter and Bill to come with him. They were pretty excited to get out of the city for an adventure and to meet a real live Indian.

---

"No one should die of hunger in the woods." That was how Fiji introduced the week-long expedition with John and his friends into Algonquin, and as John still vividly remembered, "He then proceeded to 'learn us.'"

They spent the morning walking deep into the woods until they had no sense of where they were or how far from the Weir cabin. The subject of food came up at around what the boys felt might be lunchtime. As instructed they'd brought nothing to eat with them, so they assumed they were heading towards a rustic camp deep in the woods where they'd probably have to cook their own hot dogs and eat beans off a tin plate. But when food was mentioned, all Fiji would say was, "Not yet," and they'd continue walking.

By mid-afternoon, the boys were getting anxious. Fiji listened to them talk until they ran out of steam. Then he said if they were so hungry, they should start looking. This was met with a confused silence. He told them that together they would see what they could find to eat. Off he went with the three of them trailing behind, Peter and Bill starting to grumble to John. Fiji paid no mind to this. He showed them plants and mushrooms, then said that under every rock and fallen log there were worms and bugs to eat. To show what he meant, he flipped over a rotting log and pulled a worm out from where it was trying to burrow. He gave it a quick "clean" with his fingers, then dropped the thing whole into his mouth and swallowed. He looked at the boys, who were horrified. Nobody made a move.

"John?" Fiji said. John knew he was on the spot. It was his idea to bring the other guys, and he'd got them all excited about the adventures they would have. What's more, he knew his father was going to want a full report of all that went on. So he gamely plucked a worm from the earth and swallowed. Or tried to, but it came up faster than it went down.

"You're not hungry enough," Fiji said. "Tomorrow we try again."

This was not reassuring. John swore to himself that he'd never leave the house again without his pockets full of chocolate bars. The boys went foraging for anything slow enough to lay hands on, but came up empty handed. Now hungry and tired, the adventure in the forest had quickly lost its charm. By late afternoon, the boys were ready to wrap things up and head home. It had been great and all, but they thought they'd better get back before it got too dark.

John spoke up for the three of them, just saying shouldn't they be heading home soon? Fiji shook his head and said that it was too late. It would be dark in a few hours so they'd better make their beds, then go looking for something if they wanted dinner. That put a damper on an already pretty damn damp day.

Bill had a pup tent that he had wanted to bring, but John had said no, it was against the rules. "Rules?" Peter had wanted to know. "What kind of rules?" Fiji's rules, was the answer. Too late to worry about that now. Now they were hungry and tired and it had begun to occur to them that there was a whole lot of wildlife out where they were.

Fiji got them moving again. He said once they'd made their beds they'd have another look around for food. Peter said they didn't bring sheets or pillows or anything, so he didn't know how he was supposed to make his bed. They didn't even *have* beds. No, Fiji explained. You have to make your beds from pine boughs. Pile them here and I'll get some spruce branches for cover.

Wow. John kept thinking things were getting steadily worse. But off they went looking for branches. They spread out and grabbed whatever they could. One by one, they drifted back to the clearing that Fiji had chosen and piled the stuff in front of Fiji for his approval. He picked up four or five of the pine boughs and demonstrated how you spread them out into a forest mattress. He told them to lay out a bed for each of them, and put them about twenty or thirty feet away from each other. He explained that if one of them ran into any trouble, the others would be far enough away to have a better chance.

"Is he serious?" Bill said. "A better chance? Of what?"

"And what are we supposed to do then?" Peter said. John didn't know. They really weren't happy, none of them. Not that Fiji appeared to care. The three of them never used bad language, but they knew some. During the school year they had made a pact that if something really needed a swear word, then they'd each have one that would be theirs alone that they could use as the need arose. All three words got an airing as the day wound down.

The boys grumbled but built their beds generously spaced from each other's. Then each took the spruce branches he collected and leaned them over his bed to provide modest cover from the weather. As they built their beds, Fiji's first lesson bounced around in their heads: you'll never go hungry in the woods as long as you catch your own food.

It was dark by the time they finished, and the boys were tired enough that sleep came easily.

And then it began to rain.

In the morning they were cold, wet, and hungry. The spruce branches had provided some cover, but they'd made their pine needle beds on level ground and rainwater had pooled around them. Fiji had already been up for some time and had a fire going. He told them that next time to make sure their beds were on a slope.

But Fiji showed them he had a heart. It would be worms for breakfast, but this time they would be fried. The boys were hungry enough to give them another go. Fiji had found a thin flat shard of rock with a bit of a hollow in it. He propped this over the fire to heat up, then with his knife he scooped out some muck from a little leather pouch he had on his belt and dropped it on to the rock. Bear grease, he said. Always have some. The boys nodded dumbly. Bear grease. Okay then.

The grease started to bubble and spit, and Fiji dropped a mouthful of his own spit into this, making it bubble that much more. The boys just stared at it. He had some worms at the ready. He split them down their middles, flattened them, then laid them out on the sizzling stone surface, frying them up like strips of bacon. The fat gave the worms flavour, and all three boys discovered that when you're hungry enough, your stomach is less particular. Seventy years later, John said to me, "... and believe it or not, they were delicious."

When breakfast was finished, Fiji established what would become a daily routine. They "disassembled" their beds and scattered the branches. The fire was extinguished and all traces of it were buried. The ground was checked to make sure no rubbish remained, and whatever footprint their campsite had left in the forest was minimized or removed. Then they headed off again. Fiji said that they would now head toward a lake and make camp there for the night. It was about eight miles to the northeast, and that meant that today they'd have to learn how to navigate without a compass. Bill said that they could look for moss on trees 'cause it grew on the north side. Fiji led them to a tall birch that had moss growing all around it. Clearly, that approach wasn't going to work. Fiji then showed the boys how to use sun and shadow to get approximate direction, and told them if they kept moving in the right direction they would end up at the lake. No way they'd miss it. He told them to try to remember any landmarks or points of reference; they could come in useful if they had to retrace their steps. They were to lead the way, and he would follow.

The three boys set off and walked for what seemed like an hour or more, all three spotting outcroppings and twisted or fallen trunks of trees that might be useful landmarks. No sign of the lake, though. Eventually they came to a clearing that they all said would be easy to remember. It seemed familiar to all three of them, and that would make it easy to recognize again if they had to. Peter said, "There's Fiji." John reminded them that Fiji was really good at tracking because he was an Indian. Really quiet, too. He must have been following them the whole time. Then they noticed some familiar branches and spruce boughs, and it gradually dawned on them that it was the clearing where they had pitched camp the night before.

Fiji welcomed them back. The hardest thing when you're walking in the forest is to keep on a straight path, he told them. Too many trees to confuse you. You want to keep moving, but everyone starts drifting one way or the other and you'll end up looping back on yourself. He said that when you're finding your way through the rough, first decide what direction you're heading in. Then take a fix on something a hundred yards away or so, something easy to see and remember. Keep your eye on that and walk directly to it. Don't think about it on the way there. Decide where you're going and go. When you reach your landmark, choose another and walk toward that. You're not walking in circles any longer. Check your direction, and move forward. The important thing is to keep moving.

They made their way to the lake and established a new site, but the mosquitoes were terrible. Fiji showed them how to build a fire, and then added cedar boughs to it. These began to smoke; he showed them that if you sat downwind from the fire, a little breeze off the water would gently blow the smoke over them and keep the bugs at bay. They were famished now. Fiji sent them off to look for sandy-bottomed shores of the lake, where they found clams and crayfish. He boiled the crayfish in the hollow of a concave rock until they were red and the clams until they opened, then added a little bear grease to make a delicious soup.

In the days that followed, their food included snails, clams, crayfish, and even some fish once they'd learned how to catch them without a fishing line and hook. Leaves, mushrooms, and berries were a part of the daily mix. They learned to eat the tops of green bull rushes, which tasted a bit like asparagus. Fiji dried the roots in the sun, pounded them into a paste, and then left the mixture out to dry until it could be worked into a flour. From this he made a bannock that he stuffed with worms, snails, and whatever else came to hand, then fried the whole works up on a cooking rock, making something that was pretty tasty.

Gradually, Fiji introduced new techniques, including how to lay a snare. On the fifth day, each of the boys had to lay one under his supervision, and by nightfall each had caught a wild rabbit. These were cooked on willow spits – one per person – and to their amazement, they found that even cleaning and skinning the animals gave them a real sense of pride in what they had managed to do with nothing but their jackknives and a little imagination. The boys thought that rabbit tasted quite a bit like chicken, but Fiji said he thought it tasted more like cat, which made them think.

By the seventh and last day, they'd all had a crack at navigating through the forest and had fared pretty well. Now it was time for them to learn to do it at night and, more significantly, for them to find their way back to the Weir cabin. Fiji led them through the basics such as navigating by the North Star and the other simple techniques and tricks they had learned over the week. After a few stumbling starts, walking into trees while staring at the sky, they managed to find their way. The boys were astonished at what they had done, and what they had learned to do. They were full of stories as they nattered away at Gordon, and kept referring to Fiji for not just what he had shown them, but *how* he had shown them. When they looked to see if he was listening to them, he had already disappeared back into the forest before they could say their goodbyes. That night, after sleeping on the ground for seven days, they couldn't get comfortable sleeping in beds. What a terrific week.

Gordon was pleased. The boys had learned solid stuff, important stuff. Work with what you have. Don't take things at face value. Trust what you know, not what you think or hope. Be prepared and understand what that means. Even if things get really tough, figure out where you want to go, and then keep heading straight for it until you get there. And above all, think for yourself.

Algonquin had a profound impact on the rest of John's life, just as Gordon had planned. John's education in survival had begun.

# Chapter 4

# DUTCH UNCLE

Sir John Adrian Chamier, known to his family and friends as Adrian, was born in 1883 in Fyzabad, Uttar Pradesh, India. He was the son of Amy and Francis, a British army officer then serving in India. Adrian obtained his education in England and in 1902 earned his commission from Sandhurst. He was immediately posted to the British Indian Army's Punjabi regiment in Jharkhand, India, where he remained until the outbreak of WWI. In 1914, he returned to England and enlisted in the Royal Flying Corps (RFC)[1] as a pilot, serving with great distinction. By the end of the war, Adrian had achieved the rank of Lieutenant Colonel, and had transferred to the RAF. By 1921, he had been appointed Deputy Director of the RAF's Intelligence Section, and he continued to serve with the RAF in various capacities until 1929.

Adrian had met Edwina Ratcliffe Lordly – "Ted" – in 1917, and so began a courtship that led to their marriage in February 1918. One of Ted's maids of honour was Freda Ferguson, the nursing sister she had befriended on the ship that brought them from Canada in 1915, and who had become her closest friend. Later that year Freda introduced Ted and Adrian to her own new beau, the officer she'd met in her military hospital ward: Gordon Weir.

Like Freda and Ted, Gordon and Adrian immediately hit it off. In some ways they were an unlikely pair. Gordon was an outdoorsman and athlete, but, according to his son John, barely knew how to screw in a light bulb. Adrian, on the other hand, was inventive and mechanically

---

1    In the early years of the 20th Century, the RFC was a branch of the British Army, but during the war it became clear that aviation was no longer a novelty: it had evolved to become a prominent feature of modern warfare. In August 1917, a recommendation was put forward to form a new air service that would be on a level with the Army and the Royal Navy. Accordingly, in 1918 the Royal Flying Corps and the Royal Naval Air Service were amalgamated to form a new service, the Royal Air Force (RAF).

inclined, and loved nothing more than to tinker, invent, repair, and *make* things. Yet the two shared a keen interest in world events and politics. In particular, both men – Gordon through his military and business interests, and Adrian in military intelligence – had professional reasons to be watchful of political and military developments in Europe. Germany was of particular interest, as were the simmering resentments – or perhaps seething vitriol is more appropriate – that the Treaty of Versailles had engendered across Europe.

In the years after the war, Gordon's focus returned to business and in time the development of McLeod Young Weir. Much of the firm's success was built on the sales of large bond issues, and an increasing number of international clients. Gordon made yearly trips to France, the Low Countries (Belgium, the Netherlands, and Luxembourg), and Germany. Adrian, as RAF Deputy Director of Intelligence, also travelled throughout Europe, Canada and the United States. When Gordon landed in England, he would visit the Chamiers in London, and when Adrian came to Canada he always made a point of coming to Toronto to stay with Gordon and Freda.

John considered the Chamiers to be a part of his extended family, and called them Uncle Adrian and Auntie Ted. His parents' volatile relationship often made the home atmosphere charged and uncomfortable, and having the Chamiers come to stay was always a welcome break. Uncle Adrian always seemed to have some new gadget to show John; and most significantly, John never felt like Uncle Adrian treated him like a child.

By the late 1920s, John and Nancy were being largely raised separately, John by Gordon and Nancy by Freda. John would go to Algonquin and be shown how to handle guns and live off the land. Back in the city, Freda encouraged Nancy to chart her own singular course. Take no nonsense from any male, and regard all personal relationships as her business and no one else's, was the message. This was the stuff of life that Freda felt it essential for Nancy to explore on her own terms. Both Weir children were being educated by their highly intelligent and fiercely independent parents how to develop their own points of view, how to analyze, to explore their worlds, and how to take the lead. It was a rigorous upbringing, which forged the adults that John and Nancy would become.

When the Chamiers came to visit, Nancy spent much of the time in the company of Auntie Ted and Freda. John was often left on his own while Adrian and Gordon talked with one another. One evening, however, John escaped to the back garden to catch a breather from being well behaved and unheard. He was a bit startled to find Uncle Adrian was out there, smoking a cigarette and staring at one of Freda's flowering bushes. John didn't know if he should leave him alone or not, but Adrian saw him and wandered over. He asked John if he knew the names of any of the things in the garden. John shook his head. He'd heard his Mum say "hydrangea" when she was out here, but he wasn't sure if that was one of them or not. Adrian nodded thoughtfully. John tried to think of something to say.

"You can eat worms," he said.

"Really," said Adrian. "I had no idea. Just as they come, or with some kind of sauce on them?"

"You fry them."

"Well. Imagine that. Oh, and speaking of which, Francis [the Weir's maid] has given the word that we're expected for dinner in ten minutes. We'll have to test your worm theory another time."

John gave him a nod. Couldn't think of anything to say. Adrian asked how school was. John said it was fine; he liked some of the teachers better than others. He got above average grades in physics, math, and chemistry.[2] And he was good at sports – hockey, gymnastics, that kind of thing. But he didn't know what he wanted to do when he grew up.

Adrian said he knew what he meant. After military college, he'd gone straight into India, where he'd been born, and became a lieutenant in the Indian army. But when a chance presented itself, he joined the air arm of the British Army, known as the Royal Flying Corps. Flying was all he had wanted to do since the Wright Brothers made their first flight. Up in a plane at five thousand feet early in the morning? Nothing else like it!

Flying? John hadn't known that Uncle Adrian had been a pilot. But he was too shy to ask any questions. John later recalled how Uncle Adrian had looked so serious during their conversation in the garden, making him think he was in some kind of trouble. Then Adrian surprised him by asking if he could remember how many windows

---

2    John was actually a very good student, self-disciplined and hard working – not surprising, given how accomplished and determined both his parents were. But he never spoke of this; if anything, he was self-deprecating about his education and grades.

there had been in the room where they'd had tea that afternoon. John asked if he meant the sitting room, which he did. Four windows, he said. Doors? Two. Mmmm-hmm. How many people? Counting you and me? Yes, counting us. Six. Mum, Dad, you, Auntie Ted, Nancy, and me. How many chairs? Seven. And what colours were they? John asked Uncle Adrian why he wanted to know this stuff. Before Adrian could answer there was a call to dinner, and they went in.

John was really puzzled by this odd conversation. It seemed like some kind of a game, but not like anything he was used to. But because it was Uncle Adrian, he knew it wasn't just some grownup horsing around with him.

The next morning, John found Adrian sitting alone reading the paper and asked him about the odd conversation of the evening before. Adrian told him it was a game; one he'd learned in India. He called it the "Observation and Memory Game."[3] You didn't win or lose. You played it to change the way you looked at the world around you. And with that, he challenged John again, asking specific questions about the Weir garden on Forest Hill Road. John didn't do as well that time, but now he understood that it was just a way of looking at things. Not unlike Fiji showing him how to see things differently in the forest.

---

3    John always referred to the game in this way, but it is in fact a version of "Kim's Game", which Rudyard Kipling mentions in his 1901 novel, Kim, written and set in India.

## Chapter 5

# GROWING UP

With the economies of most other western European countries still recovering from the impact of the Great War as well, McLeod Young Weir expanded their business interests to the evolving European markets. In the 1920s and 1930s, many Toronto financial and investment companies closed their doors during the summer months because their major clients frequently vacationed during those months. No point staying in the city if there was nothing happening. As the business was expanding overseas, Gordon spent his summer months in England and the continent, combining work and travel. Adrian's work with RAF Intelligence, as well as with Vickers Aviation and the BBC, also brought him across the Channel to the continent on a regular basis. He and Gordon would make a point of getting together, frequently travelling to the same cities, and sharing their observations and views of the dramatic changes that were beginning to take place in Germany. And to be more precise, both men's professional networks afforded them reasons for travel, and provided a useful cover for gathering information about the firestorm that was brewing in Nazi Germany.

Germany had been ravaged by a post-WWI depression. A crisis of national pride was engendered by the Treaty of Versailles, the political and economic penance imposed by the Allied and associated powers at the end of the war. The Treaty was the result of competing and frequently incompatible goals among the victors, and satisfied no one. Germany was neither pacified nor conciliated by its terms, and the ramifications of those terms created enormous financial, political, and social chaos in the country. This in turn forced a resurgence of nationalism and defiance, nowhere more than in the ambitious and ruthless Nationalsozialismus – National Socialist Party – that came to be known by its acronym, the Nazis.

John and his sister Nancy were frequently present during conversations between the two men, which took place around the dinner table, in the sitting room, and the library. Children were to be seen and not heard, and while this must have been dull for the energetic pair, both John and Nancy absorbed a huge amount of political and economic information in the process. John told me that although he had little interest in world affairs during those years of his adolescence, in retrospect he was surprised by the impact these discussions had on him. When war broke out in 1939, he realized that he was already familiar with most of the names and political forces that were then shaping the world.[1]

Through the 1930s, Gordon and Freda's marriage continued to fray at the edges. Freda was nothing if not independent, and the ongoing friction between her and Gordon was reason enough to spend the majority of her time in London with her daughter. There she could be close to her best friend Ted, raise and educate Nancy on her own terms, and be free to pursue her own interests and social life without being continually irritated by Gordon's sharp tongue and judgemental manner. As a result, John accompanied his father on trips to the Netherlands, Belgium, and Germany. He even spent some time attending school in France because, as he remembered it years later, he had made a disparaging comment about the French. In consequence, his father thought that a term or two at a boarding school in Brittany might help him develop a better appreciation of the language and the people. If he was going to pass comment on it, he should know what he was talking about.[2]

Sometimes Freda and Nancy would join Gordon and John on their travels (Freda often frowning at the camera in group photographs), and when possible the Chamiers as well. Because they were so much alike in temperament, Auntie Ted was able to cool Freda's sharp tongue with her sense of humour and pragmatic social sense. Neither woman felt like she had to fit anyone else's definition of "lady."

John went on his first trip with his father in 1929, just as Germany

---

1    Throughout 1941, John watched the war's progress very closely, and frequently commented on it in his journal with considerable depth of knowledge and insight. In one long entry written in October and reproduced here, he stated his critical opinion of the British attitude towards the Russian campaign, and how lacking he thought it was.

2    Gordon also thought acquisition of a second language would be very good preparation for a future career in business; this perspective was something John passed on to his own children in time.

was enjoying a resurgence in what is remembered in Germany as the "Golden Twenties" era. Economic challenges had finally been subdued and there was stability and growth again, accompanied by a tremendous cultural renaissance. These were the high times. But even then Gordon sensed there was something precarious about the state of things, and he was distrustful of the high expectations that everyone seemed to have for continued financial gains.

On that first trip, John and his family stayed at the Hotel Metropole in Wiesbaden, about 30 miles southwest of Frankfurt am Main. Staring out a hotel window, John was surprised to see a squad of young men dressed in brown shirts and black belts come marching from a side street and parade through crowds in the busy square below. This delighted him; here in this foreign country was a street full of young men who reminded him of troops of boy scouts back home. He called to his father and told him there was a parade of scouts marching through town.

"They're just like us," he said.

Gordon came over to the window and looked out at several dozen men wearing a kind of military uniform, marching through the centre of the city with arrogance and an aura of thinly veiled threat.

He said, "They're nothing like us. In time you'll see how different they are."[3]

In those early days, the Nazis were still establishing themselves as a credible political power, worthy of consideration in coming elections. For John, however, what struck him most was the blunt force and authority they imposed on an otherwise peaceful situation. It made a strong impression on him, and thereafter served as a reminder not to take things at face value.

The next four years saw a marked change in Germany's political and social atmosphere. The Nazis slowly seized control of the nation through an imposition of their power and their ruthless tactics. Foreign

---

3    The "scouts" John saw were in fact Brownshirts, members of the Sturmabteilung – the "Storm Department," or "Storm Troopers" – also known as the SA. They functioned as a paramilitary faction of the Nazi party and played a key role in Hitler's rise to power. The SA's brown shirts echoed the brown uniforms of Mussolini's Fascists, curiously known as Blackshirts. But then Fascists march to a different drummer. The somewhat sinister nicknames of Blackshirts and Brownshirts were derived simply from colours of the fabric, which in the case of Brownshirts had come to be because of the availability of a surplus of that colour cloth. The SA was eventually superseded in power by the Schutzstaffel – the "Protective Squadron" – more commonly known as the Blackshirts, or the SS, who had the German fashion designer Hugo Boss – with what must have been an intentionally theatrical flourish – create their snappy black-on-black uniforms.

nationals were increasingly treated with hostility and suspicion, as the propaganda machine reinforced fears and distrust, and instilled paranoia and aggression. John and his family were first-hand witnesses to these seismic socio-political shifts. In the summer of 1933, the family returned to Germany accompanied by Uncle Adrian and Auntie Ted. During this visit they first travelled to Cologne. There was less informality about travelling in the country now that Hitler had taken power and the Nazis had freedom to insinuate themselves into all facets of life. It was no longer safe for a boy to go out and wander around outside the hotel unaccompanied; the situation had become much more volatile since their visit in 1929. John was instructed to stay in the hotel unless in the company of an adult.

But now in his early teens and fired by a restless curiosity, John quickly got bored sitting in the room. His father had gone off somewhere with Uncle Adrian, and his mother and Nancy were with Auntie Ted. Looking out at the city, everything looked pretty peaceful and safe. It was hot in the room, and he figured it wouldn't hurt just to go across the street. He would keep the hotel in sight, and all would be fine. So off he went. He found his way to a city square just a few hundred yards from the hotel. It lay in the shadows of the towering Cologne cathedral, and was a focal point of the city. Hundreds of people were crossing through the square. He watched this unfamiliar world swirl by, staying near a fountain where he could watch people come and go and not get in the way. He remembers thinking how clean everything looked.

"Then, like something out of a movie," John said, "A swarm of uniformed men – I wasn't sure if they were police or what – came trooping into the Square, driving the people back with shouts and heiling Hitler." He stood there, unable to move, watching these soldier-like thugs bullying the crowd. A police captain – a Hauptmann – spotted John staring at them, but not "Heiling" in acknowledgment as would be expected, and stormed over to him. It was common in large German cities to deal harshly with affronts such as not offering proper respect to the governing power. Age was not an excuse. The Hauptmann strode over to John and, his face only inches away from John's, began to scream at him in German, his face red and the veins in his neck bulging with rage.

It terrified John, as he not only spoke no German, he was also just a child, alone in a strange city and certain he was about to be arrested and carted off. Not to mention that he hadn't a clue what he had done wrong.

At that moment Auntie Ted came walking through the square and caught sight of this uneven standoff. It took her a moment to realize that it was John who was caught up in it, but when she did, she acted swiftly. She immediately moved in, and stepping between the Hauptmann and the boy, she took on the German with both barrels. She had learned that when you found yourself face to face with this brand of German fanatic, they would be more attentive if you did not talk but rather shouted at them, at close quarters, and square in the face.

Auntie Ted cut a pretty striking figure and had a voice to match. To John's endless admiration, she wielded an extremely spicy vocabulary and Anglo-Saxon invective. In a bark that would do any German proud, she shouted back at the Hauptmann that John was only a child, had no passport, and was not a member of any party – all expressed in language that stunned John with its colour. To the best of his memory, what she shouted was something like, "Here's my *Goddamned* passport and he hasn't got a *Goddamned* passport because he's a *child!* We are *Canadians!* That's right, fucking *Canadians*, and we don't give a crock of coon shit for your fucking Nazi *bullshit!* You lay a hand on him, and you will live to regret it!"

John had never heard such profanity. She rounded off her tongue-lashing with a concussive *"scheißkopf"* ("shit head") that seemed to punctuate her point and satisfy the concerns of the shaken Hauptmann. He tipped his hat and walked away, too rattled to salute, let alone "Heil Hitler" her. John never liked being treated like a child, but in this instance he was only too happy to have her wade in and save him.

But this was hardly the worst of what he saw in Germany, at a time when individual freedoms were being systematically constrained and re-directed to the service of Hitler's authority. In Frankfurt am Main, now confined to the family's hotel room, John watched a swell of activity in Römerberg Square, the most beautiful of public squares in Frankfurt's Altstadt. Several thousand people had gathered to demonstrate against the increasingly violent tactics of the Gestapo and the SS, which included the rescinding of habeas corpus and other civil liberties. These were the early years when the ability to express discontent, while not welcomed, was not yet grounds for being shot, sent to a camp, or summarily guillotined (a chillingly common method of dispatch for political dissenters during the height of Nazi power). An SS officer, resplendent in black, faced off against this mob. He was in command of three armoured trucks with powerful water cannons mounted on turrets and capable of discharging blasts of water powerful enough to break bones and knock people flat hundreds of feet away.

Sizing up the situation, the officer saw the odds were against him. He didn't hesitate, but picked up his flare gun and fired two flares directly into the body of the crowd. This created some mild panic and split the mob into three smaller groups. He immediately followed this with blasts from the water cannon, injuring dozens of people and making them disperse. John would never forget that moment, and how ruthless the new German enforcers were. He would never again feel the same about what German efficiency had come to represent.

---

Gordon would say to John, "Know the facts, and don't speak until you know them." Following Gordon's example, John sought out as broad and informed a perspective as possible on any important subject, and the rise of the Nazis was a case in point. John could see the transformation of the country into a nation of fanatics. He read his father's English language newspapers, and saw that what they were reporting about the "new" Germany was frequently at odds with what John saw taking place. He asked questions of Gordon and Adrian, and began to understand how "official" reports could distort reality to better suit what the writers and publishers wanted you to see.

With Gordon going to meeting after meeting in one city after another, Adrian made a point of taking John with him on walks through various neighbourhoods and streets to get a first-hand sense of how German society was changing. Gordon was openly critical of the shape of things in Hitler's Germany, and made a point of explaining his views to John. Adrian encouraged John to absorb all that they were seeing on their explorations. He wouldn't instruct him what to focus on, just encouraging him to be attentive and aware. At the end of their days, back at the hotel, they'd have long conversations about what made a city square in Cologne distinct from one in Amsterdam or London or Paris. How did people make use of the public spaces? What was the interaction between the people and the buildings? With one another? They would discuss customs and manners of dress, curiosities of the language and the culture, always with a mind to how things were changing from when Adrian had first visited those cities twenty years earlier. Then Gordon would ask John questions and expect thoughtful answers. It was work more than social chatter, and it made John appreciate the need to really engage with the world, not just watch it pass by. (For the rest of his life John described himself as a "people watcher." He frequently used his 8mm camera on his travels, which occasionally got him into hot water in some Eastern European and Middle Eastern countries.)

Adrian revived the Observation and Memory game as a part of their walks and their conversations, and every evening he would ask John all manner of questions about places they had visited and things that had stood out in their memory. In Frankfurt, Adrian brought a new dimension to their exploring. One morning, he and John walked to Römerberg Square. Half-timbered houses from the 15<sup>th</sup> and 16<sup>th</sup> centuries lined the east side of the square, famous for centuries as the site of markets and fairs. In the centre stood the Gerechtigkeitsbrunnen – the Fountain of Justice – built in 1543, and a small Gothic church, the Alte Nikolaikirche, dating from the 11<sup>th</sup> or 12<sup>th</sup> century.

Then as now, there were hundreds of people passing through this popular part of the old city, on their way to work or simply passing the time. John and Adrian walked around the entire square until Adrian stopped in front of the church. He asked John if he had a pretty good sense of where they were. John said he thought he did. Fine. Good. Adrian said they were going to try something a little more challenging today. Not the Observation and Memory game. Today he wanted John to follow him. Like he was a detective. John wanted to know what the rules were, but there were none. Well, one. You can't let me spot you, Adrian said. You can walk as fast or slow as you want, but just don't let yourself be seen.

John was enthusiastic – this was something quite new – and so he and Uncle Adrian set off ambling across the Square. Adrian wasn't hurrying or trying to be evasive in any way. In fact, to John it looked as though he had forgotten that they were playing a game and got caught up in looking at the old buildings and the impressive fountain. As soon as John felt Adrian had walked a reasonable distance – he was about 20 yards ahead of John, and there were lots of people in between – he set off in pursuit. John told me it couldn't have been more than a minute or two before he had lost Adrian. It was like he had evaporated, which was remarkable because Adrian simply didn't look like the everyday Germans filling the square. John walked all around the Römerberg, checking down all the side streets, but nothing. Then he moved a bit further out and looked up and down as far as the eye could see, but there was no sign of Adrian whatsoever. Then it occurred to him that he didn't even know where they were supposed to meet in case something went wrong. And he certainly didn't know how to find his way back to the hotel.

He kept walking in what he was sure was the direction they had come from, and found himself staring at the River Main, which ran through the centre of the city. They hadn't crossed the river on their way to Römerberg, so he decided had better try to get back there and wait for Uncle Adrian to come looking for him.

He turned around, and Adrian was standing there. John was stunned. How did you do that? he asked, astonished. Together they walked back to the Square. Adrian talked about how a large public space was a good place to get yourself to if you found yourself stuck in a strange city. Especially if you were trying to avoid being found. A big public square made it easier to blend in with the crowd. But here was the thing: you don't stay there. Mark it out as a point of reference, but then slowly move beyond it and get a sense of the city as it unfolds around the square. Keep your eyes open for landmarks or unusual buildings. Train terminals are significant points for getting into or out of a city. Find out where the trains go. If you don't have a destination, pick one so you know where you are headed. When you're in a crowd, walk at the same speed as everyone else. Don't look back and don't steal sideways glances. Use window reflections to see if anyone is trailing you. Keep moving until you are certain you aren't being followed. Then slow your speed as you move through the crowd, doing nothing that might draw attention. When you want to change direction, slowly drift off to one side of the crowd, check the reflections again, and then move in the direction you want without changing pace or looking around.

Appearance is also extremely important in these situations, Adrian said. John's bright blue blazer had made it easy for Adrian to keep a bead on him. Most people don't pay as much attention to the face; they'll get a general impression of your colouring, and your clothing. That's where you can trip up. It's essential to wear some kind of clothing you can quickly get rid of or change. Shorten it, lengthen it, reverse it, or get rid of it. Whatever. The objective – Adrian fixed John with a stare that rattled him – the objective, Adrian said, is to never look like there's anything about you worth looking at. John had no idea what that meant, and said so.

They sat on a bench next to the wall that ran alongside the river. Watch what people actually look like when you pay attention to them, Adrian said. Look at their faces. Blank, simple-minded, bored, dull, distracted, late for something, upset and not showing it. Best of all, he said, look like you're running a bit late for something you have to do but don't care about. Like you're bringing Nancy a library book that your Mum told you to run over to her. You've got to do it, but you don't care.

John watched the sea of faces going by and could see all of these things in their eyes and the twists of their mouths. He saw one man clutching a leather case under his arm who looked like he didn't belong. He didn't know why. Adrian asked if there was anyone who stood out, and John said yes. The man with the red tie, with the case? Adrian asked. Yes, him, John said. Adrian nodded. But how did he know that? It was like some carnival trick. Then Adrian asked John to tell him why he had spotted him too. John responded that it was the red tie that had first drawn his attention, but as he looked at the man, he noticed that he seemed nervous and ill at ease in the crowd. Adrian agreed: those were good observations and just what he had noticed about the man himself. He went on to say how useful it could be in certain situations to have no notice taken of you.

"Sometimes," Adrian said, "being unremarkable is the perfect place to be."

What did that mean, John asked. "Close your mouth and open your eyes," Adrian said. "Don't say anything unless you must. You've heard the expression, too clever by half. Be the opposite."

Over the next several days, the two of them continued their evasive "cat and mouse" walks, always starting from Römerberg Square, looping around and doubling back again. John gradually absorbed an appreciation of what Adrian had meant by unremarkable. He would follow Adrian, then see him slip through a crowd and disappear. Even though he was a tall, distinctive man, Adrian had a gift of being able to make himself seemingly fade into the woodwork. If John took his eyes off Adrian for a moment during their walkabouts, he would vanish. John gradually absorbed the sense of what Adrian was teaching him, and he even became reasonably competent at slipping away when the tables were turned – not bad for a young teenage boy.

Adrian next introduced John to something he called the Contact Game. He began by asking the question: how do you exchange information with someone without being seen to do so, and without ever having to meet face-to-face if necessary? This was an essential skill when you needed to pass something to someone else with a minimum risk to yourself or your contact. Adrian described the technique of the "dead drop," anonymously and inconspicuously leaving something – an envelope, a package, anything really – hidden behind a loose brick, on the underside of a bench, or wherever it could be effectively hidden in plain sight. A discreet signal – a chalk mark on a wall or a mailbox, a carefully placed stone – would alert the recipient that a drop had been made. These were common enough tricks in the world of intelligence, but to young John they were terrific sport.

Through the week, John and Adrian practiced these exercises: tailing one another and then shaking that tail. They made dead drops, posted signals, exchanged messages. They shopped at stores that dealt in working mens' clothes, looking for simple things that could be altered in some way in a few seconds, just enough to change your appearance briefly and confuse anyone following you. On their last full day in the city, John and Adrian simply walked around Frankfurt. Adrian revisited the subject of finding your way around a foreign city, and the importance of starting in a central and public place. Determine what the city's most notable points of reference are, then create a map in your mind's eye, putting the highlights relative to one other in a way that would allow you to move around quickly if needed. Are there "safe" areas where you could go to ground? Find out the fastest and safest ways to get in and out of any city or town.

John had a natural aptitude for remembering things he had seen, and was able to recount them accurately and in detail. Practice helped, and being given specific objectives by Adrian helped a great deal more. What he didn't understand was the purpose of these games. They weren't really games at all, because there was a strict discipline to how they were played, and rules to follow. What was it all about?

The Weirs' and the Chamiers' last stop was Amsterdam. On the last day, Gordon and Adrian were talking in the lounge of their hotel. John wandered in and was invited to sit down and join them as long as he didn't say anything. John remembered how serious and intent both men seemed. Both had served in the Great War – supposedly the war to end all wars – and they talked about how that conflict might have been avoided if there had only been better communication of information in 1914. Paradoxically, the increase in communications during that war had led to an increasingly dangerous state of affairs in England – and by extension, Canada as well. After military disasters such as the Battle of the Somme in 1916 (57,000 thousand British casualties on the first day of battle), English men and women had been exposed for the first time to the horrors of modern warfare in film reels and photographs. As the war progressed, the flow of images and information increased exponentially, permanently deflating the delusion that going to war was going to be a romantic adventure. People soon realized that modern warfare meant living in trenches, often knee-deep in mud and infested with rats, and the mechanized killing of machine guns and artillery that resulted in hundreds of thousands of casualties.

---

By the 1920s, England had become steadfastly pacifist. And while Adrian understood the reasons for this, he was increasingly concerned that the country could be caught unprepared should war once again become a possibility. Now he saw Germany emerging from a very unstable decade, with a growing array of military resources at the heart of its reconstruction. The fact that Germany's rearmament was largely being ignored by Britain and America and was a direct contravention of the terms of the 1919 peace talks was cause enough for grave concern. But with the Nazi party's ascension to power in 1933, Adrian believed war was inevitable. Gordon agreed completely, and they discussed at length the crisis that would be faced unless England and the Commonwealth began to equip and prepare for war. Such preparations would act as a *deterrent* to full-scale war, not a provocation to wage it.[4]

John had little understanding of what they were talking about, but later came to appreciate that they had been discussing how their respective relationships with the Canadian and English governments had to be used to bring forward urgent information about the inherent dangers of Hitler's emergent Third Reich. The families returned to

---

4    After WWII, several German generals acknowledged that had France and England mobilized against Germany's incursion into Poland, they would have been defeated within a matter of weeks, and full-scale war would have been avoided.

England the next day and the Weirs sailed for home.

In the summer of 1935, Gordon travelled again to Germany and the Netherlands. John had finished his school term in Brittany, and Nancy had finished hers in London. Gordon had gone to Jersey, one of the Channel Islands, to conduct some business, and John met up with him there. Together they sailed to Portsmouth, where they were joined by Freda and Nancy, Auntie Ted and Uncle Adrian, and two of the Chamier children, John and Pat. The group travelled to the Continent and spent a month touring Germany and the Netherlands, which was much more of a typical holiday, at least for John. It was difficult finding time to talk alone with Uncle Adrian, and there was no time or opportunity to resume any of the exercises or games that they had played on the last trip.

But the clouds of war were forming, and Gordon and Adrian spent increasing amounts of time together and meeting with what John had assumed were business associates and clients of his father. He thought there was something very different about the people Gordon and Adrian were meeting; they were nothing like the businessmen back home. Years later, John told me he sensed there was something else going on, something a great deal more serious; but it was beyond him to understand what that was. He had learned that his father's business dealings were a subject about which he could not yet ask. But he was soon to discover the significance of what Gordon and Adrian had undertaken, and how he had become a part of it.

# Chapter 6

# THE FLYING FLEA

Adrian Chamier had officially retired from the RAF in 1929 when he was 46 years of age. He had served in India in the early years of the century, been a highly decorated pilot during WWI, and then served with the RAF in Intelligence and various other capacities until his retirement. However that "retirement" marked the beginning of what was probably the most interesting period of his life.

After leaving the RAF, Adrian became secretary of the Air League of the British Empire. On their website, they offer a brief history that melds with his personal philosophy:

> *In 1909, the founders of the Air League were concerned that Britain was falling behind other nations in the development of its aviation capability.... They foresaw the threats, both military and commercial, to the country's future wellbeing if aviation was not made central to government thinking.... History teaches that few causes, even those of vital national importance, can afford to rest on their laurels and this has certainly been the case with our on-off love affair with aviation. The country cheered the exploits of 'The Few' during the Battle of Britain, but how many knew that they also had to thank The Air League for promoting the formation of the Air Cadet Defence Corps – later the Air Training Corps – which provided a precious source of pilots and engineering personnel.*

Adrian embraced this vision. He was very concerned that Britain's aviation should keep pace with the massive and covert growth of Germany's military air force. Many people of the day considered aviation a rich man's hobby. Adrian believed that by making flying more accessible to amateur pilots and young people, it would be possible to build popular support for increasing Britain's aviation strength. This, to him, was a key component of Britain's defensive strategy against the potential future threat of a well-armed and well-equipped Germany.

While working to further the Air League's mission, Adrian befriended a Frenchman, Henri Mignet, who had become fascinated with flying and building his own aircraft from a very young age. Mignet had been a radio engineer in the First War, but flying was where his heart was. He built his first plane – the "HM 1" – in 1912, and by the early 1930s was developing HM 14, better known as "The Flying Flea" (v.4), his most intriguing and popular creation. It was an ultra-light aircraft, looking very much like a bathtub with a biplane's wings, a wooden propeller, and a motorcycle engine bolted to the tub. In 1934, he published a book, *Le Sport de L'Air*, published by the Air League as, *The Flying Flea ("Le Pou-du-Ciel"): How to Build and Fly It,* in which he included detailed instructions on how to build and fly the Flea, as well as a list of materials required for constructing the airframe.[1] He dedicates the book "To all those who dream of having wings…"

Most intriguingly, however, the book's preface is by Uncle Adrian, here more formally identified as Air Commodore (retired) J.A. Chamier, C.B., C.M.G., D.S.O., O.B.E. In the preface, Adrian writes, "Mignet has… captivated a youthful generation; he has fired them with his own enthusiasm, and he has proved that the romance and the spirit which inspired the early pioneers of flight are still with us, only waiting for some such outlet as he has provided. … I can only hope that [the]… very many young men who speak our language [of aviation] will be encouraged to follow him in this new and exciting Sport of the Air."

In 1935, after returning from their trip to the Continent, the Weirs met up with the Chamiers at Christchurch airfield in Southampton, where Mignet was demonstrating the Flying Flea at an Air Display. Adrian had built a Flea according to Mignet's instructions, and his familiarity with the aircraft and his friendship with Mignet gave young John one of the most profoundly eye-opening experiences of his life.

The Flea is a one-man aircraft, so there was no question about John going up for a ride in one. But the potential for excitement that it offered was something that he never forgot. Mignet and the Flea clearly made

---

1    Mignet: "2 wheels, 25 square meters of fabric, 20 liters of dope, laths and strips of planed wood, plywood, oddments of ironmongery, and a block of wood for the airscrew". He estimates the cost of these would total 1,300 francs, or about $87 in 1934. He goes on to add that "…a motorcycle engine of about 500 cc's is worth about 3,000 francs new, but you can often pick one up which has been overhauled as good as new for 1,000."

a powerful impression that afternoon at Christchurch, which became a part of John's view of the world. Mignet described himself in this way:

> Don't think that I am exceptional. I am over forty years old, a man of routine, a typical man in the street…. It is just because I am… a plain ordinary man that I write my book for normal people, that I will launch them, if they will follow me, not into danger but into the finest of sports, the sport of one's dreams.

In short, Mignet was insistent that anyone could fly, and from that point forward John knew that this is something he would do too. Adrian gave him a copy of the book, which he treasured for the rest of his life.

British Prime Minister Stanley Baldwin had assured the House of Commons in 1934 that the strength of the RAF would be increased – but only if the Geneva Disarmament Conference[2] should fail. In such an event, the strength of the RAF would be increased to equal that of the strongest air force within striking distance of Britain. When Hitler removed Germany from the terms of the Conference in 1933, thus signaling failure of that accord, a major expansion of the RAF followed. By the end of the decade, the number of first-line strength squadrons had been increased significantly, to a total of 128. Yet despite this, and the debut of the iconic Spitfire in 1936, the majority of the RAF's aircraft were seriously underpowered and outdated and Adrian's repeated warnings to the government fell on deaf ears.

Gordon and Adrian had one long final meeting together before the Weirs returned to Canada in 1935. John wasn't a part of their talk, but he remembers how serious both men were. Adrian had always been very approachable and welcoming of John's company, and Gordon always seemed more relaxed when he and Adrian were able to spend time together. But not now. John sensed that something very worrying was looming and darkening both men's spirits. What John remembered so many years later were fragments of conversation he'd overheard: "German rearmament", "growing threat", and "Britain's failure to acknowledge…". The prospect of war began to take on a distinct reality

---

2    The Geneva Conference of 1932 had involved 61 nations wanting a reduction in general arms. Discussions proceeded well, until Hitler came to power in 1933 and removed Germany from the Conference and the League of Nations. Progress slowed after that point, both because of Germany's distension and because many nations lost faith in the process. Most came to believe that disarmament was an unrealistic goal, and that military balance could best be achieved through treaties.

for young John.

---

Over the next four years, European friends of Gordon arrived at the Weir home, stayed for an afternoon or perhaps a few days, and then moved on. It puzzled John. These people were all extremely gracious, albeit somewhat reserved. He judged from their accents that they were mostly German and Dutch, with only a modest familiarity with English. He had politely introduced himself as they came and went, but they declined to talk at any length with him. He said nothing to anyone about this or how so very different they were from his parents' other friends. But he thought it curious.

By the fall of 1935, John was back at school at Upper Canada College (UCC), a short walk from the Weir home, where he was active in sports and various academic activities, as well as being a sergeant in the college battalion[3]. UCC was (and is) a preparatory that offered boarding for students. One of those was Hugh Constant Godefroy – Hughie, to his friends – the son of a Dutch mining engineer, Constant Godefroy. Hughie had been born in the Dutch East Indies, but his Canadian mother, Maude McLachlin, wanted him to have a Canadian education, hence his enrollment as a boarder.

Hughie's father, Constant Godefroy, was much like Gordon Weir, in that he firmly believed that the burden of responsibility for one's future rested on each individual's shoulders. There were no shortcuts to a purposeful and productive life. You had to earn your place in the world, and work for the betterment of others. To even have the opportunity of obtaining an education was a privilege; and one must never abuse such a privilege. It's not surprising then, when visiting from the Far East, Constant Godefroy was extremely disappointed to discover that his youngest son had "...a handful of first team cups and a boxing mug," but lamentable grades. The Godefroy family was descended from Dutch Huguenots, and had a distinguished lineage that could be traced back to the Crusades. But this was not a subject that Constant spoke of with Hughie. When his grandmother raised the topic of their ancestry, his father quickly put things back into perspective. He made it clear that quite possibly their ancestors had done great things, but that did not

---

3    Military training was a common part of the high school education system in Canada in the 1930s.

make either him or Hughie exceptional. What was important was what Hughie made of himself, and most significantly, what he contributed to the world. The rest was nonsense. Gordon Weir could not have put it better.

When John and Hughie crossed paths at school, each discovered a kindred spirit in the other and a friendship immediately took root. Both had strong-willed and resolute parents, and both had cultivated senses of humour to help carry them through the more stressful parts of life. Both were very athletic, albeit quite dissimilar in physique: John was quite trim and compact, whereas Hughie was almost a half a foot taller, with broad shoulders and strong arms. They naturally gravitated toward similar likes and dislikes, and within weeks of meeting one another an enduring friendship was formed. This is no idle phrase. John's affection and respect for Hughie was clear throughout our dozens of hours talking together. When I first met John in June 2001, he didn't talk about himself at all. He acknowledged that he had "…some stories about my war. But you know what? You really should talk to Hughie Godefroy. He has a terrific war record. He could tell you what it was *really* like to be a fighter pilot in those years."

Hughie – Dr. Godefroy, as I came to know him – had been widowed once, then remarried and eventually retired to Myrtle Beach in South Carolina. I spoke with him over the phone – a delightful, charming man – and made arrangements to travel down to interview him. Sadly, he was extremely ill with cancer at the time, and died before I was able to meet him. But in my phone conversation with him, and in my many conversations with John, it was clear the absolute love and regard these two men had for one another endured, almost seventy years after they first crossed paths at school.

By his own description, John was like a "fox terrier" as a teenager,[4] darting around the fields playing football or soccer or rugby, and in winter catching a streetcar at 5:30 am to go play hockey at one of the city's many rinks.[5] Hughie was always right there in the thick of it with

4    Mary MacCormack, John's future sister in law, remembers a sixteen year old John unexpectedly dropping down from a branch that overhung the long tree-lined drive through the school's grounds. She said John was a pretty well known character around their neighbourhood.
5    John had played for St. Pat's hockey club, which was a well-known 'farm' team for what became the Toronto Maple Leafs. He never sewed on the shoulder insignia, but kept it for the rest of his life as one of his treasures. Hughie had been offered a position with a professional team, which he turned down in favour of enlisting in the air force with John.

him. John told me that he and Hughie had had a featured role on the gymnastics team; a team he was quick to acknowledge was pretty thin in terms of its numbers and depth of talent. Nevertheless, they both had a knack for it and together developed several routines that they repeated in competitions around the city. They had a signature routine for which they (apparently) became very well known. It was a two-man number. John was "top" man, being more trim and compact, and Hughie was "bottom" man. John described the routine to me this way:

> Hughie stood in middle of the gym floor, and I'd back off about twenty feet or so. When we were ready, I'd run straight towards him – he was pretty tall, a head higher than me – and as I reached him, he'd outstretch his hands. I'd grab them and with his help vault up on to his shoulders. We'd still be holding on to each other's hands. Then he'd extend his arms straight up, and I'd curl up into a handstand and balance there, both of our arms straight out. We'd hold that for a couple of seconds, then I'd do a sort of somersault dismount back to the gym floor. It always got a great reaction.

> [A 1941 photograph taken of John at his squadron's base in England shows him executing a perfect handstand on the forward edge of his Hurricane's wing.]

Hughie's father worked in the Dutch East Indies managing mines manned by Javanese prison labourers. With a fragmented marriage, by the early 1930s Hughie and his older brother had been shifted from relatives to family friends and finally to board at UCC. After he and Hughie had become close, John, in his delightful and very direct way, told Hughie he thought living at school was foolishness, and so he was to pack his kit and come live in a spare bedroom at the Weir house on Forest Hill Road straight away. And that's exactly what he did, with John and Hughie living together there like brothers until they were separated by the outbreak of war four years later.

In the summer of 1936, John turned seventeen. Hughie went to Java for a summer visit with his father, and John was expected to find summer employment to earn university tuition and pocket money.

Gordon said that the important thing was the work itself. Nepotism was against company policy at McLeod Young Weir, so working there wasn't an option. What other jobs might be possible? John hadn't really given much thought to what kind of work he would like. Gordon didn't particularly care if John didn't know what he wanted to do for a living. The important thing to him was for John to figure out what it was he *didn't* want to do. And if that meant doing something different from year to year, so be it. So John tried many things – running errands for an advertising agency, copy-boy at a newspaper, and working as a clerk in Simpson's, a large Toronto department store. He hated them all, and what was worse, Hughie wasn't around as a companion for trips north to friends' cottages on Georgian Bay and in Muskoka.

Despite this, one episode did redeem the gloomy summer of 1936, and remained one of John's fondest memories of his teenage years. That summer, the school organized a six-week packhorse trip in the Northwest Rockies for the students. They would be accompanied by teachers, and would have experienced native guides. One of the chaperones was a teacher, Nick Ignatieff, who was a particular favourite of John's. For John, Ignatieff exemplified what a great teacher could be: someone who'd had an interesting life, and could help teenage boys better see and understand the world they were stepping into. These kinds of teachers wanted their students to learn to see the world for what it was – just as Gordon had been teaching John.

Nick Ignatieff's father, Pavel, was the (last) Minister of Education for Tsar Nicholas II in Russia. Ignatieff and his family had escaped the fate of the Tsar and other senior ministers through the good graces of sympathetic guards, fled to France and then on to Canada. Nick took tremendous pride in his adopted country, and placed great value on the trips to the wild with students. The year after his trip with John, he explained why in a speech to the Empire Club:

> *Last year we took thirty-two boys to the Peace River country where we crossed the Rockies into the Fraser Valley and then descended along the route made famous by Sir Alexander MacKenzie and Simon Fraser down the Peace River through the Rockies back into the Peace River Country. I believe this sort of thing has a three-fold educational value. First, it opens up the eyes of young Canadians to the romance, the grandeur, the immensity of Canada and its vast problems as nothing else can. It may teach them to think in terms of national development and inspire them with the idea of national service. Secondly, it challenges*

*them to meet hardships unflinchingly when hardships are but an
adventure and thus may help to revive the spirit and courage of the old
pioneers. Thirdly, a hard long journey of this kind teaches the value
of voluntary cooperation and comradeship – the very foundations of all
democracy – in a way this cannot be taught in the classroom, playing
field or by preaching.*[6]

That's a mission statement that could have been written by Gordon
for his son. For John, the trip was not only a welcome break from the
tedium of a summer job; it was an opportunity to refine skills he'd been
taught by Fiji, and to be challenged intellectually by Ignatieff and other
chaperones.

They rode west on a Colonist car, something of a relic even in 1936.
These dinosaurs were the most basic means of transportation, only a
small step up from hopping a boxcar. The Colonists were old wooden
rail cars that had been re-built at an absolute minimum of cost in order
to provide cheap transportation for the masses that were heading west
in the first decades of the century. They had cement floors with wooden
benches that faced one another. These could be folded down to make a
kind of sleeping pallet, with a second pallet that could be folded down
above. At one end of the car there was a toilet, and at the opposite
end a pot-bellied stove. Gas lanterns hanging from the ceiling provided
lighting, but as the windows were painted shut, there was little in the
way of ventilation. Any sour smells would linger to be shared by all
until the clerestories in the roof were opened, which in turn would let
in a whirling draft of wind generously laden with cinders blowing back
off the coal-burning locomotive's smoke stack. It was about as basic a
ride as there was.

They travelled west where they were met by their native guides and
picked up their packhorses for the trip. The lead guide, Bill, a Cherokee,
was a quiet, well-spoken man who kept to himself. To John, Bill seemed
like a kindred spirit, and reminded him of his friend Fiji. Keen to make
a connection with Bill, John spotted a porcupine up a tree and said,
"That's good eating."

Bill looked at John somewhat doubtfully, then asked him how
you would cook such a thing. John explained that you wrapped the

---

6    Excerpted from The Empire Club of Canada Speeches 1937-1938 (Toronto, Canada: The
Empire Club of Canada, 1938) pp. 263-270

porcupine in clay and placed it directly in the fire; let it cook for about four hours. The clay would turn hard as a brick, and when the time was up, you'd break it open and the clay would pull all the skin and quills off. This surprised Bill, who was by nature wary of these young people from the city. But John's enthusiasm and lack of guile bridged the gap between them, especially as he made clear that he was primed to soak up any knowledge Bill was willing to share with him.[7]

One night, unable to sleep, John got out of his bedroll and eased away from camp to check on the group's horses. They were a hundred or so yards away from the camp, hobbled to keep them from wandering off. He moved silently towards them, just as Fiji had taught him, and through the shadows he could see several elk mixing with the horses. It was magical. Then a hand touched his shoulder, giving him a start. It was Bill.

Before John could find words, Bill put a finger to his lips. When his eyes adjusted to the dark, John saw an enormous grizzly bear moving through the darkness a few dozen yards away stalking the elk and the horses. On Bill's signal, they edged away and made their way back to camp. When they were safely by the fire, Bill told John, "The thing to remember is that your grizzly will outrun you every time going uphill. Downhill's a different matter; sometimes you can beat him running down as long as you don't fall. You fall, and he'll have you. You got to learn how to turn when you run so you don't stumble."

John listened to this without comment. Bill suggested that he not come out again at night by himself, as it could be dangerous. John thought this to be a very fine idea. Bill returned to the horses to deal with the bear, while John slipped into his bedroll, still shaken but very thankful for Fiji's gift of silent movement and Bill's gentle common sense. Thinking back on the trip seventy years later, John's dominant memories were of Bill and Nick Ignatieff. Those two men were worlds apart in many ways, and yet they shared a conviction in the inestimable value of challenging yourself in life. And nowhere better to do so than in the wild. There you would learn what cooperation and comradeship really meant.

---

7    This episode was typical of John's deep and sincere interest in other people, one of the defining features of his life. He would sit rapt with attention, absorbing the stories and experience of anyone from a surgeon to a beekeeper. He was without prejudice or chauvinism in his boundless curiosity.

For years John had listened to his father and Uncle Adrian talking about the growing tensions in Nazi Germany. From 1935 onward, John became very conscious of Gordon's frequent trips to Ottawa, and the heated political discussions held in the Weir home and at the Granite and Badminton & Racquet Clubs with friends and business associates. Gordon's common theme was that war was coming, and to ignore the signs was foolish and irresponsible. It wasn't surprising, then, that when a Talent Night was announced for the boys at UCC, John and Hughie (who shared John's views) put together a satiric sketch about Hitler and Mussolini, which they performed on the appointed night in the gymnasium.

It did not go over well. John didn't recall much about it, except that he had swung from the ropes and bars in the gym doing a baboon impersonation, while dressed to look like Hitler or Mussolini or maybe a bit of both. After the performance, the headmaster called the boys into his office and reprimanded them sternly for what he felt was their flagrant attempt to provoke the other students into enthusiastic support for war. He told John and Hughie that his generation had fought and suffered in the Great War, and because of that, because of what they had experienced and accomplished, no sane nation would ever allow war to erupt again. Furthermore, anyone who thought otherwise was a warmonger, and there was no place for any such agitators at his school.

Far from feeling reprimanded, both John and Hughie became more resolute in their convictions about the coming of war. As John told me in 2007, he admired and respected so many of his teachers at UCC. There had been several, such as Nick Ignatieff, who had seen and done some remarkable things in their lives. He and Hughie were just saddened by the Headmaster's dismissal of what they had been trying to say. But it wouldn't be long before their fears were vindicated.

Freda Taylor in Toronto, 1914.

Freda Taylor (at right) with an unidentified sister nurse in the military hospital at Le Tréport, France, 1915

Freda Taylor in England, 1915. She wears two 'pips' on her epaulets indicating her rank of Lieutenant, presumably to reinforce her authority in her wards.

Freda (far left) with two sister nurses in the military hospital at Le Tréport, France, 1915.

Freda (centre) with two sister nurses in the military hospital at Le Tréport, France, 1915.

Gordon (right) with an unidentified fellow officer, England, 1915.

Freda and Gordon at the Thackeray Hotel in London at the time of their engagement, August 8, 1915.

Captain Gordon Weir in
France, 1915.

Inspecting trenches at Vimy Ridge, March 1917.

Lt. Colonel Gordon Weir, MC
DSO in 1919.

Forest Hill Village in Toronto looking west along Eglinton Avenue in 1924.

Freda with John and Nancy, in 1922.

Gordon Weir (centre right in bowler) at the ground breaking for the new Granite Club on St. Clair Avenue West in Toronto around 1923.

John in Brittany, 1928.

John in Toronto, 1927.

John in Brittany, 1930.

John and Nancy with Gordon, in Brittany, 1930.

John in 1933, looking like a character out of Huckleberry Finn.

John and Gordon in Muskoka, 1931.

Ojibway guide "Fiji", John's friend and teacher, in 1933.

Nancy and John in the backyard of the Weir home in Toronto, 1935.

Edwina (Ted) Lordly, Freda's close friend, with her fiancé Adrian Chamier in London, 1918.

A German policeman in Frankfurt, similar to the one who accosted Auntie Ted and John in Cologne in 1933.

Captain John Adrian Chamier (33rd Punjabis), India, October 22, 1912.

Brownshirts on the march in Germany in the early 1930s.

Crossing the English Channel to France in 1935. Nancy Weir, John, and a family friend, Ian Baxter.

Freda and Nancy Weir at left, with family friends the Baxters and their son Ian, in Germany, 1935. Note the Nazi flag in the background on the right.

Uncle Adrian onboard ship crossing the English Channel, 1935.

Air Commodore Sir John Adrian Chamier CB, CMG, DSO, OBE, in England, summer 1939.

Henri Minguet with his Flying Flea "Pou" at the Christchurch Air Display in Southampton, England, 1935.

The mining town of Timmins, Ontario, in the 1930s.

The "Condor Legion", which included
many veterans of the German army, fought
in Spain during the Spanish Civil War,
1936-39.

Hitler at a Nazi party rally. Hermann Göring is at the
bottom left, his chest swathed in decorations and a
meaty fist clutching a bouquet of flowers.

Lieutenant Colonel Gordon Weir at the beginning of the war in the backyard of the Weir home in Toronto.

The Palais Royale in Toronto during the 1930s.

Fran MacCormack shortly after she met John at the Palais Royale.

John (in the fedora) holds a rugby ball he and some of the other guys had been horsing around with at the Winnipeg Flying Club. On of his flight instructors stands in the aircraft's (a Fleet Finch) cockpit, February 26, 1940.

A Fleet Finch, the "trainer" on which John learned to fly in the early days of flight school in Winnipeg during the winter of 1940.

A Fleet Finch equipped with skis, the type of landing gear on which John learned to take off and land. There were no brakes.

John in a standard winter flying suit at the Winnipeg Flying Club, February 1940.

# THE TURNING OF THE TIDES

In the summer of 1937, John worked in a midtown office doing clerical work, which was just another dead end, as far as he was concerned. But he put in the hours and did the job.

Thankfully, Gordon had invited him to come on another trip to Germany – likely the last such trip before things began to erupt over there, Gordon said. The Spanish Civil war had broken out, and Hitler's Germany had become involved, supporting Franco's nationalist troops with powerful air and armoured units. The skirmishes provided the Germans with invaluable combat experience with their advanced military technologies, but Hitler saw the dangers in the conflict escalating into a world war. This was something he was not yet prepared for, so he limited the extent of German involvement. Nevertheless, Germany's meddling in another country's civil war demonstrated to many people, Gordon and Adrian among them, the direction in which Hitler was taking the reconstruction of his country.

When John and his father arrived back in Frankfurt that summer, it was clear that the scales of power had shifted, and that a new zealous nationalism gripped the country. Gordon had made plain that on this trip they would not be staying long in any one place. Two days in Frankfurt and Wiesbaden, then on to Cologne, and finally Amsterdam.

Even though John was 17, his father's instructions were firm: he was not to leave their German hotels while Gordon was wrapping up his business. Everything seemed much more rigid and constrained than any other trip they had shared. One day, after he finished his work in the city, Gordon took John to an amphitheatre outside of Frankfurt. A rally for the people was getting underway as they arrived. The stadium was packed with thousands of the Nazi party faithful, charged by adrenaline and mesmerized at the prospect of seeing and hearing the great man himself, whose arrival was imminent. Flags and banners were everywhere, John recalled, and the noise in the stadium was deafening with trumpet fanfares and the crowd chanting and singing. It was unlike anything he had ever seen or imagined.

> *I had a half-frame Leica that Dad had given me. I carried it everywhere with me on our trips. I took it out of its case to take some shots of this incredible scene, but he put his hand on my shoulder and said, "Don't. Put it away right now." I didn't know what the problem was, but people around us were staring and saying things to him. He grabbed my arm and he got us the hell out of there.*

They took a taxi directly to the railway station where they boarded a train to Cologne. They had tickets for a First Class compartment. But as John had seen everywhere they'd been in Germany on this trip, the open hostility towards foreigners had become palpable. If you weren't German, you were no longer welcome and you most certainly had no rights. The two of them were elbowed out of their compartment and forced to stand in the aisle for the duration of the trip while Germans took their seats.

After Gordon finished his business in Cologne, he sat down with John in their room. For several years, since he was about nine years old, John had been delivering notes and messages on their annual European trips in various and unusual ways. John enjoyed the challenge and thought it something of a game. What boy wouldn't? On that particular day, Gordon had written his message on a slip of paper, which he then tucked into John's shoe underneath the leather insole. He instructed John to walk down the street to such and such a hotel. Go upstairs to a particular room, knock on the door and go in if they answer. Deliver the note, and then take the note that they're going to give back to you, tuck it into your shoe, come straight back here.

John did as he was instructed, and the note was delivered. He never asked what these exchanges had been about. But he enjoyed being a part of something he sensed was important, and which had little to do with sightseeing or the world of finance.

They next boarded a boat travelling down the Rhine for the quiet final leg of their trip down river to the Netherlands. En route, the boat stopped at a town to take on supplies. While they were docked, Gordon took John aside. He told him that this time he needed John to go to the bow and look for a man with red hair, taller and heavier than Gordon. When he found him, John was to say a phrase to him – Gordon gave him the phrase and had John repeat it, although it sounded like a weather report to him – then he was to listen to what the man said, remember it word for word, and come back and tell him what the message was.

John followed this to the letter, although he thought both messages seemed pretty simple and kind of meaningless. When the ship was underway again, he asked his father what it had been about. Gordon explained that the exchange had been to establish whether or not it would be safe for them to meet a certain person in Amsterdam. He added that these were difficult times for many people in Europe, as the Nazi government was progressively imposing severe constraints on basic freedoms and rights. In short, he was trying to help some people get out of the country and begin a new life in Canada.

Then he became very serious. He said that none of this could be spoken of, either here or when they returned home. Europe, and Germany in particular, had become an increasingly dangerous place to live, and he could no longer stand idle while the governments dithered about appropriate diplomatic actions and responses. There was little being done to help, let alone prevent, the hundreds of thousands of lives being upended by the roiling politics of Germany. But Gordon knew he could help some of them. He firmly believed that if you were *able* to help, then you *must*. Whether that meant helping a neighbour whose car is stuck in the snow or a stranger who was lost: if someone was in need and you could do something about it, then you did. This was a fundament of John's upbringing, and it didn't require reinforcing. It lay at the core of his character for the whole of his life.[1]

What made an impact on him at that young age, however, was seeing the lengths to which Gordon not only stood by his convictions, but to what degree he acted on those convictions. He came to understand that Gordon's friends or clients (or whomever else he'd mistaken them for), those shy people who had passed through the Weir home in Toronto during the 1930s, were just a few of the families Gordon had been helping build new lives in Canada. He had grudgingly come to accept

---

1    Thirty years later, John still made a point of stopping to help anyone in need, even if that meant rousting his three children out of the car to help push a stranger's car out of the snow drift it was mired in.

that his government's policy of "limited liability" made political and financial support of humanitarian intervention extremely unlikely. And so Gordon undertook these actions at his own expense and at great personal risk. There would be no recognition or reward; in fact, he went to great lengths to ensure that his efforts were *not* acknowledged, let alone celebrated.[2] Among those he helped were men and women of science, Jewish families, refugees from other persecuted cultures, and members of threatened and oppressed political, industrial, and cultural communities. What was of paramount importance to Gordon was to get involved and act on what you believed in. In Europe in the latter half of the 1930s, this meant taking action against egregious abuses of human rights, and doing so as circumspectly as possible to avoid retribution and without compromising the security of his own family and those families that Gordon helped.

John was profoundly affected by his realization. He began to see the excursions in Algonquin, the observation and memory games, and the summers spent in Europe for what they were, and as having a great deal more significance than simply being the exciting "Boys' Own" adventures he had always assumed.[3] He wanted to tell his father about the exercises and games he had played with Uncle Adrian, but ultimately decided they were also possibly a test of his ability to follow instructions accurately and to safeguard confidential matters. So he said nothing.

Back in England after Amsterdam, Gordon and John stayed with the Chamiers. One morning, Gordon had gone to an appointment with some officials in Whitehall. Adrian asked John to join him in the library for a talk. He started by asking John if he had ever wondered about those exercises of the past several years – the observation and memory game, the contact game, and so forth. Which, of course, John had.

Adrian told him that through his work during the 1930s, he'd become aware that German agents were being embedded throughout England, and given the current political situation in Germany this had become a serious threat to national security in Britain. He had submitted many reports, more than he could remember, to various government

---

2    John only discovered the full scale of his father's humanitarian work some years after the war; and even then, it was not from Gordon, but from families to whom Gordon had provided aid. Gordon was also adamant that family – his family, too – came first, and their security was always a primary concern.

3    *Boys' Own* is the title of a series of magazines and annuals published from the mid-19th century to the mid-20th century mainly for pre-teen and teenage boys. They featured sports, games, nature study, and rousing tales of adventure.

departments advising them of the potentially explosive situation that was building, and the dire threat that Adrian believed enemy agents now posed. Undaunted, he continued to meet with senior cabinet members and drew up briefs for MI5 and MI6; but the government remained resolutely pacifist and unmoved. There was intelligence being circulated in London concerning the extent of Germany's rearmament, but he still believed that this explosive situation was not being given the appropriate weight. Adrian was increasingly certain that England was going to be caught unprepared for a war – or, as John remembered him saying, "caught with its pants down".

One of the reasons for this inaction, he said, was the relentless backbiting and infighting between various government ministries and agencies. In his opinion, bureaucratic jealousies and shifting government priorities and alliances were already undermining the British intelligence services. These distractions created alarming gaps in security, and all but invited ready access to German agents hunting for information about Britain's military strength, and her offensive and defensive strategic plans.

With this in mind, in 1931 Adrian began building an intelligence network that would have affiliations with British military intelligence, but would operate below official and departmental radar. This network focussed its activities on the reconnaissance and surveillance of German agents. Damage control, in essence, to limit the flow of information being appropriated due to bureaucratic inattention, neglect, and negligence. Even if the government continued to dismiss such concerns, Adrian was certain that war was coming, and as such felt he must do what he could to stem the flood of secrets to the Nazis, and begin preparing for the consequences that were sure to follow.

Large government bureaucracies were vulnerable precisely because of their unwieldy size and suffocating official procedures. Adrian's organization would focus on specific objectives of observing and reporting enemy actions, and would do so covertly and deftly. The contact game, the observation and memory game, dead drops, and all the other exercises lay at the heart of such fieldwork. Adrian told John that he had a facility for such information gathering. As John was about to turn 18, and would then be of age, would he be interested in helping out?

There was a caveat, however: if John accepted, he could never talk about any assignments he was given, nor could he speak of or in any way acknowledge the existence of any such organization with anyone but Adrian. No one. Not his father or his closest and dearest friend. What's more, he would be accountable to Uncle Adrian for the rest of his life, and there would be no turning back. The work would never be particularly easy, it would always have aspects of danger about it, and there would be no reward apart from the work itself. No one would ever know what he was doing or had done, and nor would he ever be thanked or awarded any medals or decorations. By and large the assignments would be mundane, achieving specific ends that were a small part of a much larger objective known only to Adrian. But there would come a time, as there did in all intelligence work, when John would be asked to take on an assignment that he did not want to take. Refusing would not be an option.

Adrian challenged John to take time and think very seriously about it all. If this was more than he was able to commit himself to, then he should decline. There would be no disgrace in doing so. No one would know about their conversation, nor would it be mentioned again.

John asked if his father was a part of this. Adrian didn't answer directly. He said that he and Gordon shared a conviction that although the English and Canadian governments weren't precisely hiding their heads in the sand, there were few men in positions of power who were responsibly evaluating the dangers of appeasing Hitler's Germany.[4] There was substantial information being disseminated about the vast scale of German rearmament, but precious little action was being taken upon it. Both he and Gordon had been branded warmongers by their governments, which only made them more resolved to accomplish what they could without the benefit of official sanction. "If your father had waited for a government to take action," Adrian told John, "those people he has helped would not survive what is coming. He will never speak of what he's done, and he's confident they won't either. Should you meet any of them, you might now appreciate their reticence."

John remembers something cutting short this conversation and his father returning to the Chamier flat shortly thereafter. Nothing more was said about the work his father and Adrian had been engaged in.

---

4    Ralph Wigram and Desmond Morton were two renowned exceptions in pre-war England, supplying Churchill with sensitive information about the scale of Hitler's build-up of arms that supported Churchill's unheeded warnings – his war mongering – to Parliament.

Seventy years later I asked John about Adrian's network: did it have a name, or anything else that might identify it? He said no, it was below the radar; that was the whole point of it. He had heard Adrian refer to it with one watchword in particular, but that was only in passing. "You'll never find any trace of it," he said. And I never did.

Hoping to shed a bit more light on such an organization, I wrote David Cornwell (better known by his pseudonym, John le Carré), to ask about the existence of such groups. He had been active in intelligence work with the SIS (MI6) during the 1950s and 1960s, prior to his writing career. I asked if he was aware of any such operational networks during the war. He said that he wasn't, as his service had started a decade after the war's end. He added that clandestine intelligence "cells" were, and are, created for operational security to protect identities, leadership, and objectives. Resistance cells, operated throughout Europe during WWII, and were predicated on precisely those values. With that in mind, Le Carré said that it stood to reason that such networks had been operational in England during the war as well. Ironically, their anonymity would have been the hallmark of their success.

John had completed "senior matric" (high school) that spring, and on their trip home he and Gordon talked about summer employment. John had been accepted at Queen's University in Kingston, and so there was a need to earn his tuition. This was clearly understood. Gordon had built a successful career, but that entitled John to nothing. He had to create a life for himself that he wanted, and that meant finding meaningful work, or in the interim, work that paid well.

John had tried all sorts of jobs over the past few summers, none of which he much liked. The Flying Flea had definitely made an impression on him, and thought that it would be terrific if he could find some kind of work at the at the Toronto Island airport over the summer. Wouldn't that be something.

But Gordon had an alternative. He had asked around and found an opportunity for John to work "mucking" – digging and excavating underground – in a gold mine near Timmins in Northern Ontario. Timmins is a city that was founded during the Porcupine Gold Rush in the early years of the 20<sup>th</sup> Century. In the 1930s, it still had a rough atmosphere about it, definitely a workingman's town, largely perhaps because in those years manual labour was the primary means of extracting the ore from the mines. John was not enthusiastic about the prospect of spending a summer in such a place, but there were few unskilled jobs that paid better back in the 1930s, and he had no other options with the economy recovering from the Great Depression.

Unhappy as he was about this kind of work, and where he would be spending his summer, he was still unprepared for the reception he got when he arrived at the Augite Mine in July 1938. The mineworkers depended on the mine for their income and their families' welfare, and they greatly resented the intrusion of this kid who had effectively stolen employment that could have gone to one of their sons. For the months he worked with the miners, they never let him forget that, relentlessly bullying and chivvying him, pushing him around, and generally giving him a rough time.

On his first day on the job, John was directed to a skiff that transported the miners on rails down into the mine. As he cradled his lunch pail in front of him, the other miners piled on and pushed up against John until they squashed him and his lunch. This kind of careless bullying continued throughout his time in the mine. John chose to submit to it rather than challenge the miners, although it cost him some dignity. "I was stuck," John told me. "So I had no choice but to stick it out and somehow to get through those months."

He quickly learned to do what the men told him to. This included everything from loading and unloading tools to learning how to dig with a pick and a shovel and not burn out in the first hour. But his first big challenge was fetching water from a stream in huge pails. This involved hauling the two pails back up a couple of hundred yards of steep ground. At first, he could barely lift a single full pail, and even then he had to struggle his way back up a hill to a waiting truck, one pail at a time, stumbling and spilling water the whole way. But after a week or two he found he could manage the task nicely.

Underground in the mines, his main job was mucking – digging and excavating – where the routine was to fill a wheelbarrow with damp rock and earth, and then wheel it up a ramp and dump it in a skiff to be hauled up to the surface. It was even more demanding work than hauling water. He had learned to hold his tongue, though, and went about the work without complaint. Some of the miners saw he was strong and agreeable, so they got a charge out of finding ways to make him work harder than he was already managing to do. One fellow in particular, a cocky little Englishman by the name of Harold – John never forgot his name – had taken a particular dislike to John straight off. His favourite prank was to load a wheelbarrow in a particular way such that when John went to lift it, it toppled over. Every time this happened there were gales of laughter all around, which John silently endured as he patiently refilled the barrow.

Amongst this flinty lot of men there was one exception. Gunnar, a Swede, was a hardened veteran of the mines, and he took a liking to John. He had a son back in Sweden about John's age, and was inclined to act something like a surrogate father to John. He gave him tips on how to handle a shovel properly, and how to pace himself to last through the long shifts underground. Gunnar had also watched Harold bully John for the better part of his first week, then decided to step in. Gunnar suggested John swap places with Harold for a shift, which meant John would be doing most of the heavy lifting. Harold was all too pleased to have the city kid to do the shovelling, which meant he could relax until his time came to wheel the barrow up the ramp and dump it. Gunnar lent John a hand with the shovelling, showing him how to load the wheelbarrow. When it was full, Harold stubbed out his cigarette and picked up the barrow, whereupon it flipped over backwards and knocked Harold off his feet. John said nothing, but Gunnar and the others enjoyed the joke. "Serves you right, you little shit," Gunnar said. That kind of support gave John endless admiration and respect for the Swede.

The work underground was backbreaking and dangerous. Accident rates were high in hard rock mining, and about a third of miners sustained injuries on the job each year. This was not a place for the faint of heart: it demanded a particularly determined character to survive in a place that was so primitive both above and below ground. The miners lived close to where they worked, and living conditions on every front were spartan at best.

The strange thing is that John came to like it. Not at first, mind you. He had to learn everything the hard way, and in hard rock mining everything is hard. Gunnar continued showing John skills he had learned from years of working underground. After two weeks of this, Gunnar came to John with a proposition. If they worked as a team, they could earn more by not taking their hourly wage, but by working on "piece work." If they met or exceeded a weekly quota, they stood to earn about four times as much money. John was quick to agree, and the partnership was a great success, both financially and in helping the time slip by. With Gunnar's experience and direction, and John's single-mindedness and drive, they were an effective and efficient team. Week after week they surpassed their quotas. Gunnar earned enough for return passage to Sweden, and John filled out, going from 118 pounds to 155, all of it muscle. He put on so much bulk that most of his clothes no longer fit.

That September, he started his first year at Queen's University to pursue a degree in chemical engineering. But after a couple of months of it he realized he didn't have much interest in the subject. He finished off his first term at Queen's, then arranged to transfer to the University of Toronto, where Hughie was already a student. At Varsity, as it was known, he enrolled in Aeronautical Engineering, which for John was not just studying the physics of aerodynamics. "It was also a way," as he told me, smiling, "to learn how to fly!"

Ever since he'd met Henri Mignet, seen the Flying Flea in action, and heard Uncle Adrian enthusing about the aircraft and flying in general, he knew it was something he was going to do. And there was another advantage to taking the courses at U of T: if war did come, as his father and Adrian were both forecasting, he would definitely enlist. But he had decided that he wanted nothing to do with the stories he had heard from Gordon about life in the trenches. He had seen more than enough photographs of WWI battlefields, the bodies in No Man's Land, and the misery of mud and disease you had to struggle through if you were fortunate enough not to be mutilated by shrapnel or machine gun fire.

No, if war was coming, he'd made up his mind. He was going to join the air force. He was going to fly.

## Chapter 8

# LIGHTER THAN AIR

John and Hughie had long shared a dream of learning to fly, although it's likely that John's enthusiastic talk of the Flying Flea helped fire Hughie's imagination. Mignet's book that made it all sound so accessible and fun. However, both knew their fathers expected them to complete university and start earning a living and building a respectable life, so they resigned themselves to the tedium of more years of school.

The outbreak of the war changed all that. War was declared between England and Germany on Sunday, September 3rd, 1939 – Labour Day Weekend in North America. This came as no surprise to John or Hughie, and they were eager to enlist. But an unexpected event spurred them to join up much faster than they might have done otherwise.

On the day war was declared, Hughie's girlfriend, Peggy Hodge, was travelling back to Canada from England with her sister and mother on the S.S. *Athenia* out of Liverpool. A few hours after the official declaration, a German U–Boat mistook the *Athenia* for an armed merchantman[1] and torpedoed it without warning. In doing so, they defied the "Prize Rules" of war. Prize Rules or Cruiser Rules were internationally recognized treaty agreements that had been signed by both countries many years before. They obligated the Germans, in this instance, to force the *Athenia* to stop (even if she had been a merchantman), and allow passengers and crew to abandon ship before she was sunk. But this new war was to be unlike anything the world had known before, and such treaties and rules – while not wholly abandoned – were rarely read faithfully. And so the *Athenia* was attacked without warning.

In the commotion of the torpedo hitting the ship and the subsequent explosion, there was panic and confusion among the passengers and

---

1    An armed merchantman is a supply ship that is also equipped with artillery for defensive purposes.

crew. Even though there were plenty of lifeboats, evacuation plans had been informal at best. Peggy and her sister managed to find their way to the lifeboats, but their mother either jumped or was accidentally pushed off the stern, and was lost along with 111 other passengers. Peggy was adrift in a lifeboat for 15 hours on the Atlantic before being rescued and returned to Liverpool, where she managed to reconnect with her sister.

The next day, September 4th, Hughie received a telegram from Peggy confirming she was safe. John and Hughie promptly enlisted, no doubt driven by a desire to strike back at the new enemy in light of Peggy's loss. But equally compelling must have been the tremendous excitement at the prospect of someone paying them to learn how to fly. Five friends – John, Hughie, Jimmy Jordan, Paul Phelan, and Jim Scott – went down to York Street in Toronto, just up from the Royal York Hotel, and enlisted in the nascent and barely equipped Royal Canadian Air Force. It wasn't until they were on their way back to the Weir house that Hughie said, "Uh, John, what do you think your dad is going to say about this...?"

In most military families of the time, it would have been expected that the son serve in his father's regiment. In John's case, that would mean joining the ranks of the Argyll and Sutherland Highlanders, which he already knew he wouldn't do. Hughie, on the other hand, had a different and equally daunting challenge. Constant Godefroy possessed extremely strong opinions about the battleground that Europe had been in WWI, and would undoubtedly become again in another war. He was Dutch, and they were a peaceful people; Constant was not about to allow Hugh to run off to war just to get shot up. With this in mind, Hughie thought it might make things easier if he broke the news to John's father before he told Constant.

John and Hughie were talking with Freda about their decision, trying to work out a way to tell Gordon without there being too many fireworks, when Gordon unexpectedly came in. He asked the boys to join him in the library for a talk. John told me that both he and Hughie were sure he must have somehow got wind of what they'd done.

"Boys, I've got some news," Gordon said. He went on to announce that he had pulled several strings and managed to arrange commissions for them both in the Horse Guards. They were silent.

"Alright," Gordon said, "Whatever it is, let's have it." More silence. "I haven't got all day, John."

John got to his feet and stammered out that they had signed up for the air force that morning. Gordon frowned. Then as both Hughie and John remembered it, without a word Gordon turned towards the fireplace and stared into it for a long time. Then he turned back to them and said, "We thought the last one was sure to be enough. God help you."

Adrian would have been on Gordon's mind when he said this. In the First War, pilots had been extremely vulnerable – anyone with a rifle could take shots at an aircraft flying overhead. Casualties for fliers were uncommonly high. But he said nothing more. When Hughie finally spoke to *his* father several days later, Constant reacted just as expected, calling John and Hughie's decision "monumental stupidity", especially for Hughie and his Dutch ancestry. Constant made it clear it was not "their" fight; that Holland would remain neutral, and Germany would never invade Holland in any event. But that conversation was yet to come. Both John and Hughie set aside their studies at the University of Toronto, and the day after talking to Gordon they decamped to a family cottage on Georgian Bay to wait to be called up.

Canada declared war a week later, on September 10th.

---

While the army was well established and ready for mobilization, that was far from the case for the RCAF, which had only a handful of ageing planes and no training facilities or pilot training plan. It took until December for them to organize the paperwork and personnel necessary to begin to mobilize an air force. The situation was complicated by the need to coordinate planning across the Commonwealth, which was fighting as a single, unified air force. By contrast, Germany had been rebuilding its military forces for almost a decade. They had tested their tactics and equipment in the Spanish civil war, and had high-efficiency production facilities already built and operating.

For the boys, other obstacles arose. Much to his frustration, Hughie received notice that there were problems with his enlistment. He had been born in Java, although he had spent most of his life in Canada, and had a Canadian mother. As a Javanese national, he would have to wait for the Canadian government to grant approval of an "alien's enlistment."

While they were waiting for news about their activation, John and

Hughie went back to taking classes at U of T. In December 1939, just a couple of days before Christmas, John had been invited by a friend, Peter Hart, to come along with him and his girlfriend Betty McMaster for a night of dancing at the Palais Royale on Toronto's lakefront. John couldn't remember exactly how it started, but one way or another Betty ended up on the phone asking her friend Fran McCormack to join them and be a fourth on their Saturday night out. John overheard this and tried to wave Betty off. He had been seeing a girl for a while – not quite a girlfriend yet, but he liked to dance and she did too. Still, he was (according to John himself, and in the eyes of friends who knew him then) socially innocent and somewhat shy with girls.

He remembered dreading the night out, especially as he had been relegated to the rumble seat of Peter's Model A roadster. He knew that once they picked up Fran, she would be tucked in close beside him. Not his idea of a comfortable evening. Still, when Fran climbed in, she was pretty, bright, and friendly, and John managed to make some small talk. But what made the date a success for him was at the Palais Royale. She was a terrific dancer, and he felt they had made a natural couple on the dance floor. Everything had been easy and second nature, as if they had known each other for years. At the end of the night, they drove Fran home. John hopped out of the rumble seat, helped her get down, and then shook her hand warmly.

"I had a really good time. It was awfully nice to meet you, Miss..."

And there he trailed off. Either he couldn't remember her last name, or had never been told it, but he felt pretty foolish. She didn't miss a beat, and said she'd had a good time too, and that her name was MacCormack; Frances MacCormack.

That was it for him. December 23rd, 1939. He made note of that date in the diaries he kept when he started basic training a month later, and for several years to come. For him, that was their anniversary.

---

John got his formal call-up in mid-January, and had to report to the Winnipeg Flying Club on the morning of Monday, January 29th, 1940. The war was still new enough to seem a bit of a romantic lark. That first year of the war, there was no established training program for the RCAF, and so the young men who were in the first wave to enlist were sent to a variety of civilian airstrips across Canada to be trained by local instructors in the basics of flight. There was little in the way of equipment, uniforms, or even accommodations. John, for example, stayed at the YMCA during his first weeks of his training in Winnipeg.

Apart from a few minor skirmishes, neither Britain nor Germany launched major military operations against the other for the next uneasy seven months. This curious period of waiting was referred to as the Twilight War (by Churchill), the Phony War (possibly by a US Senator), and the Sitzkrieg (the sitting war; a play on Blitzkrieg). It seemed to give justification to those who wished to avoid becoming part of a European war – at least unless they really *had* to.[2]

Germany had invaded Poland in September 1939, forcing Britain and France, Poland's allies, to declare war on Germany. But throughout the 1930s, Britain's policy of appeasement had prevented them from preparing adequately for a major European conflict. As a result, Germany was able to regroup quickly following the successful invasion of Poland, and then strike swiftly into Luxembourg, Belgium, the Netherlands, and finally France in May and June 1940.[3]

Canada's air force was also poorly equipped for war. The RCAF that John and Hughie signed up for was comprised of a handful of aging aircraft and a couple of Hurricane fighters. Hurricanes were the precursors to the iconic Spitfire, and represented a new generation of sturdy, pilot-friendly aircraft designed for air warfare. But it would be a year or more before the new pilots got to try one out.

Flight training took place in winter on the Prairies, and the new airmen were taught to fly in biplanes. The three "kites" that John and the other fledgling pilots first fumbled around in were the de Havilland Tiger Moth, the Gypsy Moth,[4] and the Fleet Finch. This initial part of their training lasted 12 weeks, and was a combination of practical flight training and lectures. The training aircraft were very stable and generally considered to be pilot-proof. Because it was winter, the trainers had

2    In his book *The Good Fight,* coauthored with Peter Neary (Copp Clark, Toronto, 1995), the eminent military historian Jack Granatstein commented that the Canadian government had adopted a policy of "limited liability" in the months leading up to the war. Canada withheld a full military and industrial commitment to a possible war effort until Britain and France declared war, and the path forward became clear.
3    After the war, German generals acknowledged that had Britain and France struck decisively against the German army in September 1939, their combined 110 divisions would have been able to suppress the 23 German divisions within a couple of weeks, and the war would have effectively been over. But it was not to be.
4    These were named in recognition of founder Geoffrey de Havilland's renown as a lepidopterist.

skis on them instead of wheels, which added a challenge to landing the aircraft. John discovered that the Tiger Moth had a tendency to slide for quite a distance when he came in to land from the west with a tail wind. The implications of this didn't completely hit home until he found himself coming in at around sixty miles per hour on a frozen field with the wind to his back. His plane's skis bumped down harder than he expected, but he didn't have time to think about that as his plane slid a couple of hundred yards further than he'd anticipated, directly toward the hangar, finally nosing up against the hangar door with a gentle "thump".

But such experiences didn't faze him. You learned by flying and making mistakes. In the daily journal he kept from his first day there, he never talks about being afraid. Rather, he writes that he is worried about passing tests, frustrated by bad weather preventing him getting time in the air, that the lectures are boring, and what's coming next. In his journal entries, he seems to have felt that the war, if not precisely phony, would hopefully wrap up fairly soon, allowing him to get back to Fran and everyday life back in Toronto.

When I first interviewed John, he talked about the ship that took him and the other RCAF airmen from Halifax to England in October 1940. He told me he got sick as a dog on the crossing, and was relieved when they reached Liverpool and could get on solid ground again. I asked him if he hadn't been bothered by airsickness, and he smiled mirthlessly and shook his head "no". To get airsick meant that you would be washed out as a pilot, and he wasn't about to have that happen. But he came close.

On February 11th, he wrote:

> I flew this afternoon and was so close to being airsick that it wasn't funny. I've been seasick like a dog before, but on board at least I have somewhere to be sick. But up in the air in a small plane there is no room to be sick, and when you can see the airport 10 minutes away and it's a bumpy ride, well it's just a toss-up. Literally. So either you win or you toss up all you have.

He had been flying for less than a week then, and the prospect of getting airsick started to haunt him. The instructors were a mixture of young and middle-aged, terse and patient. One of the more understanding ones took John aside, and gave him a tip. Bring something up with you to be sick in. And if you forget to do so, make sure you scrub your plane clean once you're down and ready to turn her back over to the ground crew. John told me that once he knew he had ways to manage the problem, he never got sick again. At least not in one of the biplane trainers.

Those 12 weeks in Manitoba don't sound like men preparing to go to war; John's class of five pilots was having too much fun together. They ate well, slept in comfortable beds with clean sheets, went to the movies a couple of times a week, had parties and dances, and were regularly invited for home-cooked dinners by the locals. During the days, they followed a routine of classroom lectures and practical flight time with their five instructors. Every week they needed to keep building up their flying hours. Each new pilot had to have 50 hours in the air to pass the course, and every flight was noted in detail in each man's flight log. Once they'd learned the basics of take offs and landings – always the most challenging and dangerous aspects of any pilot's skills – they acquired aerobatic skills like steep turns, spins, loops, and eventually how to put your plane into a stall in mid-air, and then pull it out again before crashing. (John was particularly fond of the adrenaline rush of that trick.)

One of John's biggest challenges in heading out to Winnipeg for flight training had been Fran MacCormack, the girl he had met just before Christmas, and whom he'd fallen head over heels for. He had never had feelings like that before for anyone, and they knocked him off balance. He had taken her out on January 13th for their first official date, and had realized that she was someone he wanted to spend more time with – maybe even the rest of his life. As much as he was aching to learn to fly, two weeks later he went to Winnipeg with very mixed emotions. He was the first to be called up of the four who had enlisted together on September 4th. Hughie, Jimmy Jordan, Paul Phelan, and Jim Scott came down to Union Station to see John off.

Worse for John, though, was that there was no sign of Fran on the platform to say goodbye. In the week before he left, they had spent a lot of time together. She encouraged him to buy a small diary to keep a running account of his training. He had never done that kind of thing, but the idea clicked with him. He got one and started writing in it three days before heading out west. And for the next two years, he faithfully wrote down what happened every day. In those diary entries – over 600 of them – you can see John slowly transform from a young man to an experienced combat pilot. At the outset, he is newly in love, full of the adventure of learning to fly, earning a decent salary doing what he wanted to do, and living with a group of like-minded guys. Gradually, the entries reveal his growing maturity. As he begins to assume more responsibility, his romantic notion of heading off to war slowly transforms into a more realistic perspective.

It starts in his first entries in Winnipeg:

*Sunday February 11*
It seems we only [get to] fly every other day. Today was a rotten windy day, so we had lectures all day and plenty of them too. Tonight I played stud poker. I liked it and it gave me something to put on this page.

*Sunday February 18*
Today was a half-day. The weather was useless so they let us off. If it's clear tomorrow then we fly. Lectures in the morning.

*Saturday February 24*
Boy, today was a day! I flew solo, exactly 4 weeks since I left Toronto. The instructor and me flew around three times, and after our third landing he says, and I quote: "How'd you like to take it up yourself?" End of quote. Naturally I said yes. Who doesn't want to solo? So out he got and away I went. Now I have 11 hours and a bit more. 38 to go.

*Wednesday February 28*
It's been a good month all in all; the instructors are all darn nice. Cliff the head instructor is a bit snappy, but I like him. Archie is a regular fellow. Bill is only 23 or so but he's darned nice and tries very hard to put across his lectures to us. Herb of course is a peach of a guy and has all patience in the world (or else he's awfully good at keeping his feelings to himself). How any man living or dead could endure teaching five guys

like us to fly is beyond me."

But Fran is present on every page of his diary. Throughout their courtship and the war, he called her by a nickname he'd come up with: Robin. This was because of a maid his parents had who had been with them for as long as he could remember at the Forest Hill Road house. She was like family, and unfortunately had the same name – Francis McCormick (with a slight difference in spelling). That had been just a bit too close for comfort, John told me. And so he came up with Robin because she was perky and spritely and simply full of life – just like in the popular song, "When the Red, Red Robin Comes Bob, Bob, Bobbin' Along".

At the end of February, as he was nearing the halfway mark of the flying course, he writes a plaintive diary entry about missing her, and how the Phony War is starting to make him feel frustrated:

> *Thursday February 29*
> Still having heart trouble over Robin. I'm crazy I suppose, but she'll never find out unless this crazy war stops soon.

> *Sunday March 3*
> Well, today I was (pretty nearly) a dead pigeon. I almost fell asleep in the plane three or four times. Luckily it was all bumpy and every time we hit one it woke me up. I was up an hour in the afternoon. I've now got 15 hours and 30 minutes. All's well except with my heart. How's yours?

He's always thinking of her when he writes. And although he kept the diary to himself, he makes clear why he's writing it:

> This book should be called Robin's Book – after its inspiration. I'd never keep it if it wasn't for you, Robin. Soon I'll be home to tell you what I've been afraid to tell you so far.

John's feelings for her never diminish, but he starts becoming more determined to succeed at his new trade:

*Friday March 8*
Lectures this morning, then flying this afternoon for about an hour. Practicing spins, steep turns, and stuff. 17 hours and 30 minutes not enough time until our 20 hour test, maybe on Sunday.

*Tuesday March 19*
Today we started aerobatics! Loops and slow roles – more fun, most fun yet. We had news today that we might be stationed at the Eglinton Hunt Club in Toronto![5]

*Tuesday April 16*
After an hour's flying this morning, through three layers of clouds, we took our tests and all passed!! Tomorrow we do instruments (flying by them) and then we're finished!

*Wednesday April 17*
We finished up the instruments tests and all of us passed. Just back now from a party at the Flying Club and another at the Royal Alex Hotel. We fly home to Toronto tomorrow!! Yeeeah Hooo!!!

He was back in Toronto the next day, and four days later he reported to No. 1 Initial Training School (ITS) in Toronto at the Eglinton Hunt Club, the first such school of the incipient British Commonwealth Air Training Plan (BCATP).

———

The BCATP was a massive air-training program involving Britain, Canada, Australia, New Zealand and Southern Rhodesia during World War II, and remains the single largest aviation-training program in history. It was responsible for training nearly half the pilots, navigators, bomb aimers, gunners, wireless operators, and flight engineers of the Commonwealth air forces during the Second World War. Canada was chosen as the primary location for "The Plan" due to its ample supplies

———

5    The Eglinton Hunt Club was then on the east side of Avenue Road just north of Eglinton Avenue – just a couple of blocks north of UCC, and a few blocks north of Weir's house and Fran's, too.

of fuel, wide open spaces suitable for flight and navigation training, industrial facilities for the production of training aircraft, parts, and supplies, and its proximity to both the European and Pacific theatres. Over 167,000 students, including over 50,000 pilots, trained in Canada under the program from May 1940 to March 1945, more than half of whom were Canadian.

This was actually the first formal stage of John's air force training. The Winnipeg Flying School was a civilian enterprise, and there were no barracks, no uniforms, and no military routines to speak of. The new arrivals at No. 1 ITS were to be drilled in the basics of military discipline. Actions were repeated until they were instinctive. Complex actions were broken down into simpler parts that could be refined individually and then rejoined. Drilling was necessary for military units to perform at maximum efficiency in a wide variety of situations. At No. 1 ITS, the Pilot Officer Provisionals (POPs), popularly referred to as P.O. Prunes, were being drilled to become a team.

The P.O. Prunes of No. 1 ITS were under the command of a permanent force RAF veteran, Warrant Officer First Class Firby, whose rough, working-class accent and sarcastic turn of phrase were perfect complements to his ruthless brand of drilling. The RCAF and BCATP had acquired the Hunt Club and its ageing amenities – a gym, a bowling alley, a ballroom, stables for a hundred and fifty horses, an indoor riding ring, a swimming pool, none of which the young airmen were allowed make use of – and turned it into the first air force training centre of its kind in Canada.

The spacious grounds around the buildings were the main attraction, providing plenty of space for drills and parades. Firby marched his young charges relentlessly back and forth across those grounds, unsuccessfully struggling to get them into some kind of synchronization. That man loved his whistle, using it incessantly to signal pattern changes in close order drills. After two days of frustration, Firby still saw only marginal improvement in the POPs. On the morning of the third day, he lined them up alongside the swimming pool, barking at them that they could use the pool's edge as a guide by which they could recognize what a straight line actually was. In no uncertain terms he outlined what his plans were. He was going to march them and drill them until their feet were bleeding and they had, through sheer brute force if nothing else, become the best-trained Prunes that their superior officers had ever seen. He made it clear that he was going to have them jumping around the CNE grounds like "…a bunch of monkeys fucking a bag of tacks."

Firby's personal recommendation was that they pay very close attention, because he had entered them into a drill competition on the Exhibition grounds in two weeks time. As an afterthought, he added that they had bloody well better win or they would all repeat their four weeks in ITS. Was he making himself clear? John thought it might be amusing if he said, "Beg pardon?" but thought better of it. One of the young POPs was not so wise, and took umbrage at Firby's treatment. He stammered that his father was a very important person in the Government and that this was no way to talk to provisional officers. Firby listened to this, nodding his head with sympathy and understanding, and then toppled the boy over backwards into the pool. When he came up for air, spluttering, Firby was staring down hard at him. He told the young man that they would continue their talk in his office in twenty minutes in a dry set of clothes or he would be grounded permanently. Firby then regarded the others with his thin smile, and asked if there was anyone else who wanted to talk about his dad. There wasn't.

Early in their first week of drilling, their first uniforms arrived. This was very exciting, because for the past three and a half months they had been wearing their own clothing. Having a uniform meant they were actually in the air force, and they knew how girls love men in a uniform. The tunics, however, left something to be desired. Hughie Godefroy remembers getting his first one: the shoulders were more or less the right width, but the pants were six inches too big in the waist and about 3 inches too short in the leg. But any such imperfections could easily be rectified. Most of the boys wasted no time in tracking down a tailor to have appropriate alterations made. There was a general inclination among them, since they were having things adjusted in any event, to add padding to the shoulders to give the tunic a dramatic and dashing silhouette.

Inspections were part of the daily discipline routine. Belts, buckles, buttons, and shoes all polished, trousers crisply pressed; everything had to be just so or God help you. The purpose was to erode any sense of individuality and to inculcate a culture of mind-numbing conformity. Firby was not pleased during a morning inspection in which the new and improved uniforms were proudly on display. He wasted neither time nor words. Taking a straight razor from his pocket, he sliced open the shoulder pads of one boy's tunic and pulled out the superfluous stuffing, silently dropping it at the boy's feet. He noted acidly that when the rest of the misguided matinée idols had also removed their stuffing and returned their tunics to regulation form, they would then reassemble in formation and resume the inspection. Furthermore, they would remain on parade at attention until he was completely satisfied that order had been restored.

John remembers that he and his buddy Paul Phelan listened very attentively to this as they had both unwisely had their shoulders extended about a foot on either side. They did their best to slouch in the vain hope of escaping Firby's scathing eye. They caught a break when Firby turned on his heel and dismissed them, at which point Paul and John hustled out to have their uniforms restored. At inspection the next morning, Firby moved up and down the line, making no comment about the uniforms but tugging on the fringes of hair on the backs of their heads. "What a lovely bunch of chorus girls," he said. "Let me now tell you what we are going to do." He blew a sharp note on his whistle quite close behind John's head, making his ears ring for some minutes afterward. He informed them all that the next time they heard the whistle each one of them would get themselves to a barber and get a man's cut. Regulation short. And if it were not regulation short by the next day's inspection, then the corporal would see to it that whatever hair was left on their sorry heads would be removed. He finished by saying, "And, ladies, neither you nor your boyfriends will like the results."

Discipline was not about how long your hair was or how you tailored the uniform: it was about responding without question or thought when acting on order. No second thoughts: attack the objective. A career soldier, Firby had been raised on such discipline, and was determined to make his mark in the close order competition at the Exhibition grounds. With not much war on yet, it was also a good way to make these boys smarten up and lose their fantasies of being war heroes.

Over and over and over again they practiced their drill patterns, Firby's whistle signalling each change with the same insistence that whistles drove soldiers from the safety of their trenches into the line of fire during the Great War. It worked. Firby's No. 1 ITS won the competition handily that spring. It was a bright spot during those early months of the war, when the training seemed to extend beyond the comprehensible future and the increasingly restless Prunes were impatient to get into the fight. But the European war, as it was often thought of in the early months, still seemed like a bit of a charade to some, John among them. Regardless, it would still be many months before they would be sufficiently prepared to step into the fight.

A few days after the competition, John and fellow provisional pilots were shipped off to Service Flying Training School (SFTS) at Camp Borden near Barrie, north of Toronto, to learn how to become combat pilots. They spent the next four months learning the fundamentals of flying modern aircraft, or as modern as the RCAF could get. These were Ansons, Oxfords, and Harvards, which were already out of date in 1940, but were nonetheless much more powerful then the biplanes they had learned to fly in Winnipeg.

Furthermore, now they would be flying over a much greater range of country: urban areas, mountains, and large bodies of water. This meant learning visual flight rules, the guidelines used to fly around visible objects, such as trees, buildings and other aircraft, without colliding with them. As basic as that might seem, not heeding such rules was one of the major causes of accidents in training. The new pilots had to internalize what they learned so their actions and reactions became automatic: pedals, stick, airspeed, altitude, flaps, rudder, prevailing winds, and visibility. There was a daunting amount of memory work, quite apart from additional considerations such as learning to use aircraft instruments, navigational aids, armaments, and tactical skills.

Anyone who can drive a car can probably steer a plane. But flying fighter aircraft was like learning how to drive in a fourth dimension. Just learning how to get off the ground and get back down again in one piece separated the living from the dead. The close calls, the unpredictable winds, the bad landings – for John, this was all part of the excitement. His first time soloing at Borden gave him an ecstatic high that he never lost; in fact, it became an addiction.

I soloed today for 40 minutes! The first time I have even flown one alone. It didn't have breaks or steerable tail wheel, so it was a bit hectic on the ground.

I was up for one hour and five minutes in a Fleet [Finch] and had a pretty good session – mostly trying to learn about the aircraft – I did my first roll off of a loop today, more accidental than anything else. But it rolls beautifully!

John told me that he felt as though he became a part of the plane when he left the ground, and from the start he knew in his heart he was good. It didn't really matter how good he was: he had endless faith in himself as one of the best, and that's what often kept good pilots alive.

By the spring of 1940, those who hadn't been washed out or killed were moved on to intermediate training as bomber pilots at the Trenton air force base in Eastern Ontario. This was a much more demanding kind of flying because the planes were larger and less forgiving. As a bomber pilot you were responsible for the men on your crew, and some discovered that they were now gambling with their friends' lives.

The trainee pilots were flying the Fairey Battle, a light three-man British bomber of questionable repute that had been pulled out of front line action after Dunkirk in May 1940. It was slow, limited in range, and highly vulnerable to attack, making it a challenging and often unnerving airplane to go to war in. The Battle could also be archaic and unpredictable to fly, as John discovered during his months at Trenton. All pilots have bumpy landings, and John had a red-letter one while racking up hours flying on his first Battle. His friend Paul Phelan was onboard as a gunner when John attempted to touch down on the landing strip from somewhat higher off the ground than he had intended. About forty feet too high, he cut back his airspeed, bringing the plane back down to earth with an impact akin to driving a large American sedan off the roof of a two-storey house onto a grassy lawn. A ton of whining metal and Perspex hit the runway with a "whirrrrr-BANGGGGG!" And Paul, who was removing ammunition from the machine gun at the time, was bounced around the inside of the plane like a gumball. The plane came to a shuddering stop, and John glanced back and saw Paul's bloodied nose and bugged-out eyes. John scrambled out of the cockpit and beat a hasty retreat to the barracks, where he lay low until Paul eventually cooled down.

But such experiences didn't deter John. All he wanted to do was fly, and imperfect landings weren't going to keep him out of the air. Over the next week, he flew endless hours alone to smooth out the rough edges of his technique, logging a few more flight hours in the never-ending hope of being allowed to fly something better and faster than the old tubs they were stuck with. As he came in to land from his third "review the essentials" flight, he noticed that his Battle's engine had (not untypically) caught fire. He dropped altitude and managed to get his plane back on the ground just as the engine blew, spraying the engine-cooling glycol back over the cockpit and John. Reeking of anti-freeze, he scrambled out of the plane, an unholy mess but otherwise no worse for wear.

Three days after this close call, a dress parade was called for the POPs to be inspected by a visiting English RAF Group Captain. The POPs had only been issued one uniform, so John had no choice but to go on parade in his stained and battered tunic. The glycol had bleached it into an alarmingly mottled amalgam of greens and greys. In addition he had put on some weight, straining the jacket visibly at its seams and requiring him to reef his jacket's belt off to one side in the vain hope that it wouldn't give way.

As the Group Captain moved down the lines of smartly turned out airmen standing to attention, something caught his eye. He paused as though to confirm what he'd just seen, then ambled over to John, looked him up and down, and said, "And who might you be?" John owned up to the fact that he was POP Weir. The Group Captain turned to the base's CO (commanding officer) with a quizzical expression as though he was missing the joke, but received no clarification. He sized John up and down again, just to make sure, then turned back to the CO and said, "Rather a scruffy looking individual, wouldn't you say?" And then carried on with his inspection. There was a ripple of chuckles from John's friends down the line, but the name stuck. From that moment on, John was known as Scruffy.

## Chapter 9

# CIRCUITS AND BUMPS

Hughie had been called up at the end of April 1940, and was now out in Saskatchewan at No. 2 ITS in Regina doing his initial training. He and John stayed in touch through letters and an occasional leave. By the summer, Scruffy had been placed in a training stream headed for Bomber Command, which depressed the hell out of him. He wanted to fly fighters; he didn't want to be responsible for someone else getting killed on his airplane. But it didn't much matter what you wanted, the odds were you wouldn't get it anyway.

There came a point in the Initial Training that some of the boys were told that they weren't going to make the cut. Hughie saw how the anger and disappointment of the unlucky could be devastating for those who'd dreamt of nothing else. Hughie had been one of the fortunate few.

> *If I hadn't been chosen [to be a pilot], I think I would have died.*

And he went off by himself to absorb his happy news. But when he returned to the barracks he learned that one of the new pilots had been more than a little thoughtless. As Hughie remembered, it,

> *This lad [who'd been chosen as a pilot] had run straight to his barrack room on the third floor. Most of his barrack mates were already there, and most of them were now going to be gunners [meaning they hadn't made the cut].*
>
> *I'm going to be a pilot! I'm going to be a pilot!" he sang out gleefully. The others listened in silence for about two seconds, and then, unable to endure it any longer, they pounced on him and dragged him to the*

*window. "Okay, fly boy, let's see you fly," they shouted as they threw him out. From the third story he wasn't killed, but both legs were broken. We had suffered our first casualty.*[1]

At least John was still in the pilot stream. He accepted his regrettable shift away from fighters, and transferred back to Camp Borden to start the final stage of his training, flying newer two-man bombers, Oxfords, and the docile and forgiving Ansons, dubbed "Faithful Annies" by those who flew them. It was still anyone's guess what kind of aircraft would have the most impact in this war, which meant all options had to be explored and pilots trained accordingly. For the time being, the training would consist of lectures, cross-country flights, night flying, combat tactics and aerobatics, and generally racking up hours in the air toward getting your "wings."

For John, the great thing about being back at Borden was that he was close to Fran. At Borden he was just an hour's drive from home, and despite strict regulations forbidding leaving the base while in training, he determined that he could dash down to the city to see her in the hours when no one was paying as much attention. But on the days he couldn't get away, he still managed to stay in touch with her. One of his tricks, when they were flying cross-country sorties, was to write her a love note, bundle it up in a small weighted bag with an improvised parachute made from handkerchiefs attached, then fly down over her family's house in the city and drop his notes from the plane. His aim was usually pretty good, but even when he was a few houses or streets off, the neighbours came to know that it was John doing this and would collect the errant notes and deliver them to Fran's house. He also loved to visit her when she was vacationing on Georgian Bay. He would figure out what cottage she was at, then come screaming low across the lake in a Harvard, its deafening Pratt & Whitney radial engine roaring as he swooped in 20 feet off the water. It left a lasting impression that still had Fran laughing 70 years later.

John and Paul Phelan roomed in the same barracks at Borden, and had worked out a plan to skirt regulations so they could slip away on Saturday nights and duck down to Toronto to see their girls. When it was Paul's turn, John would stuff Paul's bunk to make it look like he was sound asleep under a tangle of bedclothes. And when it was

[1] From Hugh Godefroy.

Scruffy's turn, Paul returned the favour. One warm June night in 1940, John had gone down to the city and was too slow to start heading back. He didn't get around to leaving Fran's until about 4:30 am, which meant it was going to be nip and tuck if he hoped to make it back to Borden for the 6:00 am roll call. Being AWOL – "Absent Without Leave" – was a serious infraction, especially for provisional pilots.

He went tearing north through the towns and villages scattered between Toronto and the base in his Mercury convertible. The roads were quiet, which was a blessing. On the outskirts of Barrie, he passed a sedan heading in the same direction. Scruffy caught a glimpse of the driver out of the corner of his eye and saw that it was his flight instructor. He slumped down in his seat, stepped on the gas, and managed to put some distance between them. He skidded up to the base's front gate with no one in his rear view mirror. The guards knew Scruffy from all his after-hours excursions and waved him through. He dumped his car behind the barracks, ran inside, and jumped into bed fully dressed, burying himself underneath his blankets to blend in with the other sleeping bodies.

Ten minutes later the lights snapped on and the flight instructor strode in, barking that roll call was in fifteen minutes. Heads stirred and the boys rolled out of their beds and toward the showers. The flight instructor added that there was no need for Mr. Weir to feel the need to dress if he didn't want to, as he was damned sure that he was dressed already. John stumbled out of his bed and mumbled out an explanation, which the instructor cut short. He'd heard enough of John's explanations in the past. As the other men filed out for morning parade, the officer held John back and informed him that his hooligan nights not only showed disregard for regulations, but an equal disrespect for the other men he was flying with. He was forthwith being transferred out of the section.

John was shattered. This meant he'd been "washed out," and would likely be sent to No. 1 KTS (Composite Training School; yes, I know, the initials don't match the acronym) at Trenton. This was the demoralizing final destination for any unfortunate airmen who didn't make the grade in their training. Every new recruit in the air force wanted to be a pilot, but only a few were chosen. The other options were to become an air observer, or navigator; a bomb aimer; a wireless operator; or an air gunner. Each was a good and challenging trade with its specific set of skills.

However, being sent to KTS meant that you had been jettisoned from those positions as well. Not only would you never pilot an aircraft, you would now be stuck indefinitely with a bunch of other guys who had washed out, too. You were nothing until psychologists interviewed and evaluated you, then hopefully gave you a pass. Once they had, flight instructors would make a final decision about whether there might be any simpler role that you could able to fill in the service as a third-stringer, a replacement from the slow learner's class.

In short, you were officially a failure.[2]

John struggled with how he was going to break the news to his father, Hughie and, maybe worst of all, Fran. He wondered *what* he was going to tell them. When he found the nerve to approach the flight instructor, he asked when he would have to report to KTS. Maybe if he had a bit of time, he would be able to come up with a good story to tell his family. But the Flight Instructor dismissed the question with a shake of his head. He said it was too late for KTS; he'd arranged a transfer for John to singles – fighters – where he felt John's independent spirit and aggressive flying style might be put to better use. He cut short the burgeoning smile on John's face by saying the transfer was meant as a punishment. But for the record, he added that it had been John's skills and confidence in the air that made this move an obvious one. John saluted, thanked him, and went to collect his gear.

That transfer may well have saved his life. At that point in the war, Allied bombers and their crews were having the stuffing knocked out of them, and casualties were high. Fighters were literally and figuratively playing catch up. Two months later, at the end of August 1940, Scruffy had earned his wings and shipped overseas to England to join the first Canadian fighter squadron, RCAF No. 1 (subsequently renumbered RAF No. 401). France had fallen to the Germans two months earlier and the gravity of what had been the threat of German invasion had become a very real danger. Operation "Sea Lion" – the Nazi plan for the invasion of England – was well underway, and the battle to save Britain had begun. Sea Lion was an orchestrated series of aggressive raids that the Germans directed against Britain in preparation for their invasion.

---

2    I spoke to one KTS graduate in 2001. He had washed out and been sent to KTS for re-evaluation, later becoming an air gunner and eventually reassigned to a combat bomber squadron. But for the rest of his life, he never lost that profound sense of shame at having washed out the first time round.

The first stage was to cripple shipping; then radio transmission towers would be knocked out; and finally the Luftwaffe would sweep over and destroy all RAF fighter bases across the south coast of England. At that juncture, Nazi forces would flood across the Channel and occupy the country. It was the very worst of times to be tossed into combat.

All that Scruffy had been through up to this point – with his father, with Fiji, with Uncle Adrian, the trips to Europe, the brutal work in the mines, Hughie and he and their shared dreams – might have seemed like good training for all that was now unfolding. But the world he was stepping into outstripped anything he had prepared for, let alone imagined. The largest, most professional and most heavily armed military force in the world – in history – was sweeping across Europe and conquering it. And while most did not want to admit it, Britain was now poised precipitously on the brink of defeat.

---

It took the better part of a year to train a pilot, and by the time the POPs arrived in England they were champing at the bit to get some hours in a real fighter. Those who had made it this far loved flying, and the idea of sliding sideways through the air strapped into a ton of metal awash with lighter fluid was their idea of fun. Instructors kept an eye out for new pilots who demonstrated a sure hand on the controls, even in the trickiest situations. John was one of them.

There were about seven times as many German fighters as there were Allied fighters at that time in the war. Worse, the German planes were almost all newer, faster, and more lethal; but the new boys were happily ignorant of this. Almost everyone in those early years was eager to jump into the thick of things. There was so much that was so startlingly new that for a long time they had simply put out of mind where they had come from or where they could be headed.

Scruffy arrived in England, along with a few hundred other newly minted airmen, onboard the *RMS Duchess of Athol*, an aging Canadian Pacific steamer known colloquially as the "Duchess of Asshole" by the men onboard because of her decrepitude. She was more tellingly known as "The Drunken Duchess" due to her proclivity to pitch and roll at the same time.[3] Scruffy was just glad to get off the tub and back on solid

---

3    The *Duchess* had been built for work on the St. Lawrence River. She had a flat bottom for sailing in shallow waters, but no stabilizers. Ill-suited to the rough North Atlantic, she pitched and rolled constantly.

ground. From the second day, he had been sick as a dog – damned hard not to be on a ship like that on the North Atlantic, he said. Even the huge Cunard liners, the *Queen Mary* and the *Queen Elizabeth*, would list back and forth as they zigzagged their way across the ocean dodging U-boats. The issue of seasickness was of some concern because of the unofficial RAF policy to ground you if you were inclined to upchuck while flying. There were too many other would-be pilots with cast iron stomachs waiting in line behind you to take your place. A weak stomach in the air force was like admitting you were gun shy. Scruffy was not about to let something as mundane as a bit of queasiness keep him from qualifying as an operational pilot. Whether it was mind over matter or fierce determination, he never suffered from nausea once he set foot in England.

The *Duchess* chugged into Liverpool harbour in the middle of an air raid during what came to be known as the Battle of Britain.[4] The air raid left the city on fire, and it was the next morning before the ship was able to approach the docks and the passengers disembarked into this new world at war. In his journal, Scruffy wrote about their arrival.

> *Friday October 25*
> Here we be at Liverpool. Arrived about 3:30 in the afternoon and sat in the river all day. At 8:45 pm the air raid sirens were sounded and nothing happened for about an hour. Then we had some crashes of guns and stuff but no bombs have been dropped as yet (10:25 pm). A very poor show considering all the advertising it has had. One thing is certain though – when they say blackout they mean blackout – gosh, it's black – not a light showing anywhere.

In the morning, the new arrivals were herded on to small, slow-moving trains and transferred to aircrew manning pools outside of London. Manning pools were transit camps where new aircrew would be collected for a week or so before being shipped off to the various bases around Britain where they would learn how to fly combat aircraft in battle.

---

4   In May 1940, shortly after the fall of France, Churchill told the House of Commons, "The Battle of France is over. I expect the Battle of Britain is about to begin." What followed was the relentless and sustained air offensive of the German Luftwaffe that began in July 1940 and lasted through the autumn.

*Saturday October 26*
We started for Salisbury Plains and have been on the train for over 12 hours. The blackout is really black and since I'm damn tired I think I'll just tell you about it tomorrow – there's the air raid siren now. No signs of bombing. Got here and there were no quarters for us. Slept on the floor in the Officers' Mess. Tomorrow we move into tents.

*Sunday October 27*
Cold? Wow!!! A dreary day with nothing doing to speak of. We were allotted our tents today. Our beds consist of a bunch of hay in the form of a mattress wrapped in blankets. The running water we get is when it rains or else we do the running. It's really quite fun, 'cept it would be a lot more fun to be here together. Wish you were here!

*Monday October 28*
Got tin helmets we did nothing else except freeze this morning when we got up.

*Tuesday October 29*
We were paid! £20 and got leave to go to London. I'm staying at the Regent Palace Hotel. You can really see the effects of the bombing – one whole block knocked out alongside our place.

From the hills around the village where Scruffy's lot were billeted, they could watch the vapour trails of German Junkers 88s and Messerschmitt 109s over the English Channel, and see the RAF fighters that chased after them. On a clear day there would be hundreds of trails crisscrossing the sky, the short skirmishes often ending with one of the planes spiraling down in a plume of smoke and extinguishing like a lit match as it dropped into the water. It was all a little unreal to the new arrivals, but that would soon change.

London was only a short train ride away, and when the boys had a bit of leave they took advantage of the chance to see some of the big city – for most of them, far and away the biggest city they had ever seen. Even though London was being hammered by nightly air raids, this didn't deter the airmen from swarming into the city to see and enjoy what was on offer. Uncle Adrian and Auntie Ted had a flat in Kensington, and John was often invited to stay with them when he was in town, an offer that he gratefully accepted. Most airmen were not so lucky, and a weekend in a London hotel was a big deal. One of these was Geoff Marlow, a Canadian pilot from the bomber stream who was waiting to be posted to an Operational Training Unit (OTU) where the hard skills of combat were taught. He had met a girl at a tea dance in Bournemouth, and after they'd been out a few times he invited her up to London to see a show and stay in a nice hotel.

They met at Charing Cross station and walked a couple of blocks east to the Strand Palace Hotel. Geoff went to the desk to check in while the girl waited beside him. He asked for a room, and gave his name and the name of his "wife." As the desk clerk filled out the registration card, Geoff looked over at his girl and saw that she had turned as white as a ghost. He took her aside to ask what was wrong. She explained as best she could that she had never thought they would be sharing a room; it was something that she had never done, and she couldn't start now. Geoff was deeply disappointed, but said that of course he understood. He said he couldn't afford a second room at the Strand Palace, but he promised to behave himself if she was okay with them sharing the room for the night. She was, and they spent a happy evening out on the town and a quiet and chaste night with him sleeping in an armchair.

The next morning over breakfast, they talked about what they were going to do that day. Geoff said that first off he had better find a less expensive place to stay and book a couple of rooms for them that night. He found a small family hotel near Victoria Station, and with that in hand they had a lovely day together in the city. They returned to their new hotel late, said their goodnights, and made their ways to their separate rooms.

As Geoff lay in his bed, he couldn't help but feel a little disappointed at the way things had turned out. Not that he hadn't had a wonderful time: he'd just got his hopes up a little too high. He sat smoking a cigarette, watching people walking past on the street below for a while, then turned off the light and lay in bed staring at the ceiling tiles. His eyes were just beginning to close when the sirens started wailing, and the anti-aircraft guns opened up, sounding so close it was as if they were down the hall. The blackout curtains did a pretty good job of keeping the light out, but the noise was something else. Geoff burrowed his head under a pillow and hoped he would eventually find sleep. He had just dozed off and begun to dream when what seemed like a warm body – a warm female body – slipped under the covers and cuddled up next to him. It was his girl, terrified at the pounding and shaking from the guns and bombs, and who had come to his room to find reassurance.

On his way back to Bournemouth the next morning, Geoff smiled and thought that sometimes a night visit by German bombers wasn't such a bad thing after all, depending on where you were sleeping of course.

––––––––––––

John liked London. He had often been there before the war with his father and Adrian, but the world was different now. When he went out on the town with friends, they would see shows and have drinks, often staying out well into the night. What startled him was the social life. Or more specifically, sex. An astonishing number of professional girls seemed to be offering their services. It seemed to John that just about everybody was happy to hop into bed with anybody else at the drop of a hat. This was not a type of social situation he'd had any experience with, and it rattled him a bit. In his diary, he wrote:

> The same ones [are all] after the same stuff which is all well and good, especially as they are so frank about it. But I don't like it much. I guess I'm just a stuffed shirt. The more I see of it the more certain I am I'll stay faithful.

But London also offered a peaceful respite for many servicemen. I asked one veteran about what London had been like during the war years. He had been a Royal Canadian Naval officer in Intelligence, and had spent two years living and working in the heart of the city. He thought about my question, and smiled a little wistfully. He said what he loved about London during the war was that it was so quiet. There were free concerts in the parks, very few trucks or cars on the roads, and you could walk safely everywhere. It was a peaceful, beautiful city. What about the air raids and the bombing? I asked. Oh, he said, there were *those* of course. But you got used to that. Apart from the air raids, it was a wonderful place to be.

Air raids were indeed a part of every day life, but they failed to bring the city to a standstill as German High Command had hoped. As the posters displayed around the city advised, *Your Courage, Your Cheerfulness, Your Resolution Will Bring Us Victory.* You simply had to exercise common sense. When the air raid sirens started, you had to get to a shelter. And if you couldn't, then you had to stand flat in the doorway of a solidly constructed building. The most important thing was not to get caught out in the open.

On one leave in London in early November 1940, John was walking back to his hotel up Regent Street when the sirens started wailing. Seeing no shelter signs, he quickly ducked into a doorway and flattened himself against the stone. At that moment, a man who had been walking across the street from John also reacted to the sirens. He looked around for shelter, then panicked and started running up Regent Street. John yelled at him to find cover, but the man showed no signs of having heard. Bombs started falling and exploding, and one must have hit high up on one of the buildings on the street, as stone and concrete shrapnel came raining down. From the doorway where he was huddled, John watched as a fragment hit the man and clipped off his head as neatly as a blade of grass. That was the first person John had seen killed.

Moments like these turned the abstraction of war into a real if impersonal threat for the newly arrived soldiers and airmen. There had been the occasional training accident back in Canada, but no one among John's bunch had been killed. However, within the next few weeks of operational training, three of the boys that had shipped over with John were killed in flying accidents. In one diary entry at the end of November, he wrote, "Bill killed today. Really a nice guy."

On November 5th, John was told to report to Operational Training Unit (OTU) Sutton Bridge, an RAF fighter base 200 miles northeast of London, where he would receive the final stages of his training. There, he would become familiar with flying the aircraft that in a couple of months he would be taking into action. Ten days later, John received a letter from Auntie Ted and wrote this in his journal:

> Today I got the worst news I've had for some time. Pat [Chamier] was killed doing a cross country [flying exercise]

in southern Rhodesia. He had just got his wings too. Gad, it seems impossible but it's true. Auntie Ted must be almost crazy over it. I vow I won't rest until at least 4 Huns pay for it.

For John, the real war was about to begin.

# Chapter 10

# BATTLE ORDERS

In those early days, Scruffy thought of little other than flying, and Fran. At Sutton Bridge, he learned that he was going to fly the Hurricane, a robust single-wing fighter that was the foundation of the RAF in the early years of the war. Long overshadowed by the more romantic Spitfire, the Hurricane provided the lion's share of Britain's air defenses during the Battle of Britain, seeing more action and making more enemy kills than any other aircraft. Like most large mechanical things, the plane had a very distinctive personality to which you had acclimate yourself. The Hurricane was vastly more powerful than the biplane trainers that the guys had learned on, so everything the new pilots had learned about flying had to be unlearned. It was like having driven an old VW bug for years, then being buckled into a souped-up hot rod ten times as fast on a road with much more liberal speeding rules. It was an intoxicating experience. The Hurricane was built like a truck yet was highly manoeuvrable in combat. It was a serious step up from the planes Scruffy had trained on, and he loved the fact that he could beat the hell out of them and they'd still keep flying. It was a terrific plane to go to war in.

*November 25*
[John's good friend] Jeep's undercarriage collapsed while he was landing, and he ploughed in nose first – unhurt – that boy is lucky. It's the 4th plane he's racked up since we've been here. [Eugene 'Jeep' Neal flew in the same squadron as John, and became a lifelong friend.]

*November 30*
Had my first crash in the air force this month. The clouds

had closed in right down to the ground, and I was forced to land because of bad weather in a peanut-size farmer's field. Couldn't see much of anything. The wet grass made my brakes useless, and some bad judgement by me, and I ended up in a hedge on my nose. That will be my last! [Author's note: It wasn't.]

After the pilots had gained confidence in the basics of flying the Hurricane, they were trained to fly in formation: twelve planes flying in groups of three at slightly different altitudes from one another. Groups of three were "flights," with a leader and two wingmen. The pilot of each aircraft provided cover for the others in his flight. One man would watch in front, a second would watch behind, and the third would watch for peripheral attacks. Formation flying was a constantly evolving strategy for encountering the enemy in the air, as well as for attacking them on the ground.

During the six-week training period, the sprogs[1] were constantly on training missions in formation. Typical assignments included cross-countries, which were reconnaissance flights at about 5,000 feet, during which the pilots would sharpen their skills at identifying specific villages, rivers, and railways, and any other landmarks they could use as points of reference. Whatever the mission, the objective was to give them as much flight time, in as wide a range of conditions, as possible, to prepare for whatever situation might be thrown at them.

Once the pilots had passed these final training hurdles, they were transferred to "operational" status and assigned to squadrons to be eased into action. On a fighter squadron, the day-to-day work entailed several types of missions. The most straightforward was a Sector Reccie (short for reconnaissance), where the pilot flew from one aerodrome to another, touched down, then took off again and flew around to identify key landmarks and characteristics of the base so that when they returned they would have their bearings. Reccies were also flown at night, so the pilots had to develop some very clear points of reference to keep oriented in the dark.

Combat sorties, also known as shoot-ups or rhubarbs, were more interesting, certainly with 401. A single plane would be sent out across the Channel to attack "Targets of Opportunity" – shipping, trains,

---

1    "Sprog" was a term often used by more experienced airmen to describe new pilots.

convoys, trucks, or airfields. The pilot would fly low to the water across the Channel to avoid being spotted. When he reached the coast, he would pull up sharply to avoid anti-aircraft fire ("ack-ack"). Once past the coastal guns, he would swoop down again to see what trouble he could stir up. If a line of trucks or a train were spotted, he might attack and try to "give them some squirts,"[2] and then dash home across the Channel again. On such operations, the pilot would typically be in the air less than an hour. If he got into a skirmish, the pilot went full bore, which used a lot of fuel. Then the problem would be making it back across the Channel. Most experienced pilots tried to be conservative in their fuel usage, because once they got into a dust-up they wouldn't have time to watch their gauges. A lot of guys ran out of gas simply trying to make it back home across the Channel and had to ditch over the water. Many of those who went in the drink couldn't be rescued in time. It was either your day or it wasn't.

There were also reconnaissance missions, known as sweeps, to get a sense of the enemy's positions. These were typically two- or three-plane flights, sometimes only a single if that's all that was available. If the planes spotted an aerodrome, they might swing down and attack. But they'd have to make sure they could get in and out quickly. Learning how to interpret what you were seeing on these sweeps provided key tactical information for the squadron. In those first few years, the air war was the only offensive arm that the Allies had against what had become Fortress Europe, and fighter sweeps were invaluable in learning where the "Krauts"[3] – the Germans – were dug in, what their strength was, and even what their objectives might be.

The war was a rich cornucopia of acronyms, nicknames, shorthand, slang, and jargon, all arising out of the need to say a lot with a little. John's nickname, Scruffy, is a good example, encapsulating something of his story as well as a bit of the spirit of the man himself. In the air, pilots couldn't chatter on R/T – radiotelephony, their radios – when

---

2     Slang on the squadron for machine gun fire.
3     "Kraut" is a somewhat derogatory slang word that was used by the Allies for the Germans. "Kraut" translates as "cabbage", but the slang word is actually a centuries-old term derived from the diminutive of pickled (sour) cabbage, or sauerkraut, which was popular in German cuisine and elsewhere. For centuries, sea-going nations used sauerkraut as a vitamin-rich preventative against scurvy on long naval voyages. The British eventually came to use citrus fruits – especially limes – while the Germans and other nations continued to use sauerkraut. This inspired another derogatory sobriquet: the term "Limey", used by Germans for the English.

they were flying. The RAF had a strict R/T procedure. If and when there was talk, everything had to be boiled down and reduced to the minimum language. Scruffy was flying a reccie in Lincolnshire, and as he came up over the brow of a hill, he was greeted by a panorama of military confusion. A bunch of "Brown Jobs" – army types – were thrashing about in the throes of one of the innumerable training schemes that were conducted both to train the soldiers and to stave off the boredom of waiting to get into the war. It was a "Red Army attacks Blue Army" type of affair, and thousands of men and vehicles had come to a dead stop at a crossroads, no one willing to back up and admit responsibility or defeat. Scruffy, who had to report on any such situation he encountered, radioed in a one-word report to describe what was happening: FUBAR. Made famous in Spielberg's *Saving Private Ryan*, this was an acronym for "Fucked Up Beyond All Recognition." The other two words pilots commonly used on R/T were SNAFU – "Situation Normal, All Fucked Up" – and the most delightful, which he used the next day on his follow-up report, SABU, which translates to "Self-Adjusting Balls Up," indicating that the FUBAR situation had resolved itself without intervention. (The word designating the worst state of affairs was TUIFU – "Tooey-Foo" – meaning, "The Ultimate in Fuck Ups.")

The exception to talking over the radio was if you were in action engaging the enemy. Should a man on your flight spot an enemy plane threatening your tail, he could break in with an abrupt, "Yellow Leader, mind your ass!" at which point, if you were on your toes and still alive, you'd punch your throttle, flip the aircraft over on its back into a dive, and pray. Things happened extremely fast in the air, flying 300 miles per hour or more toward your enemy.

When Scruffy completed his operational training at Sutton Bridge, he was given a week's leave before reporting to his first fighter base. He had been posted to No. 1 "City of Westmount" Squadron RCAF, which had distinguished itself flying with the RAF during the Battle of Britain from August through October of that year. The squadron had suffered substantial losses in equipment and men, and in October 1940 it was withdrawn to Prestwick, Scotland to rebuild, and then on December 7th to Castletown, the most northern RAF station in Scotland. The squadron's duties were to protect Scapa Flow, the main base for the Royal Navy, situated near the Orkney Islands in the extreme northeast of Scotland.

John arrived in Thurso, the town nearest to Castletown, on December 17th. He wrote,

> Arrived here at 9:40 this morning. Thurso is a very small
> town in the very north of Scotland – just on the coast opposite
> the Orkneys. Gads what a place – quiet is putting it mildly.
> The rumour is that the Germans are planning to "pay us
> back" for [the Royal Navy's attack on] Taranto and give
> Scapa what for. Also [the English] are still pretty scared of an
> attempt to raid the Isles by an invasion on Scotland, which
> is very vulnerable at this point. So we are here on a dual
> purpose – to prevent a successful invasion as well. It's going to
> be very interesting here if things start to happen – they'll be
> happening fast and furious!!!

It was the squadron's responsibility to fly cover for navy ships coming and going from Scapa Flow, and intercept any German aircraft that could pose a threat to them. Most of the squadron's work was reconnaissance and recognition. In his first few weeks posting there, Scruffy logged many hours of flight time, in the air every day refining his flying skills. Then and later he did a number of flights for the army along the east coast of Britain to show whether their camouflage was effective or not. After a couple of such trips, he made the recommendation that the army use colour-blind spotters: it stood to reason that they would be less likely to miss oddities in camouflage. It was an extremely effective technique that the army adopted immediately.

One of Scruffy's regular missions was being "scrambled" (called into action at a moment's notice) to try and intercept "Weather Willy," a Luftwaffe pilot who flew his JU-88 fighter over Scapa on a mind-numbingly predictable schedule to report weather conditions back to German High Command. As England's chief naval base, Scapa was always a prime target for attack. Willy always flew at 10,000 feet and always at the same time: you could literally set your watch by him. Scruffy had been trying to catch him for weeks, but he was flying a Hurricane and the JU-88 was a hell of a lot faster and could outrun anything flying at Scapa. But as frustrating as it was, Scruffy liked the challenge. He devised a plan where he would scoot up to 15,000 or

16,000 feet and wait for Willy to show up at his usual time. He would then dive down from behind, hard and fast, and open fire with his kill shot before Willy knew what had hit him.

A promising day arrived, with clear skies and minimal wind. He took his Hurricane up to 16,000 feet and marked time until Willy showed up right on schedule. Scruffy watched him from a safe distance, then opened his throttle, going into a steep dive and pushing the Hurricane past its top speed as he lined up Willy in his sights. Just as he came into range, his radio crackled and a German-accented voice said, "OK, Yellow Leader, you may pancake now." Then the JU–88 spat out a couple of puffs of black smoke, flipped over, and disappeared into the horizon.

Scruffy was stunned. Willy had not only anticipated him being there, but had used the RAF term "pancake" as well as Scruffy's call colours – Yellow Leader – and that was highly secret stuff. It meant there had to be someone at the base who was transmitting this secret information to the Krauts. He landed, baffled, angry, and determined to do something about it.

At this point in the war, Adrian was officially known as Air Commodore Sir Adrian Chamier, and had offices at Adastral House, the Air Ministry's headquarters in London. Adrian supervised the Balloon Barrage Command over London as well as the Air League's air cadet program. But his position at Adastral House was also ideal for monitoring the ebb and flow of much of the RAF's flow of intelligence during the war.

The intelligence network he had created was, by design, essentially non-existent. There were many military intelligence departments operating under the auspices of the War Office in England during the war, such as MI5, MI6, and so on – nineteen "M's" in all, each with a separate mandate.[4] Adrian had created an organization that would operate below the radar of these agencies, all but invisible, cloaked by the more public activities of the government's secret intelligence services. With no offices or traceable pattern of communication between its agents and its objectives, Adrian's circuit of intelligence operatives were able to pursue their work silently.

4    The "MI" is an acronym for "Military Intelligence". MI6, however, is more properly known as SIS, the Secret Intelligence Service.

There were no shared secrets, no conference room briefings, and no paper trail; in short, there was no common, traceable thread connecting its agents – with the exception of Adrian. The greatest strength were the secure and untraceable lines of communication. Simply put, no one knew anyone else.

The roots of this silent network predated the war. Given the British government's reluctance to respond to the rise of the Nazi threat in the 1930s, Adrian had been determined to do whatever he could to track and identify potential German agents who were living in Britain, and answering to the Abwehr, the German Intelligence Ministry. What the CIA was to the FBI, and what MI6 was to MI5, so the Abwehr was to the SS: the international versus the home front.

German agents who had managed to embed themselves in England were typical of the world of espionage at that time. Some may have been die-hard Nazis, but most were questionable characters living on the fringes of society. Many were borderline criminals who recognized a once in a lifetime opportunity to peddle their modest resources in a seller's market. If their superiors in Berlin or Paris were desperate for information, these agents were in a unique position to provide reports on everything from troop movements to the kinds of food that was served in the RAF messes. Early on, nothing was too small or insignificant to flip into a moneymaking opportunity. These were men and women who had discovered loopholes in the flow of information and capitalized on them. Most significantly, it was a business that delivered ready cash, which satisfied the impulse for instant gratification that had driven so many into this dangerous line of work.

In 1940, Churchill (with Hugh Dalton, one of his Cabinet ministers) created the Special Operations Executive (SOE) as a covert force to counteract the perceived threat of a network of German spies laying the groundwork for an invasion. With the admonition to "…Set Europe ablaze!" its objectives were to encourage and create sabotage and espionage behind enemy lines. It would also serve as the core of resistance in England in the event of invasion, a very real prospect at that point in the war. Adrian was aware of these plans, and worked with the SOE in refining the parameters of how to best implement its field strategies. The SOE came to have great impact in the European theatre of war, but in its early years it could be painfully inept, sabotaged by bureaucratic logistics and departmental infighting, as Adrian had forewarned. He intentionally kept his organization's operations in an autonomous orbit, working common objectives with the SOE, but secure from its vagaries and vulnerabilities.

One of the Abwehr's most significant incursions into British Intelligence and the newly formed SOE was the infiltration of a Dutch resistance circuit in the third year of the war. Circuits were the networks of resistance agents that were supplied and facilitated by SOE's London office and its field agents. The "Baker Street Irregulars" (the SOE's offices were at 64 Baker Street, near Sherlock's fictional stomping grounds) had devised a simple and seemingly foolproof system to confirm the identity and status of field agents in their wireless transmission signatures from occupied countries. When an agent established radio contact with England (via Morse code), they were to key in two acknowledgments of their identity. The first was a "bluff" (false) identity codename, and the second was the confirming or true identity codename. If an agent had been captured and was being forced to transmit, only their first bluff identity would be sent, thereby alerting HQ in London that the agent had been compromised. Bad luck for the agent, but it ensured the integrity of the resistance circuit.

Unfortunately a keen but inexperienced officer at SOE headquarters had been placed in charge of receiving these communications in the early months of the SOE's penetration of occupied France and Holland. He had the unfortunate tendency, upon receiving only the first bluff check from a compromised agent, to ignore the implicit message conveyed by the single transmission, and to radio back, "My dear fellow, you only left us a week ago. On your first message you go and forget to put your 'true' check."

One can only begin to imagine the rapacious delight of the German interrogators to have discovered such a gaping hole in the armour of British intelligence, through which they could now confidently extract key information from captured agents. Once they had coerced the captured men and women into coughing up their true identity key codes, it was a simple matter to establish false communications back to England, and from that point on the Germans held all the cards. The most chilling part of this leak was that for more than a year London was unaware that their circuits had been broken. This afforded the Abwehr the opportunity to send a continual flow of false reports back to London, allowing the Gestapo to arrive early at secret drop zones to wait and collect the new agents as they parachuted into France. The result was the capture, torture, and execution of dozens of agents and hundreds of members of the resistance, and the near destruction of the majority of resistance circuits in France and Holland.

According to the few SOE agents who were caught and somehow managed still to be alive by the end of the war, the Abwehr's interrogation centre in Paris had wall charts detailing the SOE chain of command from the head man and woman, right down to the names of the various resistance circuit leaders and their contacts. It is small consolation to know that both sides suffered from such lapses in judgment and security. But it is a vivid illustration of how it was often the small things at the sharp edge of war that determined how you lived and how you died.

MI5 did not intrude on MI6's areas of operations, nor did MI5 have any sovereignty over police matters, which were Scotland Yard's concern. The SOE worked in both domestic (MI5's arena) and foreign (MI6's arena) theatres of war, but there were innumerable conflicts of interest and refusals to cooperate and share information. That is precisely why Adrian's organization was able to achieve its success and remain invisible: its ability to operate outside of formal channels of procedure. Adrian had devised his network with an understanding of what a shoddy and dangerous business wartime espionage was, at least in the early days. While the stakes were extremely high, the game was largely peopled by civilians of dubious character and mercenary motives, barely controlled by their Abwehr handlers. Most were amateurs so guileless that they were willing to wander into a city, town, or village and just assume that they would blend into the crowd. Which, of course, by the very nature of their nonchalance, often proved to be a very effective method of slipping through the cracks of English security.

Adrian's senior rank in the RAF made him privy to the flow of intelligence, and able to initiate certain actions to gather information. Now that John's[5] training was complete, and he was on active duty, Adrian was able to activate him as a field agent with the code name "Collette." Thus began John's shadow war.

Before John left London for Thurso, he met with Adrian and was briefed on communication protocols. His orders would come through

---

5    John Weir was known to his family as John, but to his fellow pilots on the squadron he was known as "Scruffy". In this book, I refer to him as John when he is interacting with Adrian or other members of his family, but as Scruffy when he is with other airmen.

his commanding officer on the squadron, Deane Nesbitt[6], and there would never be any other communication. Deane would never know the true reason for the assignment; he would just receive an order from the Air Ministry to send John to a particular place at a particular time. When John had information to get to Adrian, he was to go to a neutral telephone, away from any RAF facility, and then telephone Adrian directly at Adastral House.

John remembered those early missions well – and that there seemed to be nothing mysterious or covert about them. Typically, his CO Deane Nesbitt would issue orders for what seemed to be a straightforward mission, along the lines of, "Scruffy, you're airborne in twenty minutes and flying toward the heat. See what you can see, then head back and report." John was given the vectors he was to fly, which was the extent of the information that Deane had. He simply conveyed orders that, unknown to him, had originated from Adrian at Adastral House in London. John's instructions from Adrian were also simple and direct. He told John that on such missions he was to keep his eyes open and report back if there was anything that caught his attention. If there was, then he was to deliver the information and forget about it. It was in this way that John's covert activities were made possible.

RAF Castletown was a small, isolated, and quite primitive air force station when No. 1 RCAF was stationed there. The winter of 1940-41 was one of the worst that Scotland had seen for many years. The men lived in draughty Nissen huts with concrete floors and a small stove for heat. On such remote air force stations, the Navy, Army and Air Force Institutes (NAAFI), a British government-run organization, provided modest catering services to servicemen from boxy vans that became a familiar sight all over Britain during the war. At Castletown, the NAAFI "mobile canteens" were driven directly onto the grounds adjacent to the runways. The van's side would lift up, creating a small canopy and revealing a service window from which the staff sold rationed sweets, soap, and cigarettes, and handed out cups of tea and warm buns. These were particularly welcome during that bitter winter.

The vans were staffed by NAAFI enlisted men and women (members

6    Coincidentally, Deane – a highly decorated pilot and greatly admired officer – was the son of Arthur Nesbitt, who cofounded Nesbitt Thomson, later Nesbitt Burns, a Canadian stock brokerage firm not unlike McLeod Young Weir.

of the Royal Army Service Corps and Auxiliary Territorial Services), and occasionally supplemented by willing volunteers. John remembered a friendly girl with rosy cheeks who worked behind the counter who deflected all romantic overtures with good humour, and the matronly woman who managed the operation with a sharp tongue but a generous heart. They were occasionally lent a hand by a grey-haired vicar in his 60s, who was never without his dog collar and well-worn tweeds, his battered Trilby perched on his head, and tufts of hair sprouting from his ears, making him look for all the world like a Father Christmas in a Giles cartoon. Like most of the pilots, John would stop at the van and get a cup of tea after a mission, and then be debriefed by Herb Norris, the squadron's intelligence officer.

A few days after John's encounter with Weather Willy, he had returned from a routine patrol and stopped at the NAAFI van for his tea. The day was warmer than some, and John lingered a bit making conversation with the rosy-cheeked girl doing the serving that day and a couple of other men getting their tea. As he walked away, he was startled by what he thought sounded like a muffled voice speaking German. The voice grew steadily louder as he approached the hangar. At first, he thought it must have been his imagination, charged up by his encounter with Willy. But as he was walking back to the mess to talk to Herb he thought he should have another listen. He walked to the side of the hangar and put his ear against the metal, but all was silent inside. He circled around the building to head back to the mess and as he came around the corner, he saw the vicar walking away. The man gave John a warm smile, which John returned before heading to the mess to submit his flight report.

In their meeting, Herb remarked on how serious John looked. Given what had happened a few days earlier with Weather Willy, John said he was sure that someone was leaking information on the base. Herb wanted to know if he had any idea of who it might be. Scruffy said no, but he wondered if there might be anyone new on the base. Maybe a tradesman, or somebody new on the ground crew? Herb said he couldn't think of anybody like that. Then as Adrian had instructed him, John walked from the base into Castletown and placed a call to London to give his report.

A week after he called Adrian, Deane called him into his office and told him there were orders from Adastral House for John to report to London for 48 hours starting immediately. On arrival, John went directly to the Chamiers' flat. Young Pat's death had devastated Auntie Ted and she was staying with friends in the country; the house was empty but for Adrian and John. Adrian got right to the point. John's vicar had been picked up and there was no question he was the source of the leak, he told John. They had managed to extract a good deal of information from the man. Later, the vicar had an unfortunate accident,[7] so that was the end of that.

But then Adrian cautioned John. What he'd done was very useful, but also extremely dangerous. He had made himself something of a target by talking to Herb at Scapa. A completely trustworthy fellow, of course, but reports might have been filed and notice taken. Adrian then described some techniques for reporting threats like this vicar character without John making himself so vulnerable. Then he asked John if there had been any others he'd come across that he thought suspicious. John mentioned two men he'd crossed paths with at other bases. Again, there was nothing specific, just something about them that didn't fit: a kind of arrogance that John had seen so much of in Germany during the Thirties. Adrian thanked him with a warning to be more circumspect.

John was back into his routine at Castletown the next evening.

---

7    This being a euphemism, of course.

# THE END OF THE BEGINNING

Increasingly, Scruffy found himself singled out on the squadron for special duty flights. Requests would come in for one man to go on a mission – there were never specifics about what the mission was – and it always seemed to be Scruffy who was assigned. He had flown a wide range of aircraft, and was considered to be very experienced and capable of handling any kind of plane and flying condition. He was repeatedly called on for such missions because he had a particular gift for observation and recognition. His excellent memory earned him a reputation for returning from missions with reports that were invariably accurate and uncoloured. He frequently found the missions puzzling, but he knew that no questions were to be asked. His flying orders came from the squadron, but his covert orders were conveyed directly from Uncle Adrian via phone calls. He would receive a telephone call and when he answered, a voice would recite a string of numbers. He had been taught to disregard the first five of them and then dial the remaining ones, which would typically ring a neutral call box somewhere in London. Someone – usually Adrian himself – would answer and convey the requisite information to him. Adrian had trained John in covert communication using "Trojan Words." These were familiar phrases and colloquialisms, all familiar and seemingly innocuous, but which contained a hidden message. Dead drops were used to exchange written reports or materials. Adrian was the only contact that John had; he never knew anyone else who was a part of the organization. It therefore required enormous trust and faith.

There were rare occasions where John had a glimmer of the larger purpose of a special duty operation. In April of 1941, Adrian spoke with John on the phone and told him, "You're going to be invited to a party, and the party is private." Which meant that he could speak to no one about what he saw on the mission to which he was about to be assigned. Not even Deane or the squadron's IO. No more than an hour after this phone call, Deane called John into his office and gave him the order to fly cover for the English aircraft carrier, HMS *Ark Royal*. The *Ark Royal* was one of England's premier aircraft carriers, an essential defense in providing air cover for the vulnerable merchant convoys bringing supplies to England. She was an extremely tempting target for the German navy because of her size and the numbers of aircraft (around sixty) that she would be carrying at any given time. As Scruffy approached the coordinates he'd been given, he realized something was odd: what he was flying cover for wasn't the *Ark Royal*, but an old rusty tanker that had been given a makeshift stage dressing to make her appear – at least from a distance – like the *Ark Royal*. The objective was to use the old tanker as bait to draw out German E boats – extremely fast motor torpedo boats – and U-boats out from secret ports on the French and Norwegian coasts. Scruffy flying top cover was to add credence to the whole pantomime.

The scheme was a great success. The tanker was sunk, while an RAF fighter squadron attacked the deluded Germans with resounding success. The day after the mission, with MI5 having already leaked false intelligence to the Germans, the British newspapers reported the *Ark Royal's* sinking. (An interesting exception to the newspaper industry helping with matters of national security was *The Times*, who politely refused to publish a single paragraph that would help support such deceptions, because the publisher refused to insert any items of news that it did not believe to be true.)

On another occasion, John and Hughie were scrambled early one morning to fly cover for a huge convoy of ships off the east coast of England. Hughie recalled their nearly disastrous mission with typical wry humour:

> One morning John and I, after putting on our damp clothes and dousing the sleep from our eyes in our washbasins, stumbled over to breakfast. We flopped in the back of a panel truck which rattled and bumped its way to Dispersal. Norm Johnson, the Flight Commander, while writing names on the readiness board said: 'Weir and Godefroy on first readiness.' This announcement brought both of us to life. We ran out of the door to our aircraft where the riggers had dispersed them the night

*before. We taxied them back in front of Dispersal, put our helmets over the stick. Having plugged in the cord to the radio and the tube to the oxygen outlet, we hung our parachutes over the leading edge of the port wing with the straps hanging down, then ran as fast as we could for the Hut. The reason for our haste was that there were only five beds. Six pilots were on readiness. The last one in had to sleep on the floor.* [1]

*We arrived back at the Dispersal Hut at the same time, and were fighting over the last bed when the Tannoy[2] blared out, '401 Squadron Red Section scramble.' John and I bolted out still half asleep, blaspheming the controller. One minute later we were roaring across the field in formation. The controller's voice sounded quite cheerful as he gave us a vector, and his clear precise order somehow emphasized the fact that we had the sky to ourselves... Ordinarily a formation leader like John would have had a chance to get the letters of the day before taking off. These letters were changed each day and were used by pilots to identify themselves as friendly aircraft if challenged by ground or sea forces. If challenged, the formation leader was to tap the letters out in Morse code on the identification light on the belly of his aircraft... As these letters of the day were top secret, they could not be transmitted by radio as our radio transmissions were monitored by the Huns. John [had gone] airborne without them.*

*In silence we followed our vector which took us straight to the east coast and out over the sea... We must have gone about sixty miles when shapes began to appear. They were ships, hundreds of them, large and small, freighters, tankers, and large armed merchantmen. Around this enormous convoy, turning and twisting were the ever-vigilant destroyers, their guns bared suspiciously following us as we circled. It gave one an eerie feeling seeing all those ships quietly stealing through the mist... John looked over at me and said, 'Have you got them?' [The letters of the day.]*

*I shook my head. He raised his eyes to heaven. At that moment we got*

---

1 Pilots on first readiness were expected to be airborne within a minute and a half, so all of those preparations were essential. 401 Squadron's best time from lying down in Dispersal to being airborne was forty-five seconds, the fastest in the RAF at that time.
2 "Tannoy" became a household name referring to public address systems as a result of the manufacturer, Tannoy, supplying speakers and PA systems to the armed forces during the war.

> a challenging series of flashes on the Aldis [signal] light from the lead
> escort vessel. John did a gentle turn away from the convoy and gave
> them a belly side view of us, then hesitantly reached to his light key and
> tapped out a random sequence of dots and dashes.
>
> [John then] immediately raised his hands to his ears, and ducking his
> head, closed his eyes [anticipating the fireworks that were about to erupt
> around them]. Every armed ship in the convoy opened up. In an instant
> the sky was full of black puffs, and enough curving orange Bofors3 shells
> and tracers to look like the twenty-fourth of May. The escort leader was
> taking no chances and had no intention of letting us come anywhere
> near the convoy without giving the letter of the day. John had only one
> recourse. We had to fly back to Digby and get them.[4]

Scruffy was happy flying regardless of what the missions were.
Sometimes, however, his work for Adrian made him feel conspicuous
because he was so often singled out for special duty. But as the squadron
rebuilt and increasingly saw more action, on most operations a few men
would be lost; so the focus back at base was what had happened, not on
John's absence. Furthermore there was no regularity to his assignments,
which were intentionally kept erratic to avoid any discernible pattern.
John mentioned to Adrian that he occasionally got funny looks during
his frequent disappearances. Adrian's response was short and to the point:
"You know how to handle it. You are the dumbest fellow I know. So
just continue, and do not even *think* of turning down an assignment."
When you were a part of such a network, you were with it for life. So
he continued to fly special ops, and to polish his routine as the happy-
go-lucky guy who wasn't the sharpest tool in the shed.

There was virtually no down time for him. When he wasn't flying,
he was taking commando training at Achnacarry, in the west highlands
of Scotland, or travelling down to London to meet with Adrian.

He flew Hurricanes up to 40,000 feet, higher than they'd been built
to fly; he flew wearing a gas mask and other extraneous gear to test
thefeasibility of flying under those conditions. He flew aerobatic drills
demonstrations – flying circuses – all the while maintaining his position
on the squadron.

---

3    A well-known anti-aircraft gun.
4    From Hugh Godefroy.

He also took courses in special operations skills and techniques, building on the training he had received from Adrian. How to hide in plain sight. How to quickly rearrange clothing to change one's appearance. Never to glance behind yourself while moving through a city; to do so would make even the Archbishop of Canterbury look shifty. A limp could be a disguise in itself, and could be produced by tucking a small stone into your shoe. Never speak to strangers, never get drunk, and if you were stupid enough to pick up a girl (or a man) in an occupied country, then you were bloody well on your own.

Rules of war allowed that an agent who was arrested wearing civilian clothing could be considered a spy, which meant interrogation, torture, and probable execution. With this in mind, the agents were never in doubt as to the risks inherent in their vocation. They were volunteers, not conscripts, and to prepare them for what they might face, they could be dragged out of their rooms from a dead sleep, tossed into a cell, and then aggressively interrogated by two SS officers (played by instructors of the school). They learned that under such questioning, they should always stick as close as possible to the truth. The truth came cloaked in a cover story that had been developed to closely mirror the life of the agent and the experiences and places he or she had come to know. In this way, under interrogation, the agent could answer with as much ingenuous confidence as possible, buying some much needed time.

Under interrogation, the trainees were taught to speak slowly, and as they were taking their time finding their words, they should try to anticipate what questions might be coming next. Be vague by all means, but never tell an unnecessary lie. The challenge was to assume an air of befuddled innocence, maintaining a consistent story, so the interrogators were unable to trip you up with simple details. If the questioning became more brutal, there was never anything to be gained by being brave. The idea was to reveal inconsequential information so the interrogators felt they were getting something. If the pain levels increased substantially, then make some noise; let them hear you scream. It helps deal with the pain while convincing the interrogators that they are getting results. The most important skill of all, which John was learning and re-learning, was to make oneself unremarkable. That was the perfect place to be in this line of work.

Training also included more mundane skills: how to slip a lock silently, how to attract attention to yourself to be followed and then to lose the person tailing you. Blending into crowds, using soot as make up: so much of it was familiar ground he'd learned with Adrian, his father, and even Fiji from more than a decade before. He had learned how to walk and breathe silently when he was a boy; he had even learned to control his breathing so as to avoid snoring – an obvious vulnerability when sleeping out in the open. Nothing was ever to be left behind when you were on the move; any trace of fire, paper, or food had to be buried before moving on. And in dealing with the enemy, never underestimate them, and never try to short-change or cheat anyone that you might be fortunate enough to befriend. The wisdom that he was being taught was that while amateurs study tactics, professionals study logistics. Surviving was all about knowing where you were, knowing how to get what you needed, and knowing what you must do next.

---

Being so isolated, Thurso didn't have many visitors. So when an RAF officer from Adastral House appeared at the office asking for "Scruffy" Weir, "…just to say hello," John's guard went up. The men on the squadron called him by his nickname, but no one else did. Certainly not his family or any officer he'd ever met outside of the squadron's small circle. More significantly, no officer would ever be so informal, let alone travel 700 miles, to drop in and say hello. Something was wrong. He went looking for the man, and found him in the mess – an unremarkable middle-aged RAF officer, with nothing to set him apart except his misplaced sense of self-importance. He greeted John, shaking his hand and calling him Scruffy, and congratulated him on his good work spotting the vicar (and other suspicious characters that he had drawn to Adrian's attention. John listened carefully, responding with calculated deflection, but saying he had no idea what he the man was talking about. The officer said it had come to their attention that "Scruffy Weir" might be quite useful to them. John said that some mistake had been made and he started to walk away. The officer stopped him and told him it was all right. He understood that Scruffy received his instructions from a special source.

"You take your orders from Aerial."

John smiled politely, repeated that he had no idea what he was talking about, and asked the officer who he was.

"Who *you* are is the question," the officer said.

John was shaken because this stranger had used Adrian's code name, Aerial, a serious breach of security regardless of who he was. No legitimate intelligence officer would dare drop such a thing as casually as this man had. John walked away from him, leaving him standing there, and went directly to a call box on the outskirts of the base to telephone Adrian. Adrian told him in no uncertain terms that he had neither sent this man nor knew anything about him. He instructed John to have nothing more to do with him. Before he rang off, he asked where the man was now, then finished the conversation by saying they would take care of him. By the time John found his way back to the mess to have something to eat, the stranger had disappeared. John never heard another word about him. But he was now very aware of how vulnerable he had become.

---

By late spring 1941, back at strength and with the war being lost to the Germans, No. 1 RCAF Squadron – now renumbered as 401 Squadron RAF – was moved south to Digby in Lincolnshire. Here they were thrust back into the thick of the action, flying sorties day and night. John caught up with Hughie Godefroy in June that year. Hughie's transfer to 401 Squadron had been posted, and John got permission from Deane to fly down to Sutton Bridge where Hughie was completing his OTU stint. John strolled into the OTU mess just as the men were sitting down to lunch, shouting out, "Is there a P.O. Prune Godefroy here?" Hughie turned around and couldn't believe his eyes. It was a most welcome reunion. John told Hughie that they were in the same squadron and on the same flight together. In four days, Hughie would transfer down to Digby, and John told him categorically that from that point on they would be flying together. He wasn't about to trust anyone else flying on his tail as his Number Two.

At that time in the war, the life expectancy for new fighter pilots hovered at around six hours; six combat hours, but still, absurdly bad odds. Yet for the majority of pilots, the idea of being shot down never entered their heads. No one thought about dying. When Hughie arrived at Digby, John greeted him and showed him to his quarters: Hughie's was room number thirteen across the hall from John. John explained that the room had previously belonged to Paul Henderson, someone they both had known from UCC and had both liked. When Hughie asked where he'd been transferred, John said off-handedly, "He pranged himself the other day. Too bad. He was a nice guy. See you in the mess, Hughie." To prang meant to crash, more than probably killing the pilot and any crew. Hughie knew John well and was startled by how casually he had passed along the information about their friend Henderson's death. But the general thinking on the squadron – and for most that were active on the front lines – was that if someone bought it, it was best to just keep moving and not look back.

It helped Hughie that he and John flew together through the summer of 1941, with Hughie flying as his Number Two, or wing man, to John's leader. Hughie had sharp eyes and John had six months more experience flying ops, and together they became an extremely effective team. Both enjoyed the exhilarating atmosphere of an operational squadron's fraternal day-to-day life, where your job was to skate the fine line between skill and the dangerous side of luck at up to 300 miles per hour. Doing this with men you liked and trusted was just about as much fun as you could have with your flying helmet and pants on.

They loved racing into action – the mad dash to your aircraft when the siren sounded. Pilots on "first readiness" were the first to be called in a scramble. They were required to sit in the dispersal hut, dressed in full uniform, tunic, tie, flying boots, and Mae West, playing chess or bridge or darts – anything but drinking. Then the scramble would be called, and they would sprint to their planes. The ground crew started the aircraft, the men slipped on their chutes, clambered into their cockpits with the ground crew buckling them in, and they would be off. Possibly because 401 Squadron were the first Canadian fighter squadron, they prided themselves on having the fastest "scramble time" in England, an honour they held for a long time. They also had the cleanest planes with the fewest service problems. The ground crew loved their work every bit as much as the pilots, and took immense personal pride in what they considered to be "their" aircraft, immediately fixing anything that seemed to be amiss.

Wartime friendships are unlike any other.[5] A few months after Hughie was posted to the squadron, John encountered another childhood friend. He had been in the mess when someone shouted out, "Johnny!"

---

5    A common phrase in my interviews with veterans was "we were blooded together".
They considered themselves more than a band of brothers; they were blood brothers.

No one on the squadron called him Johnny, but he recognized the voice. The lanky figure approached him and he saw it was his old friend Wally Floody. They had known each other back at Sunday school in Toronto. Wally had been born in Chatham, Ontario, then moved with his parents to Toronto and attended Northern Vocational. In 1936, he headed north to Timmins to work in the mines as a mucker, as John had. And like most of the guys on 401 Squadron, Wally wasn't afraid of getting into a fight in the air; he was in the war to win. It didn't matter who was assigned to a sweep; Wally was always ready to go too.

There were new friends as well. Ian ("Ormie") Ormston met Scruffy on 401 Squadron in the early months of 1941. Another good friend, mentioned in Scruffy's journal entry of November 25, 1940, was Eugene "Jeep" Neal. Jeep had a tendency, when he got excited, to unconsciously flip back and forth between French and English (his father was Anglophone and his mother was Francophone). Jeep was shot down a half dozen times but never captured, and made it through the war with only a couple of broken bones.

Scruffy was still like a fox terrier, always in the middle of the fun and quick to make friends with new arrivals. Ironically, this was one aspect of squadron life that worried the brass: some pilots were becoming too friendly and too connected. Deane Nesbitt, Scruffy's CO, was nine years older than Scruffy, and had seen literally hundreds of pilots come and go. In that summer of 1941, Deane pulled Scruffy aside and warned him it was time for him to stop making friends. This surprised John, naturally outgoing as he was, not to mention that the squadron was really their only social circle. Deane told him that if he kept buddying up to all the new men who showed up on the squadron, then saw them killed in combat, it would eventually kill something inside John as well. Hughie, Ormie, Jeep, Wally – fair enough, those guys were his friends already. But he should ease up on new ones if he knew what was good for him.

Taken aback, Scruffy thought of the many friends, and the dozens of men whose names and faces he could now barely remember, who had joined the squadron and been killed. He had trained himself not to think about those who'd bought it, but Deane's mentioning of it had hit home. From then on, he followed Deane's advice. With each new wave of replacements, he would make a point of connecting – "Hi, nice to meet you" – and then he would go on his way. It stood him in good stead through the summer and the fall of that year. He began to focus on honing his skills and stopped trying to be everyone's pal. With so many men he'd known now missing or dead, the war felt less like a grand adventure and more like a game of last man standing. Scruffy was now truly at war.

In the following months, Scruffy continued flying special duty. Hughie usually flew as his number two, never questioning what the mission was. The amount of combat flying was increasing, flying day and night, and no one took much notice of anything other than their own sorties. The war was slowly being lost to the Germans, and the odds against the pilots surviving increased every time they scrambled and went into battle. There were a few who cracked under the pressure, and were subsequently shipped off to a "Glass House" for LMF – Lack of Moral Fibre. This was a terrifying threat to the pilots. It was worse than washing out: to be designated as LMF meant being branded as a spineless coward. Those labeled LMF became pariahs in their squadrons. The other men wanted nothing to do with you – you had become a liability. You had two choices: to be returned to Canada in disgrace (although not discharged); or to be sent to a Glass House and have it drilled out of you.

RAF command played on this notion as an intentional deterrent to pilots considering withdrawing from active duty without incontestable grounds. There was an unspoken but widespread belief among aircrew that LMF was contagious and could eat through the heart of a squadron if left unchecked.

Glass Houses were anonymous bases that dealt with airmen who had repeatedly choked in combat. The Glass House routine was one of brutal discipline: you would be awakened at five in the morning, run to the can to do what was necessary, then run to the mess for breakfast where you had five minutes to gulp your meal. Immediately afterwards you were hustled out for a 10-mile run carrying a full pack. On your return, you had to run to lunch, run to the can again, run to pack drill in the afternoon for two hours of marching, run to dinner, and then finally run to your barracks and bed, knowing the whole routine would be repeated the next morning. The objective was to drill the consciousness of fear out of the men who had seized up in action.

This grueling routine sounds sadistic, but it served an essential purpose in maintaining the structure of the flights within a combat squadron. At the beginning of the war, the RAF deployed flights of three, while the Germans were using flights of two. 401 Squadron came to the conclusion that the Germans were right: flying in "twos" – with a front man, or leader, and a wing man – each man's role was clear. But this put a great deal of pressure on pilots, knowing that their survival depended on their flight partner. Some panicked, and their panic soon grew to a gnawing terror. After taking off, they'd rattle off excuses, such as, "My oil reservoir was zero", "I ran out of gas", or "My gun panel was loose". Then they'd cut out of the formation and fly back to base, leaving their flight partner alone and exposed to attack. If a pilot pulled this more than a couple of times, he would be designated LMF and shipped off to a Glass House.

The location of these "re-training" bases was kept secret, partially in order to remove any potential contact with their squadrons. John discovered that there was a Glass House not far from where 401 Squadron was stationed. He had known some men who had been sent to one of them, and he was curious to see what they were like. He found his way to the base and approached the officer on duty at the gate, who duly gave him hell for nosing around. He warned John that if he didn't bugger off, he would report him as being "sympathetic", which meant he'd be grounded immediately. John's sympathies didn't run that deep, so he beat a hasty retreat. But word travels fast in wartime, and he received a crackling phone call from Uncle Adrian who had caught wind of John's snooping. He tore a strip off John with the warning that it was none of his damned business what went on at the Glass House or with the men who were afraid to fly, and that if he didn't have anything better to do with his time Adrian would be happy to speak to a few people who would take care of that.

The day you join the service, John told me, discipline is hammered into you. You learn to do what has to be done without asking questions. At each turn, you are taught to suppress your sense of self for the good of the whole. And while fear is hard-wired into everyone as a survival mechanism, the military seeks to short-circuit that wiring to focus on objectives and not emotions. That doesn't mean that men and women in the line of fire weren't fearful; they simply learned how to do what they had to do in spite of their feelings. Youthful bravado and ignorance are the most common balm against fear. Most soldiers and airmen simply thought they would never be the ones who would get hit; it was always going to be the other guy.

Some men psyched themselves up to deal with their nerves before heading into action. One Spitfire pilot worked himself into a lather of hate for Germans before taking to the air – in just the same manner he had worked himself up before his football games at McGill. An accomplished group of Luftwaffe pilots with whom I spoke admitted that they rarely went up in their fighters sober. The pure oxygen they breathed in their aircraft sobered them up fast enough, and once in the air they were swept up in the moment. But while on the ground, waiting to go into action, they spent much of their war with a pleasant buzz on. This made it possible for many of them to see going into combat as a kind of game, and not the daily life and death struggle that it really was. Self-delusion can be an important survival skill in some instances.

And then there were the men who were without fear. These curious beings weren't recklessly and theatrically brave, but were simply unable to recognize danger, in much the same way a colour blind person can't see colour in a normal way. One young soldier from Kamloops, Robert Laroux, was just such a person. He was a private with the Princess Patricia's Canadian Light Infantry (the PPCLI, or Princess Pat's) who was happy soldiering and never had any interest in winning medals or moving up in the ranks. He was tough and uncomplaining and lacked any sense of fear. His platoon sergeant tried to dig out of him why this was, but it was beyond Laroux to explain. He simply didn't know what fear meant or what it felt like. On patrols or in combat zones where they were being shelled and shot at, he was aware of the danger but felt no sense of anxiety or self-preservation.

While moving up the line in Italy, Laroux's platoon came to a river that they had to cross by wading or swimming. Like the other men, Laroux was carrying about ninety pounds of equipment when he went in. It was pouring rain and the river was swollen above its banks. And even though he didn't know how to swim, Laroux walked straight into the water with no sense of the dangers that the river presented. That was the last anyone saw of him until a few days later when his body washed up downstream. It had no wounds on it; it looked like he'd simply gone to sleep in the water. He had drowned because of his dedication to duty and his inability to experience fear.

Scruffy was something else again. His point of view was that if his ticket had been punched there wasn't anything he could do about it, so there was no point wasting time worrying. Youth certainly played a part in his confidence, but there was more to it than that. In the hundreds of hours of flying time that he had logged, he had come to respect the speed at which things happen when you're flying. He never stopped developing his skills; he wanted what he did when he was flying to become as automatic as breathing. From experience, he knew that was how it must be. As soon as you started worrying about what might happen when you were in action, it was probably already too late. He measured the risks he took in the same way that he had learned to find his way through a dense forest. Focus on the objective until you reach it. Don't take anything for granted. Act only on what you know. John was not blind to fear. Rather, his courage was something that he had learned; it was the use of discretion in the face of danger. Courage meant understanding the dangers and still being able to face them head on. (There were many examples of this during his civilian life as well. Friends and family remember him reacting instantly to challenges, rarely hesitating to weigh pros and cons.)

––––––––––––––––––––––––

Uncle Adrian's official wartime duties as an Air Commodore included two that were less onerous. One was overseeing the British Balloon Command (barrage balloon) defenses. These were dirigible-like affairs about fifty feet in length, inflated with helium and tethered with metal cables, and intended to serve as a defense against low-flying enemy aircraft. The second duty was one in which he took great pride: his work with Air Cadets as Second in Command (2IC) of the Air Defense Cadet Corps. Working with teenaged boys helped balance the stress of his more official work.

In the summer of 1941, the Air Cadets had gathered for their annual fête at Spalding, Lincolnshire, not far from where 401 Squadron was stationed. Adrian was to visit them, give a welcoming talk, and inspect their ranks on parade. He planned to work in a visit with John at 401's base, but it was not to be. Early in the afternoon of the first day, John received a phone call and a string of numbers. He called back and Adrian answered, telling him that "… you're going to be given an appointment tonight, but you are not to complete the rendezvous."

That evening, a flight of German bombers came on the attack, their targets on the east coast of England. Scruffy was the only pilot scrambled, with orders just to observe. He flew up to 12,000 feet and watched from a distance as the Germans came in. As instructed by Adrian, he did not engage – he did not complete the rendezvous – even though the Germans appeared to have little opposition. They dropped their bombs on their targets and then returned to the continent. The next day Uncle Adrian arrived at the base to speak to John. They went for a walk, with Adrian being uncharacteristically quiet. John gave him a report of what had happened the night before, and how frustrating it had been to keep at a distance and watch impassively. Adrian finally spoke and told him that about four hundred of his air cadets had been killed in the raid. He told John that there was nothing that he could have done to prevent it, and he was glad John had understood his message not to get involved. English intelligence had intercepted and cracked German coded messages about the raid, and so the RAF knew when and roughly where it was likely to happen. Had the bombing raid been intercepted, it would have tipped off the Luftwaffe that their secure communications had been breached. It was essential to keep the transmission of coded messages flowing, even when it meant putting lives at risk. No one had anticipated the Air Cadet's fête being in harm's way; and it was improbable that a single aircraft could have done anything of any significance in their defense. But Adrian had been adamant, and knew John would follow orders without question.

Having intelligence such as advance notice of the German raid, without having the ability to act on it, haunted John. He considered requesting a transfer from the squadron to the Merchant Marine, which was recruiting pilots to fly Hurricanes off armed merchantmen. Merchant ships were essential in maintaining the supply line from North America to Britain, but even with defensive guns and sailing in convoys they were extremely vulnerable to attack from the air. The solution that was created was to mount a giant catapult amidships. If the ship were attacked, the catapult would launch a single Hurricane fighter to engage the enemy. It was an effective defensive measure, but once the fighter had exhausted its fuel, it had to ditch in the ocean, and the pilot along with it. John felt that his piloting skills might be very useful in such a capacity, not to mention that he would be back and forth between Canada and Britain every few weeks. Perhaps Fran might even be able to come down and meet him. But by this point, John was a senior man on the squadron and badly needed there. He stayed with 401.

By September 1941, the squadron had been re-equipped with Spitfires, which had come into their own as the premier combat aircraft of the RAF. They were much faster than the Hurricanes and about equal in speed to the German Messerschmitt. But a Spit could almost always out-turn a Messerschmitt 109, which usually flipped if it tried to match the Spit's aerobatic agility. The Spitfire could fly up to 30,000 feet, but Scruffy and Hughie usually flew between 24,000 and 25,000 feet. John explained to me that the Messerschmitt had a two stage turbo-charged engine that cut in at high altitudes – between 24,000 and 25,000 feet – and made them faster when they were flying at heights where there was less oxygen. But this feature also offered an advantage for the British pilots. When the Messerschmitt's supercharger engaged, there was a momentary loss of power (and a telltale puff of black smoke), which made them vulnerable for a few seconds. So hovering between 24,000 and 25,000 feet, Spitfire pilots could force the 109s into stalling for an invaluable moment and then strike. This let the Spits get more of the ME-109s than the Hun got in return.

Scruffy, Hughie, and their friends on the squadron had become veteran combat pilots by the simple virtue of having survived long enough. The more experienced pilots were moved into separate flights to break in the new arrivals, but that had the result of weakening the teamwork that had developed among the men. The losses were mounting, and at times the squadron seemed barely to be holding its own. The reality was that they were living a charmed existence in the face of the high casualty rate that was the lot of fighter pilots. It was no longer a question of *if* you might get it; it was now a matter of *when*. Acquiring experience flying in combat at that time in the war depended a great deal on blind luck. The RAF was so short of pilots that young, inexperienced men were constantly being brought on to the squadron as replacements to keep manpower at strength. The first time they scrambled, many had never flown in formation with the veteran pilots, let alone in combat. All that could be done was to tell them, "Keep an eye on your tail and keep an eye on my tail." Experienced pilots like Scruffy and Hughie knew that most of the newbies didn't stand a chance, being so desperately inexperienced. John had his wing man killed on the pilot's first combat flight with the squadron. The irony was the longer you flew unscathed, the steeper the odds were against you. It was simply a matter of time until you got hit.

Scruffy had accumulated four hundred plus hours of operational flight time by October 1941, and undertaken something over a hundred special operations above and beyond his logged flight time. RAF HQ in the person of Uncle Adrian felt that he'd been too lucky – which in fact was the case – and that the odds were running against him now. Adrian summoned John to London to discuss his flying career. He told him it was time to transfer out of 401 Squadron, and as it happened he had another assignment he wanted John to take on.

John refused, the one thing he'd sworn not to do. His argument was that the squadron needed him now, as they were already so desperately short handed. He was Flight Leader, Hughie had been transferred to a different flight, and the squadron was having to spread its ranks extremely thin to cover their losses and fully man all the aircraft. The RAF was beginning to get a foothold against the Luftwaffe that fall, but 401 Squadron was still getting badly hammered, flying daily missions out of Biggin Hill airfield southeast of London where they were now posted. Adrian listened, but was unmoved. He explained to John that it wasn't just his unreasonable number of flight hours. He was also the common thread linking him to five German agents who had been arrested, agents John had identified. Sooner or later someone would connect the dots and John would have his own accident. He had been too busy and wrapped up in the work of the squadron to be thinking about the repercussions of his "spy catching" work. Still, John was reluctant. Adrian challenged him, asking if he felt he was irreplaceable, or if he was actually refusing. John acknowledged that if Adrian ordered him, he would transfer. And that was the end of the discussion. Adrian told John to report to Adastral House for assessment pending reassignment.

With deep regret, John left the squadron and reported to Adastral House. John had good French and German, which he would need for the new assignment. Furthermore he had extensive training in special operations, making him an ideal candidate for re-deployment. There were going to be nine agents parachuted in to North Africa, all dropped in individually, but working towards a common objective. John would be briefed with his specific assignment once he had met with the handlers at Adastral House.

Once there, he was subjected to a battery of tests. His field skills were tested, as well as his fitness level, his ability to navigate interrogation, and his fluency with languages. At the end of five days, he received outstanding reports in all areas apart from his languages. Both the French and German assessors reported that he was more than adept in their respective tongues, but that his accent was laughable and the odds were that he would be picked up right away if he tried to pass himself off as a local in any French or German speaking country. Two days later, he received a curt message from Adrian: "The party's off."

The mission went forward, and within the month all eight agents were dead. Their circuit hadn't been broken. There was just something about the way they dressed, or walked, or acted that caught the Germans' attention. In the early years of the intelligence war, it was these small telltale errors in judgment that got an agent killed. Agents from North America were particularly susceptible in this regard, as were the well-fed outdoorsmen typically recruited by the SOE. They lacked the pale, drawn look of someone in an occupied, food-scarce country. Scruffy was confident in his survival skills, but was acutely aware that he wouldn't have fared any better than the other unfortunate eight. He simply hadn't understood what the real dangers were.

This episode behind him, Scruffy was thrilled to get back to the Squadron and back to doing what he knew best. The squadron was off balance, though. Ormie and Jeep were on leave when he rejoined, Wally Floody had been shot down a couple of days earlier, and Hughie had been transferred to another flight. This meant that Scruffy found himself flying with replacements without a fraction of the combat hours he himself had flown. In that first week of November 1941, the squadron lost ten pilots out of twelve, and was losing new pilots as fast as they could replace them. The squadron was practically all newcomers, and it made Scruffy nervous.

## Chapter 12

# STRANGER IN A STRANGE LAND

On November 8th, 1941, Hughie, now in "B" Flight, returned from an exhausting dogfight over the Thames Estuary. Discouraged and weary, he turned in his kit and reported to the IO, who informed him that Scruffy had gone missing. Hughie was devastated. Many years later, thinking back on those days, he said,

> *I never worried about John. He was always there, always had been there since school. He had spent a good part of his life trying to keep me out of trouble. I thought of how we used to meet at 5:30 every Saturday morning at the streetcar stop with our hockey sticks and skates over our shoulder on our way to play hockey. Half the time, he would forget his shin pads, but would play anyway. Tough as nails and a perpetual clown. I can see him catching that pass I was supposed to throw to somebody else in a football game against St. Andrew's, and how he ran zigzag all around the field with half the St. Andrew's football team after him while he avoided their tackles with little bursts of speed. It seemed impossible. He was too fast; they couldn't have got him.*

Now he could picture John's mother Freda, and Fran, now John's fiancée, re-reading the telegram they would be getting in a day or so: "We regret to inform you that Flying Officer John Weir was reported missing in action over enemy territory." Hughie wrote the Weirs a letter, even though he couldn't think of anything useful to say. He kept hearing Colonel Weir's voice in his head: "Okay, Hughie, just give us the facts and forget the trimming." He went through the next few days in a fog. Air Commodore Chamier contacted him after about a week and invited Hughie to dinner in London and to spend the night. Hughie went through the dreadful task of pulling John's things together to send home. He knew that some of the more personal correspondence might make it past the censors if it was sent with Uncle Adrian's assistance.

Adrian met Hughie at Victoria Station, and they rode in a cab back to the Chamier flat in silence. Once inside, with a large whisky in hand, Hughie blurted out what little he knew about what had happened. Adrian listened in silence. Spotting the bag with "F/O JOHN. G. WEIR" printed on the side, Adrian asked, "Do you want me to take that?" Hughie gratefully passed it to him, glad that he wouldn't have the painful task of sending it home to Toronto.

On Saturday November 8th, a few days before Hughie met with Adrian, Scruffy was flying sweeps over Abbeville in Normandy with a young pilot freshly attached to the squadron. This was a dangerous mission: Abbeville was one of the main Luftwaffe bases along the northern coast of France, with as many as a thousand fighters stationed there. Scruffy was trying to keep an eye on his wing man who was new to flying in "twos" – two planes flying as a fighting unit – and this was worrying him sick. Would this guy know what to do when they were attacked? It's the wing man's responsibility to watch his Flight Leader's back as well as his own, and as Flight Leader, Scruffy's responsibility was to keep his eyes peeled for enemy aircraft in the sky ahead. But he kept glancing back at his new partner, Gardner, double-checking to see if he was in position. He should have been paying full attention to what was going on in front of him.[1]

A flight of Messerschmitts appeared in the blue haze silhouetted by the sun behind them. Scruffy glanced back to check that Gardner was in position, and when he looked forward again the Krauts had already swung up and around. They attacked from behind, and Scruffy and Gardner were trapped. Everything happened so fast John didn't have time to think. He heard Gardner scream, and a split-second later an ME-109's cannon blew John's wing off, and then raked his instrument panel with machine gun fire, ripping out the panel and piercing his upper fuel tank. Luck was with him, after a fashion, in that his tank was full, so it didn't explode, but merely caught fire.[2] The gas sprayed

1  John ruefully called his actions "nurse-maiding" this new man. He made a point of saying to me that his attention should have been focussed ahead, and not worrying about Gardner, the Sergeant Pilot flying as his wing man.
2  A full gas tank burns, while a partly empty tank will explode.

back into the cockpit and over Scruffy, then erupted into a merciless fire that enveloped him and the cockpit. All of this occurred in about seven seconds.

John described to me what happened next.

> *My plane began to spin out of control. I slid back the canopy, my battle tunic, gloves and helmet on fire and, at 26,000 feet, I bailed out. I knew I had to be very careful with my breathing. Hughie and I had talked through what would happen if you were hit and there was fire in the cockpit. If you gasped for air, you would breathe in raw oxygen and gasoline into your lungs. So the thing you must not do was to take a big breath; you'd be dead in seconds. We decided that if you got into trouble, you should hold your breath and then get out of the aircraft as fast as you bloody well could.*

Pilots were advised not to pull the ripcord on their parachute right away for fear of the chute deploying and becoming entangled with the falling aircraft. But John was frantically pummelling at flames that were incinerating his uniform and he was afraid of losing consciousness, so he pulled his ripcord the moment he bailed out. He cracked his head against the Spitfire's tail fin as he tumbled out of the fiery aircraft. A pistol that he kept tucked into his left boot was lost when his parachute popped open and the slipstream and sudden jolt ripped both boots off.

At 26,000 feet the air is extremely thin, and more pilots jumping at such heights died than survived, asphyxiated from hypoxia. This is a condition in which the body is deprived of adequate oxygen supply, causing unconsciousness and often death. Scruffy had gone through special operations training, including numerous high altitude parachute jumps. During that training it had been determined that he had a slow heartbeat and a very low metabolic rate, which required less oxygen than was common for a young man his age. Still, hypoxia would have been rapidly impacting him moments after his parachute had deployed, and he would have been dangerously close to blacking out. But his body was likely adrenalized from his extensive burns and other injuries, and that is quite possibly what kept him conscious and breathing.

John had had jump experience, so he wasn't overly panicked. He held his breath for as long as he could to get clear of the flames, and then started to breathe very slowly. He used all his strength to focus on controlling his breath and to remain conscious.

For a man of Scruffy's height and weight, falling in a standard RAF parachute from that height would have taken a very long time before landing. He was later told that it took between 20 to 25 minutes for him to touch down. Airmen that I've spoken to who have fallen from heights of only 12,000 to 15,000 feet described their experience as hallucinatory, almost surreal, certainly in part due to the oxygen deficit. What was most curious, John told me, was that at about a thousand feet he started to hear noises: a rooster crowing, a dog barking, on top of a disorienting silence. He realized he had been hurt in one way or another, but he felt no pain; only a sense of there being a lot of heat coming from somewhere.

At about 500 feet he began to hear two men talking in the field below, and he watched them watching him come down. He had some small sense of where he was – about 20 miles southwest of Caen – and thought with a bit of luck he could make it west to Dinard in Brittany, where he had been at school a few years earlier.

When he landed, he landed hard, his uniform in tatters, bootless, battered, and badly burned. He immediately set about burying his parachute as he knew the Germans would have seen him coming down and would already be on the hunt for him. If he had any hope of escaping capture, he had to get moving as soon as possible. Airmen had been warned that if they were shot down behind enemy lines to never approach two or more civilians. If you needed help, try and find someone who is on their own. You were advised to try and stay away from main roads and away from houses and villages.

The two men he had heard talking walked towards him. They looked as though they were farmers and seemed harmless enough, but you couldn't be sure so he decided to keep his distance. As they approached he gave them a simple, "Bon jour," trying to look as nonchalant as possible given his ragged state, and started walking in what he hoped was the right direction for Brittany.

As he walked, he checked himself over. He knew he had suffered some burns in the cockpit fire, but he didn't feel any discomfort, which was good news. His eyes felt like they had dust in them and he had to squint to see anything in the bright midday sun. And his hands were sensitive, and felt like he had scraped them down a brick wall. But he'd felt worse before, so he kept moving.

After about twenty minutes, a lone figure appeared on the road walking towards him. That morning, John had been given the Maquis 'call words' for the day for the day as part of his briefing.[3] He gave the man the phrase and saw recognition register in his eyes. Now they knew they could trust one another.

The stranger agreed to help. He told John to keep heading west on the road he was on, and not to stop for anything or let anyone see him if he could avoid it. He said he would catch up with John shortly with something for him to wear. It was early November and John had already been walking in his stocking feet for some time; but fortunately it had been a mild autumn so far and his feet weren't too sore or cold. After about 30 minutes, the man returned riding a bicycle. He brought with him civilian clothes and shoes for John, which he changed into them gratefully. His uniform had been largely burned off, and there was little left of it. He removed the remnants and handed them to the resistance man, who promised to get rid of them.[4]

He looked at John, then asked him how well he was able to see. John admitted he was having the devil of a time doing so. If he tilted his head back and squinted he could make out blurry shapes, but the bright sun was making it hard to focus on much of anything else.

What the man could see was that John's eyelashes and eyebrows had been burned off. He had been wearing his flight helmet, which protected the top of his head, but left a distinct outline contrasting where the skin that had been covered and the skin that had been exposed and burned so badly in the fire. What was left of his eyelids were blackened and virtually fused closed from the flames, and the skin across his face and neck had been scorched a blistering red. With the deceptive comfort of shock and in his haste to get moving, he had not given much thought to his injuries. He put his fingers to his face, but his seared fingers had lost any sense of touch. The sympathetic but pragmatic Frenchman led Scruffy to a stump and sat him down. He told him frankly that there was nothing he could do for him:

3    The Maquis were French resistance fighters in the rural areas of occupied France. Call words were codes used to identify members to one another, and were changed daily. These were casual phrases, typically a remark that could be worked into a sentence quite easily. That day, the call words Scruffy had been given were, "Where is the British captain?"
4    Three years after the war, the Maquis fighter wrote to John in Canada and included a pen that had been in John's uniform. He apologized and said he had had to burn the uniform, but thought he might like the pen back. John tried to get back in contact with him, but without success.

"Je suis désolé, mais je ne peux pas vous aider. Vous êtes aveugle."[5]

He told John that the only sensible option now would be to wait for the Germans who were bound to be coming along shortly looking for him. They could give him the medical attention he badly needed. Expressing his regrets, the man rode away on his bike.

A few minutes later, a patrol of German soldiers with dogs arrived. They had been tracking John since his plane had been shot down. "For you, the war is over," a sergeant smirked at him. (Even as early as 1941, this phrase had become a smug cliché of the conquering Germans, as they went from strength to strength rolling across Europe.)

He was escorted to a nearby Luftwaffe squadron barracks for a brief interrogation. Its brevity was due in large part to his unsettling appearance: ghoulishly blackened slits where his eyelids had once been, much of his facial hair reduced to charred wisps, and the skin on his face and neck red and puckered from the flames. These were the kinds of injuries that airmen feared most, and they undoubtedly induced some professional sympathy from the German flyers.

---

He was sent to a hospital in the small city of Saint-Omer in Nord-Pas-de-Calais for treatment. The hospital was spartan and ill equipped, and the resources for dealing with injuries like John's were minimal at best. Without anesthetic, disinfectant, or antibiotics such as penicillin (then still an experimental drug), Scruffy began to appreciate just how serious his injuries were. A pilot from his squadron, Brian Hodgkinson, who had been shot down on October 27th (the same day as Wally Floody) was also in the hospital. He later recalled seeing John with his head swathed in bandages. When the bandages were removed, he said,

> *[John's head] was swollen to at least three times its normal size, and so puffed up and inflated were the cheeks and forehead, bloated with poison and pus, that the poor soul's eyes were barely visible... his mouth was no more than a slightly flexible gash, which you couldn't have thought capable of forming the sounds of the language... [his cheeks were]... so bulbous [that] they protruded beyond the tip of the nose.*[6]

---

5   "I am sorry, but I cannot help you. You are blind."
6   Hodgkinson, Brian. *Spitfire Down: The POW Story.* Edited by George E. Condon. Newcastle ON: Penumbra Press, 2000, pp. 36, 63.

Hodgkinson didn't realize it was Scruffy Weir, but John recognized Hodgkinson's voice and called out, "Hodge! It's Scruffy! Don't you recognize me?"

He hadn't, and was deeply shaken for months afterwards by seeing the condition John was in. The German doctors, having precious little to work with, improvised a burn salve by mixing boric acid with petroleum jelly. First thing in the morning they smeared this mixture over his face, neck, and hands, and then bandaged him up. Having this applied was very painful, but once on it was cooling and provided some relief. It was when the bandages were removed and air hit the raw flesh that the pain became excruciating. His skin would peel off like so many layers of tissue paper. He felt like he was being flayed alive, yet he didn't have even as much as an aspirin to take the edge off the sensation. This rudimentary treatment went on for two long months until new skin had regenerated, and the danger of infection had passed.

John remembered those first few weeks.

> I was blind [in the hospital], so all I could go by was feel, which probably magnified things. But there was this other fellow, Hodgkinson, who was terribly burned in the crotch and couldn't walk. So I used to carry him on my back since he could see, and together we could get around.
>
> When I got some sight back, the greatest shock to me was the fellow that was the most gentle of all the bandage removers and had a deep, deep voice, I pictured him as being a heavy-set short guy and he was about 6' 6" and built like a gorilla, and hands, huge hands, and yet he was most gentle. I don't remember his name or anything. It was quite a revelation. I got all these preconceived ideas [when I was blind].

> One day the Germans decided they would see if I was blind or not. They came in and got my eyes open. I could only see a blur, but the doctor must have seen the pupils move so he knew that I wasn't blind. That's when they decided to ship me off to Dulag Luft for interrogation.

In January 1942, Scruffy was transferred to Luftwaffe Dulag Luft just outside Frankfurt-am-Main. This was a transit camp for Allied POWs where virtually all captured Allied airmen were sent for processing and interrogation before being assigned to a POW camp. More significantly, Dulag Luft was a collection centre for the massive amounts of information extracted from those men in seemingly innocuous fragments. Skilled interrogators would meet all the new arrivals, gently and obliquely extracting bits and pieces from them – details of the planes their squadrons were flying, radio frequencies being used, maybe a useful name or two – most often in the context of friendly and casual conversations. Through a relentless sifting of details and fragments of intelligence, the Germans gathered a staggering amount of information, which they carefully reassembled into a vast canvas of the Allied air war effort.

One RCAF Spitfire pilot was having a chat with an interrogator, who mentioned that the pilot's squadron was being moved to Sutton Bridge; he then named the commanding officer and where he'd trained. The pilot smiled at this ham-fisted attempt to draw him out. He shook his head and said, "I don't know where you heard that stuff, but it's wrong." The interrogator said, "No, it's all quite true," and produced a copy of the previous day's *Toronto Star* that mentioned this news in a small article. Then the interrogator went on to give the pilot a verbal travelogue of his movements from the day he enlisted two years earlier to the day he was shot down. The stunned pilot later said, "He knew more about me than my mother..."

Although it eventually became more elaborate than other POW camps, Dulag Luft's appearance was unprepossessing: low slung wooden barrack-style buildings, with twelve foot high barbed wire fences that enclosed the grounds. The Germans knew the Allies would never bomb the camp as long as it could be identified from the air, so there were large white rocks that spanned the length of the front lawn forming the words PRISONER OF WAR CAMP. The same identification was painted in white letters across the roof of most buildings, thus ensuring that the acquisition of information could continue without fear of interruption.

The welcoming committee at Dulag Luft was a combination of Gestapo and intelligence officers. The captured airmen would first be submitted to basic questioning – name, rank, and serial number – and then were placed in solitary confinement, typically for one to two weeks. While the Geneva Convention forbade torture, the Germans did have ways of softening up their guests. One of the more popular methods was to keep a man in his cell all day and night, a space about four feet by seven, with nothing in it but a bunk, perhaps one small sealed window, and a huge radiator. Food and drink were slid in through a trap in the door twice a day – usually dinner was something resembling vegetable mush soup, with an occasional piece of black bread (frequently padded out with sawdust), and an unforgettable ersatz coffee made of burnt barley and other odds and ends such as acorns. It tasted terrible, but at least it was warm and provided water. You were escorted to the toilet twice a day.

The softening up process began while in solitary. The radiator would be turned off until the temperature dropped and the occupant was left shivering beneath a single thin blanket. Then the rad would be cranked up again and the cell would heat up like a sauna, off, on, off, on, for a seemingly endless number of days. While it might be argued by the Germans that this was merely inefficient climate control, more than one POW found himself wondering if he was going to be spending the rest of the war flip-flopping between shivers and sweat in his small cell. During this softening up period, each prisoner was carefully observed to discover his habits, likes and dislikes, and his ability and inclination to resist. Accordingly, a suitable method of interrogation was determined, and the administrative machinery was set in motion to break down the prisoner's mental resistance in the shortest possible time. If he showed signs of fright or nervousness, he was threatened with all kinds of physical torture, some of which were carried out, typically very roughly. Others were bribed with the offer of luxuries: clean clothes, better living quarters, decent food, and plenty of cigarettes, exchanged for answers to particular questions. Those who could neither be swayed nor bribed were treated with respect, but were made to suffer long miserable hours of solitary confinement in the cells.[7]

The interrogators were very inquisitive with John but didn't manhandle him as much as they might have, possibly because of how wretched he looked. He offered them his name, rank, and serial number, but they already knew he was Flying Officer John Gordon Weir of 401 Squadron based at Biggin Hill, who had been born and raised in Toronto, Canada. No mention was made of his "spy catching" work in England with Adrian, for which he was thankful. He remembered Adrian's admonition about having drawn attention to himself by openly identifying the German spy at Castletown. He realized that there was every possibility they were aware of this and were simply biding their

---

7    Some of this description is echoed in the book *Kriegie*, by Kenneth W. Simmons, although Mr. Simmons was at Dulag several years after John.

time until he slipped up. He resolved to follow Adrian's advice—to keep his mouth shut and act as dumb as a stone fence.

Having visited Frankfurt several times before the war and being familiar with the city, he might have thought seriously about trying to escape if he had been able to see properly or had full use of his hands.

But he was in no shape to do anything of the kind.

John receiving his Wings at Camp Borden, June 1940.

John and Fran in the backyard of the Weir home on Forest Hill Road, September 1940.

John with his father Gordon in the rear of the Weir home on Forest Hill Road, shortly after John received his wings.

A Fairey Battle, one of the outdated aircraft that John flew at RCAF Base Trenton. This was the aircraft in which John made a very hard landing with his pal Paul Phelan bouncing around in the rear seat.

The Harvard MK II that John flew during his initial training at Base Borden in 1940.

Harvard aircraft on the tarmac at Base Borden, with a Fairey Battle in the foreground.

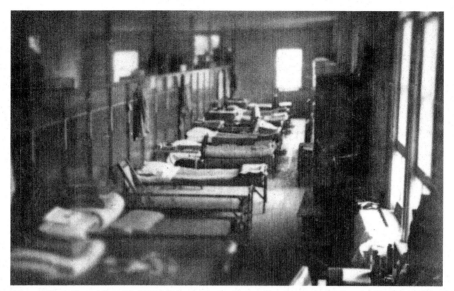

Pilot Officer Provisionals' (POPs') barracks at Camp Borden, to which John went dashing back while AWOL after lingering too long with Fran one evening in Toronto during the spring of 1940.

The Toronto Hunt Club on Avenue Road, located two blocks north of Eglinton, shortly before the RCAF transformed it into BCATP No. 1 ITS.

Vapour trails from a dogfight over the English Channel, 1940.

A photo taken by John of Tower Bridge in the mist during a week's leave in London shortly after his arrival at the end of October 1940.

The POPs' temporary (and very cold) living quarters on Salisbury Plain, November 1940.

Geoff Marlow (far left), the pilot who invited his girl to London for a weekend. He's in the pilot's seat with his crew in their Lancaster bomber during a mission over Germany.

A Hurricane with enemy machine gun damage on the forward edge of its wing.

Hank Sprague of 401 Squadron, Salisbury Plain, November 1940. Hank was shot down a year later on November 7, 1941, the day before John. They reconnected in Stalag Luft III, and survived the gruelling Winter March together.

John in front of his sleeping quarters on Salisbury Plain, November 1940.

Jack Pattison and John in front of John's Hurricane in Prestwick,
Scotland, November 1940.

A diagram of a ME-109 that was
displayed in 401 Squadron's quarters to
highlight the aircraft's vulnerabilities.

Castletown Station RAF, Castletown, Scotland, January–February 1941.

Squadron Leader Deane Nesbitt, Commanding Officer of 401 Squadron, in his Hurricane.

A Junkers 88 (JU-88), the type of aircraft that "Weather Willy" flew over Scapa Flow in January 1941.

A plane crashes and explodes on take-off during a "circuits and bumps" training exercise.

The fragments left after a plane dove nose first into the ground.

HMS Ark Royal 1941, the ship that John thought he was flying cover for during a secret mission for Uncle Adrian's intelligence network.

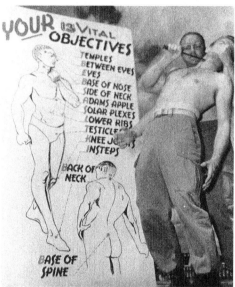

SOE hand to hand combat training exercise, highlighting vital objectives for disabling and killing an enemy.

Hughie Godefroy, John's best friend at home and on the squadron, Digby, summer 1941.

Jeep Neal (left) and Ian Ormston, Digby, 1941.

Jeep Neal.

Wally Floody at RAF Station Biggin Hill, October 1941. He was shot down a couple of weeks later on October 27th.

Hank Sprague at Biggin Hill, October 23rd, 1941, two weeks before he was shot down.

A barrage balloon being wrestled into position by two servicewomen.

Scruffy on First Readiness,
mugging for the camera.

401 Squadron scrambling
into action in Prestwick,
Scotland, 1940.

John holding up someone's
sketch of a pin-up girl
(artist unknown), waiting
to be called into Readiness
(standing by to go into
action), spring 1941.

Hughie Godefroy in his
Hurricane II, summer 1941.

401 Squadron on First Readiness at RAF Station Digby, April 8, 1941. John can be seen smiling at the camera, centre. The men wear all their flying gear to be ready to sprint to their planes when the call to action comes. Being on First Readiness typically meant long hours of tedium, broken by frantic minutes of adrenaline and raw nerves.

John's snapshot of a Spitfire VB, the latest model of that iconic fighter, which 401 Squadron was equipped with in September 1941.

John doing a handstand on the forward edge of his Hurricane's wing, RAF Station Digby, April 1941.

401 Squadron Spitfires flying in formation over RAF Station Digby, Summer 1941.

Pilots scramble into action.

ME-109s flying in formation. This is the type of fighter aircraft that shot down Scruffy and his wing man on November 8, 1941.

The port city of Stettin, Germany (now Szczecin, Poland), where John sought refuge in a brothel after his escape from the POW train taking him to Stalag Luft III.

Gestapo officers, much like the officer John and Michael had their run in with during their escape attempt in Stettin.

Members of the Maquis in La Tresorerie, near Boulogne-sur-Mer, France.

Dulag Luft, the Nazi interrogation camp for Allied airmen outside of Frankfurt.

*Photograph courtesy of the US National Archives.*

Chapter 13

# EVADER

After a week John was taken from his cell and herded onto a truck with no information about where he was going. He and a few dozen other weary prisoners were driven to a train station and escorted onto railway cars, becoming a part of the increasingly efficient machine that dealt with enemies of the Fatherland. The train's destination was Stalag Luft I[1], a dilapidated POW camp outside of Barth, Pomerania, on the Baltic Sea in the north of Germany. By the end of January 1942, there were about 1,000 men in the camp – half officers and half non-coms.[2] John was catalogued as "Kriegie" number 715, Kriegie being the nickname the prisoners coined from their official German designation as "Kriegsgefangener" – literally, war-prisoner. The prisoners referred to the German guards as "goons," which puzzled them. When asked, the POWs were inclined to explain that it was a simple acronym for "GERMAN OFFICER OR NON-COM", which they apparently believed and happily accepted, even occasionally referring to themselves as goons, to the delight of the POWs. What the boys had in mind, of course, was Alice the Goon, the oddly proportioned, hirsute, and unintelligible creature from Popeye cartoons.

Stalag Luft I had been built quickly, like all other German POW camps at that point in the war. The huts were constructed roughly

---

1    Hermann Göring was Hitler's Deputy Fuhrer and the head of the German Luftwaffe, or air force. He believed that there was a tradition of dignity in the air force, and therefore POW camps housing airmen should not be under the aegis of the SS or Gestapo, whom he viewed as brutal thugs. His pride in the air force led him to create a system of camps designated expressly for air force personnel, and therefore solely under his control. He named these "Stalag Luft" (air force camp) and Oflag Luft (air force officer camp). ("Dulag Luft" means air force transit camp.) At this point in the war, John is on his way to Stalag Luft 1, the first of these POW camps designated for airmen.
2    A non-com is a non-commissioned officer, someone holding the rank of Sergeant or below. A commission, earned through promotion, courses and training, is what defines an airman or a soldier as an officer.

and cheaply. There 15 and 20 rooms in each hut, and each room accommodated nine men in three triple-decker bunks. As the war progressed, the Germans managed to squeeze in twelve men to a room. The cottage-like buildings were raised off the ground so the goons could search underneath. The huts had no insulation to speak of, and the temperature was usually much the same inside as out, apart from the modest heat provided by a smallish pot bellied stove. The prisoners were supplied with a small amount of crushed powdered coal each day, which they would eke out as long as possible. As one of the early arrivals, John found that the rooms weren't crowded to overflowing, as they would become in the last year of the war. He was assigned to a nine-bunk room with four other flyers. To his great delight, his old friend Wally Floody was one of them. This was the first he knew that Wally was still alive and breathing. The others were Hank Birkland from Calgary, "Pop" Collett from New Zealand, and Zbischek Gotowski, a Polish air force officer. A couple of weeks later they were joined by Jens Müller, a Norwegian pilot who had trained in Canada at Little Norway, a Royal Norwegian Air Force training camp then located on Toronto's waterfront.[3]

Barth was potato country, and so their diet at Stalag Luft I relied heavily on that starch for every meal, supplemented by watery turnip soup, black bread, and a dab of a margarine-like substance. The men were also given a drink called "surface beer," which was skimmed from the top of commercial brewing vats and given to pigs and other livestock. And to the men in Stalag Luft I. Surface beer contained very little alcohol – between 1 and 2 per cent – and the Englishmen wouldn't drink it. But it also contained small amounts of yeast and malt, and the four Canadians and one Pole in John's room knew the value of anything that might give them some protein. So they took the whole block's ration and "drank and drank and drank". You couldn't get drunk on it, John told me; you'd just pee your brains out, but it was a good flushing for the system and provided a minute amount of nutrition.

The men were also given German newspapers, which John read carefully in an attempt to polish his German. Once read, the papers were carefully collected and used for an entirely different purpose. It was a cold winter, so John and the others managed to make starch glue

---

3     Later in the war, Little Norway was relocated to Gravenhurst, Ontario, where there is now a memorial to the pilots trained there.

from their staple diet of potatoes. They used the ones that had gone bad for the glue, and then lined their uninsulated walls with newspapers plastered on with the potato paste. Theirs was soon the warmest room in the hut. So they were comfortable – hungry, but comfortable – and probably used a lot less energy trying to keep warm than the others. It didn't take long for the rest of the prisoners to pick up on this neat trick.

Escape committees at Stalag Luft I were in full swing in early 1942. It was a good place from which to attempt a break, close to the coast. If you managed to steal a fishing boat, it would be possible to make it the hundred or so miles across the Baltic to Denmark. There was a double perimeter fence enclosing tangles of barbed wire laid on the ground, and guard towers on at regular intervals. Guards with dogs patrolled on foot day and night. An Escape Committee was already in place and had determined that tunnelling was the only feasible way to make it out. The problem was that the tunnels were collapsing as fast as they were dug. Being so close to the sea, the soil was all sand and the water table was barely six feet down. There was constant flooding, and they were essentially trying to tunnel through mud. Wally, Hank Birkland, and Scruffy had all worked in mines in Northern Ontario, and talked about how the tunnelling could be improved using the basic techniques they had learned.[4]

A meeting of the camp's Escape Committee was called. These committees were integral to life in a POW camp, and would provide information, supplies, and support if they felt that someone had a plan that was workable. Although he was in no shape to escape, Scruffy had been invited (along with Wally and Hank) to this meeting. This struck him as odd at the time, because he was a newcomer to the camp. Usually such meetings were only for familiar and established faces.

At these meetings, everyone was expected to contribute whatever skills, ideas, or information they possessed. Wally was going to raise some questions about the tunnelling, but the opportunity never came up. The discussion that evening focussed on rumours that they were going to be moved to another camp. Stalag Luft I had been opened in November 1941 as a British officer POW camp, but was quickly becoming overcrowded. Word had it that the Germans had built a

4    A recent publication about the Great Escape erroneously suggests that John was digging tunnels while he was interned at Stalag Luft 1. John made it clear that doing anything of the sort was impossible because of his badly burned hands – he couldn't grip anything with any strength – as well as the bitterly cold weather, and the unstable wet and sandy soil.

new escape-proof camp near the Polish border in Silesia. The isolated location alone would be a prime factor in discouraging escape attempts.[5] Security at Stalag Luft I had become extremely rigorous, fueling the rumours of changes coming. The general opinion was that they would be shipped by train south from Barth to the port of Stettin and then on to Berlin before turning east towards the Polish frontier.

The Committee pored over a map of Stettin and its surrounding area. Located on the Baltic, it would be the last opportunity to escape into a port city, and with some luck, find a ship with a sympathetic crew. Travelling by train meant less security and more opportunities to make a break. Ideas and information were pooled. Someone knew the rail routes well. He described how at the first station south of Stettin the train had to climb a rise, which forced it to slow down. This would be the best place to jump, but no one knew what kind of security there would be on the train, let alone how difficult it would be to walk into Stettin in the dead of winter without being picked up. Listening quietly in the corner, Scruffy memorized the details of the map and the other fragments of information he heard tossed around. Even though the burns on his hands and face hadn't fully healed, and his eyes without their lids were sensitive to light and cold, he was determined to try an escape.

The move came the next day, sooner than anyone had anticipated. Hundreds of RAF and Fleet Air Arm officers were told to collect their belongings, then marched to the train station on the outskirts of Barth. In the rush to pull their stuff together and to dress for the winter weather, talk of escape was forgotten. Dark had fallen by the time they were loaded on to the cars, and by 11:00 pm that night surviving the logistics of the trip to the new eastern frontier of Germany was all anyone was

---

5   For hundreds of years, the concept of prisoners of war escaping had something of disgrace associated with it. There was a general feeling amongst professional soldiers that personal surrender in wartime was a dishonourable action, and that even to be captured could be regarded as being a disgrace. As with so much else, the Second World War dramatically revised the accepted preconceptions of what it meant to go to war. Just as high explosive shells in the First World War had removed some of the stigma of being wounded in the back (which historically as something that only happened to cowards attempting to flee), in WWII the rapid evolution of the air war and such revolutionary strategies as the German Blitzkrieg transformed the shame of being captured into something much more like regrettable misfortune. And with that shift of perception and opinion, the brightest and most resourceful young PoWs of Stalag Luft I and Stalag Luft III could see their capture as a great opportunity to turn escaping into ambitious acts of resistance, and no longer as a black mark on one's military career. Knowing this, their German captors strove tirelessly to create escape-proof camps. Stalag Luft III was the first of these.

thinking about: how to stay warm and how to find enough food to eat. Even the few guards posted on the train were preoccupied with the discomforts of a long winter train ride and the uncertainty of what there would be at the far end. They were fortunate in that the cars, while rough and unheated, had bench seats and windows, although these were wedged shut. It was relative luxury compared with the Germans' other means of transporting prisoners.

The Germans assigned the prisoners to railway cars alphabetically, so that Scruffy was separated from Wally and his other friends. But that didn't deter him from working on a plan to break out. Once he was settled in and the train started rolling, he examined the windows and saw that they hadn't been nailed or secured with screws. They had been "locked" by two wooden wedges jammed in between the window and the frame. With no guards at his end of the car, he patiently worked away at one of the wedges and after about 15 minutes was able to work one free. He loosened the second one, then switched seats with the man sitting opposite and started working on another window. About an hour out of Barth, he had managed to free up two windows.

The three men sitting around him had been watching silently with some interest. When he was finished, he spoke to them quietly, explaining that he was planning to jump out of the window when the train slowed down at the station outside of Stettin. Michael Sextus Wood, whom he knew from Stalag Luft I, was game to go with him. A representative from the Red Cross listened warily. Scruffy laid out the basic plan. As the train slowed coming up the rise into the station south of Stettin, they would dive out the windows and lie flat in the snow until the train had passed. Then they would follow the train tracks back into Stettin, and make their way down to the harbour.

"What about food?" Michael asked. Scruffy said he'd drum up some supplies and they'd put these in a kit bag, and get someone to toss it out after them so they'd have their hands free. The Red Cross guy said he'd be willing to lend a hand.

Everyone seemed to think it could work. Scruffy went foraging up and down the length of the car – there was only one guard and he was dozing – and he managed to pull together enough odds and ends of chocolate, bread, and cigarettes to hold the four of them for a couple of days while they were on the move. Looking as ragged as he was, many of the other guys in the car thought he was out of his mind to try, but they humoured him with contributions. He stuffed all the supplies into a kit bag, which he gave the Red Cross man to hold. John and Michael were facing one another in their window seats, with the Red Cross man sitting beside Michael, looking increasingly anxious. Scruffy went over what they were going to do, and the signal he'd give to make their move.

The train slowed through the station at Stettin, and then as it left the outskirts of the city it headed south and began to climb a hill as it approached the next station, just as predicted. Outside were dark, snow-covered fields. Scruffy reminded Michael that once they hit the ground, to roll away from the tracks and then lie flat until the train had passed. The train slowed almost to a stop, and Scruffy handed the bag of food to the Red Cross man, reminding him to toss it out immediately after them, then slam the windows shut.

They opened the windows, and Scruffy hissed "Now!" They both dove out the windows and went tumbling down an embankment beside the tracks. They lay flat in the snow without moving, watching to see if the train slowed or stopped. It didn't. Scruffy stood up cautiously to see where the kit bag had landed. He spotted Michael right away because of the luminous white belt he was wearing, and suggested he get rid of the offending article before they were spotted. But where was the bag with all the food? The Red Cross guy had been right there at the window behind them.

Scruffy and Michael searched the icy embankments, and it soon became clear that for whatever reason, the kit bag hadn't made it out of the train.

So now it was just the two of them, standing alone in a snow-covered field at midnight, in March, somewhere in northern Germany.

# Chapter 14

# AN UNSENTIMENTAL EDUCATION

Scruffy and Michael ran north from the tracks until the train was out of sight, then turned west and started the walk back to Stettin. It was just after midnight; the sky was clear with a full moon, and Scruffy was able to get his bearings, drawing on his memory of the map the escape committee back at Stalag Luft I had been discussing. After walking for about twenty minutes, they felt safe enough to turn south again and follow the railway tracks to the outskirts of Stettin. It was "as cold as charity", John recalled, and after an hour of walking they were desperate for shelter. The tracks broke off into an industrial-looking part of the city, so they found a road and kept walking, looking for someplace they could rest and hide. Before long, they came upon a large public garden that they thought might have some outbuildings they could sleep in. Scruffy spotted what appeared to be a tool shed at the far side of the garden. It had no sign of life inside it, which was promising, so staying close to shrubs and trees they made their way across the snow-covered grounds.

Scruffy tested the door and it wasn't locked. The shed was small, about the same size as the cells back at Dulag Luft. Various gardening tools leaned up against the wall; but in the corner there was a pot-bellied stove with a small supply of wood and matches. At night the smoke wouldn't be noticed, so they built a fire and slowly started to thaw out. Scruffy scoured the shed for whatever could be found and turned up two thick glasses. Before jumping from the train, he had stuffed two large chocolate bars in his pockets as an afterthought, and now it was all that they had to keep them going. He broke off two cubes and put one into each of the glasses, then covered the cubes with snow and set them on the stove to heat. It wasn't much, but the hot watery chocolate was warming and they were able to fall asleep with something in their stomachs.

When they awoke, it was daylight. The fire had died, and once again they were shivering and hungry. Michael was in particular distress with hunger pangs. Scruffy told him to tighten his belt – as tight as it would go – because it would stop the howling in his belly. It was an old but effective trick. They couldn't light the fire for fear of smoke being spotted. Scruffy sketched out the plans for the day. They would have to sit tight for at least another day because the goons would be out looking for them, and if anyone saw them, someone would put two and two together. Michael huddled down to make the most of the scant warmth of the shed, while Scruffy cautiously peered out of the grimy window to see what could be seen. As he did, a ragged teenaged girl walked by the window of the shed leading two children by their hands. He froze, watching her as she passed. She looked directly in the window at him, but showed no reaction. He knew she must have seen something, but she just continued walking with the children down to the bottom of the garden, dropped them off at what was presumably a school, then walked back up past the shed again without showing interest in who might be inside. Then Scruffy noticed a distinctive blue triangular patch sewn on to her coat. It meant she was probably a Polish or Russian national, now working as forced labour for the Germans. She wouldn't be likely to give them any trouble. But it was only a matter of time until someone did. Scruffy decided that they had to move that night.

They huddled in the shed for the rest of that day, fighting off the gnawing cold and hunger, restlessly waiting until it was dark enough to light a fire again. It wasn't long before they had used up their small supply of wood, so they began to snap the wooden handles off all the garden tools and managed to keep the meagre fire alive with this new fuel. About one o'clock in the morning, they each ate a small cube of chocolate and melted what was left with some snow in their stubby glasses over the dying fire. When they were finished, they tightened their belts and headed off. Everyone would be asleep at that time of night, or at the very least dozy, so Scruffy felt it was their best chance to slip through the city and down to the harbour without being stopped.

As they set off, Scruffy replayed the Escape Committee meeting, and remembered that they would have to cross a bridge over the Oder River that separated the greater city from the lower harbour district they were heading for. Finding a ship with a crew who were sympathetic to Allied evaders was a major gamble but their only hope. This meant moving through the centre of the city and down to the water as inconspicuously as possible. As Michael had no languages other than English, John told him that if they met anyone to keep his mouth shut; play deaf and dumb. He would do the talking.

Michael was wearing the remnants of his Air Force uniform and other scraps of clothing he'd picked up since being shot down; and Scruffy was in a battered Polish army uniform he'd been given when he left hospital. He looked like any one of the thousands of POWs who were scattered around Germany working as forced labour, and his outfit might pass muster at night should they be stopped and questioned. With the bridge in sight, a soldier on a bicycle rode their way and shouted, challenging them. They managed to run into the woods before he could catch up to them. They circled around in the direction they had come from and found their way back to the bridge. The soldier on the bicycle had disappeared, but now there were guards posted at either end. They shuffled up to the first guard, Michael hovering silently behind. Scruffy and the soldier exchanged a few words about how cold it was and how miserable army life was. The guard let them pass without question.

They moved on across the bridge and went through the same small talk with the other guard. It was too cold and too late for these poor boys stuck on graveyard shift guard duty to care about two ragged labourers walking into the city. Who in their right mind would be out in such weather unless they had absolutely had to be?

With that first hurdle cleared, Scruffy and Michael headed straight down to the waterfront, taking care to use darkened streets and moving as though they knew exactly where they were going. Scruffy had given Michael strict instructions to walk alongside him, and to keep his eyes focussed forward. He kept watch on storefront windows for reflections in case anyone was following them. Fortunately, the streets were quiet and deserted. Scandinavian ships were frequently in Stettin's port, and that's what Scruffy was looking for. He was certain he could talk his way onboard. Surely any captain from Sweden or Denmark would willingly hide them onboard until the ice broke in a month or so, and then take them back to a neutral country. By about 2:00 a.m. they had found the harbour. Clouds had rolled in, obscuring the moon, so it was difficult to make out any telltale markings on the two large ships that were anchored in front of them. Neither had gangways lowered, but the first ship had a mooring cable that ran right down to the quay. It would be a simple enough matter for one of them to clamber up to the deck, size up the crew, and try and make contact. Scruffy told Michael that he'd have to do it. His own hands hadn't fully healed and he still couldn't grip anything with any strength.

Michael started to shinny up the hawser, about a thirty-foot climb. As Scruffy's eyes adjusted to the light, he noticed a rippling of barbed wire running along the gunnels of the ship. Then he saw a German guard appear with a rifle in hand, walking along the perimeter of the ship. He realized what it was and started hissing up to Michael, "Come back... *Michael!* For Chrissakes, it's a prison ship...!" Michael looked back down at Scruffy, not able to understand what he was saying. An awkward silence was broken by the laughter of the guard, who was now looking over the side of the ship at the sight of these two confused tramps trying to sneak into his jail. Michael scrambled down as fast as he could, and the two of them ran across the quay and ducked into an open warehouse out of sight of the ship. They stood there in the darkness, listening for the sound of footsteps or voices. But all was quiet.

Scruffy was weighing their diminishing options. Looking for another ship was a possibility, but they were both rattled and Scruffy wasn't ready to make any move until he was more certain of what was out there. He found himself staring down the length of the warehouse, its far end open to the harbour. He could see a large tube shape bobbing gently in the water. Peering through the gloom, for the life of him he couldn't make sense of what he was looking at. A guard appeared at the far end of the warehouse, walking in from the harbour entrance. This man was not the jolly middle-aged sort who'd been on the prison ship; this guard was dressed in a crisp greatcoat and carried a machine gun. A hollow metallic "clank" from the hull of the vessel in the water caught the guard's attention. He reflexively cocked his machine gun and swung to face the direction from which the sound had come. Scruffy realized that they had wandered into a hidden U-boat berth in the middle of a busy industrial harbour, away from watchful eyes. He grabbed Michael's sleeve and starting backing away slowly. Whatever they did, they had to get out of there. He whispered to Michael not to say anything and not to look at the guard. Just keep moving.

They managed to slip out of the building and into the streets of the lower city. Running through the dark streets near the harbour, they noticed a three-storey row house with its lights on. Scruffy remembered hearing about a whorehouse in the lower city,[1] and thought this might be the place. They watched the house from the shadows, and saw a couple of workingmen scuttle out and disappear down side streets. Scruffy felt it was very promising – and at this point their only option – so he reviewed what they should expect before they headed in.

Small European hotels seemed to have a common layout: inside there would be a reception room off to one side, then a long hallway that ran the length of the house to the rear. From there a staircase led up to the upper floors. Scruffy looked at the house and guessed that it would be much the same. He told Michael, "Do exactly what I do. I'll walk in and go straight to the back and up the staircase to the second floor. You wait two minutes and then follow after me. Look straight ahead. Don't look left or right." Michael agreed. They wanted to look like they were there with a purpose – to find a girl – and that's what they had to focus on.

Scruffy tried the door and it was unlocked. That was a good sign. He opened it and went in, the layout much as he had expected. He walked straight down the hall to the back of the house. From his peripheral vision he noticed a bar on his right, but he kept going. He reached the stairs at the back and heard the front door close. It was Michael. Scruffy was starting up the stairs when he heard a sharp, "Halt!", and the unmistakable sound of a pistol being cocked. He stopped where he was on the stairs, then heard a German voice call to him, "And you."

He came back down the stairs and returned to the front of the house. In the bar, Michael was standing with his hands up, a Gestapo officer holding him at gunpoint. The bartender was visibly shaken. The officer turned to level the gun at Scruffy, and said, unsmiling, "Who are you, and what are you doing here." Scruffy admitted that they were POWs on the run. He told the officer about trying to scramble up the hawser of the prison ship, and the Gestapo officer started to laugh.

Then he asked what their plans were. Trying to get home, Scruffy said. "You're home now, my friends, and you're not going any further," the officer replied. With no apparent irony or threat, he went on to say that they were not going to enjoy the next couple of days in the

---

1    The whorehouse was said to be populated by Polish girls, the daughters of families who had given the invading Germans problems back in the old country. In a typical retaliatory manner, the Nazis had the girls shipped off to this remote seaport to service the Germans and atone for their parents' crimes against the Third Reich.

Gestapo's custody. He was simply letting them know what was likely to happen. He would take them to the interrogation centre a few blocks away, and unfortunately the Gestapo there "would not be so pleasant".

Scruffy's gaze fell on the bartender, intently polishing glasses behind the bar. The man had been silent throughout the lively exchange, but now caught John's eye. He's trying to tell me something, Scruffy thought, but he didn't have time to ponder it; the Gestapo officer was already leading Michael to the door. The bartender immediately turned away and made himself busy at the sink. John thought no more about it.

The officer took them to an old jail that the Gestapo used as their headquarters. Michael and Scruffy had a few hours to get warm and dry, and to catch up on some sleep, which was something of a relief. Interrogations started the following morning.

In this Gestapo centre, the standard debriefing process began with inducing a psychological regression in the prisoner, removing all sense of autonomy of judgement and action. Nothing could be done without the guards' express permission, and in precisely the manner dictated. The prisoner was escorted to his cell where there was a bunk folded up along the wall. It stayed there until permission was given to lower it. Prisoners were issued a chamber pot and twice a day the guard opened the cell door. The prisoners had to run to a trough on the far side of the room, empty the pot, and run back to the cell. If you didn't run fast enough, you got hit with a rifle butt. If you talked, you got hit with a rifle butt. If you disappointed the guard in any way, you got hit with a rifle butt.

The tricky part of this for many was that what few instructions there were, were issued in German, of which Michael understood not a word. It didn't seem to trouble him, but his relaxed manner in the face of these professionally sadistic men did not serve him well. When taken to his cell, he flipped his bunk down before he was supposed to and was beaten. He didn't follow the proper sequence of the morning routine and was hit with rifle butts. He didn't understand any of the orders barked at him and was kicked and thrown against the wall. And when Scruffy tried to whisper to him what he was supposed to do, the goons beat the hell out of both of them. All in all it was "an educational stay", John told me later. He had never been in jail, and found the experience oddly intriguing. He focussed on what was going on around him with a certain emotional detachment, accepting it for what it was, absorbing how systematic the Gestapo were in their methods, and making note of the particular culture of these secret state police.

The most basic of comforts – water, shelter, a bit of food – kept him comfortable enough. The pain from his burns had largely disappeared. Perhaps he was less abused than some other prisoners because of his unnerving appearance. Without eyelids, he had an unblinking stare that suggested a kind of vacant innocence. Remembering Adrian's admonitions, he played the role of a simple-minded flyer who didn't know enough to hide anything. His interrogations were straightforward, and he responded with information that stuck to the broad lines of his experiences, taking care never to be vague or to tell an unnecessary lie. This was part of the training he had had back in England. You had to remain consistent in your story, talk slowly and try to anticipate where the interrogation was going so you could stay a question or two ahead.

He was well aware of what lay in store should he raise any suspicions. The final stop for prisoners even suspected of subversion of the State was "The End Room." This is where the men and women whom the Gestapo felt were being uncooperative were brought for their final interrogation. At the conclusion of this interview, if the desired information had been extracted, the prisoner would be sent back into the system and transported down the line to another camp where he or she lived or died. However if the desired information had not been obtained, then the prisoner was either (a) shot, or (b) burned with a blowtorch and then shot. Scruffy sat uneasily listening to one poor German man, screaming, *"Ich bin Deutsch! Ich bin Deutsch!"*[2] – which in Scruffy's opinion he was. But that was rather beside the point in the end, as the Gestapo had already decided he was a spy or a collaborator who had chosen not to talk. So they roasted him within earshot of the other prisoners, and then shot him. Such tactics made you think carefully about what you would say to them if and when your turn came.

In this jail, John had plenty of time to reflect on the events of the last few days. Were Wally and the others at the new camp yet? How was Michael holding up? Were there any Allied agents embedded in the area, who might be able to help? Then a thought struck him. "That bartender," John said later, "maybe he was one of us."

John continued to play his part, and Michael's incompetence in German and in learning the prison routines simply irritated the Gestapo

2    "I am German! I am German!"

into seeing him as nothing but a dim-witted Englishman, which didn't stop them from beating him almost to death. The two of them were considered small change; just a couple of POWs on the run. A decision was made to send them on to their original destination in Sagan. They were held in solitary for a week, but the beatings had stopped and the food was marginally better than starvation. During one of their daily exercise outings, John was pleasantly surprised to see a tall, blonde Polish girl grinning at him, and shouting across the barbed wire that separated them. They exchanged a few friendly words. She smirked and told him she was in for a short stretch because she had given one of the "meatheads" the clap. She was one of the girls forced into prostitution at the whorehouse, and knew all about John – that he'd been at Barth, had been picked up at the whorehouse in town, and that he and his friend Michael were about to be shipped out. John was surprised at how much she knew. It made him question what other kinds of information the Gestapo might already have.

Two very long and restless days later, John was taken from the jail alone and loaded on to a train with hundreds of other recently captured airmen. He lost track of what happened to Michael.[3]

---

By nature, John was not one to dwell on the past. And yet he couldn't help wondering what, if anything, he might have done differently. Badly burned on his face, neck, and hands from the fire in his Spitfire's cockpit, he was sitting on a train's wooden bench seat, contemplating a long ride across the snow-covered plains of eastern Germany. He had been at war for a little less than a year when he had been shot down. His raw hands were only just beginning to be elastic enough to form a fist, but – incredibly – his sense of humour was largely intact.

John embodied the idea that given the will and determination you can survive almost anything. Even without eyelids. It was April 14th, 1942, and his guards were escorting him to the prisoner of war camp that would be his home for the indefinite future. The newly constructed Stalag Luft III was located in the eastern reaches of Hitler's "New Germany," so far away from friendly faces as to make the prospect of

---

3    Michael survived the war. After leaving the Gestapo jail, he was transferred to Stalag Luft III but was placed in a different compound than John. He and John met up again in London in 1947, and had a good laugh remembering their whorehouse visit in Stettin.

escape all but hopeless. But John was never without hope. In fact, he saw his predicament as an interesting challenge and was already beginning to consider options for escape.

In these early years of the war, the Germans were going from strength to strength, sweeping across Europe and conquering everything in their gun sights. They were, as a result, arrogant and patronizing but nevertheless relatively civilized in their treatment of their new transports from the west. (Bad luck if you came from the east.)

John's trip had two stages: the first was a 100 mile run south to Berlin, where they would turn east and head another 150 miles across Germany into what is now Poland – a dishearteningly isolated place. The railway car in which he was riding had been stripped down to the basics: a toilet at one end and a stove at the other. But even so, it was better than being herded across country on foot, as so many people displaced by the Germans had been and would be. He was relatively comfortable, safe, and dry. And he was resourceful.

While waiting for the train to leave, John struck up a conversation with the grey-faced German guard who sat a few seats away looking as unhappy about the trip as everyone else. John had the gift of being able to talk to pretty much anyone about pretty much anything. He learned that this quiet man, presumably assigned to guard duty because of his age and non-combative personality, had been a professor at the University of Berlin before the war. As they talked, the train started to pull out. The professor seemed happy enough to pass the time talking. He was indifferent to John getting up and stretching his legs, wandering down the length of the aisle, or watching the scenery float by through different windows. John was marking time, taking stock of the situation: two guards in his car, no one paying much attention to anything. He judged that escape would be a simple matter of requesting permission to go for a pee, slipping out the door at the end of the car, and then jumping from the moving train. Make a run for it back to the harbour. This time he would know what to avoid and what to look for.

Stettin has a tangle of rail lines unravelling in a dozen different directions out of the city. As the train lumbered through the neighbourhoods, John calculated he wouldn't have much time before they reached the city's outskirts. After that, there would be nothing but an occasional town or village for fifty miles before the tracks angled off. Then it would be hundreds more miles of dense forest on the way to Berlin. His plan was to make the jump while they were still near the city and then find his way back to the port to look for a Scandinavian ship. But if he had any hope of pulling this off, he would have to jump soon.

Talking to the guard, John glanced out the windows, silently marking the thinning of the city and keeping up his small talk, gently taking a measure of the man and the lay of the land. It was always safe to ask about the other guy's girl or family, so he decided to try that. Calculating he had about ten minutes to make his move, John asked the guard about Berlin and if his family still lived there. The professor talked about what a beautiful city Berlin was, with its neoclassical buildings, the magnificent Brandenburg Gates leading to the tree-lined Unter den Linden, the river Spree; such a civilized place to live and far enough from England that it wasn't in much danger of air raids. There had been a few, but these hadn't had much impact in terms of damaging the historic sites. As the professor continued, it emerged that his wife and children had been among the few German casualties in a small raid the previous November. When John heard this, he could see that this gentle man was biding his time, waiting for this prisoner to try something rash, giving him a reason to carve out a little revenge. So John sat tight, murmuring his condolences, adding that war was a terrible thing. The professor was silent after that.

Hours passed with nothing worth looking at. Towns crept by, drifting in and out of the window frames. John watched the blank stares of men and women standing on platforms and wondering why the train wasn't stopping. As night came on, the black of the forest enveloped them and the murmur of conversation in the car dwindled into silence. After hours of dark monotony, Berlin was suddenly all around them, lights blazing and showing no signs of damage or even being at war. It was a living monument to the vitality and strength of the German nation, almost taunting these prisoners to acknowledge the futility of their war against such a powerful adversary. The train stopped for coal and water, then began to move again just as daylight began to break. They headed east, travelling across a landscape of little more than snowy fields, forest, and an occasional stone building. The countryside looked increasingly feudal, almost primitive, as if this part of Germany had only a passing acquaintance with the 20th century.

No one on the train knew anything about the new camp apart from its approximate location, situated so far from anywhere familiar as to make escape a daunting proposition. In fact, attempting escape would entail travelling hundreds of miles across Nazi-occupied Europe in the dead of winter. There would be no reasonable way to disappear into a crowd or find a sympathetic soul who might compromise their life by offering refuge. In the Germany of 1942, such an act of kindness was tantamount to a death wish. For John, this kind of assistance was improbable in any case. His RCAF uniform was gone and he was now wearing the tattered clothes of a Polish soldier, presumably the victim of an earlier campaign. He looked like any of the millions of refugees being shuffled back and forth across the war-torn continent.

Yet he wasn't discouraged. Throughout his eighteen-hour train ride to the village of Sagan, he had thought about little else than how and when he would find his way back to England to get back into the fight.

---

John was among the first wave of Allied air force prisoners being transferred to this remote corner of the expanding German empire. The train arrived at Sagan on the afternoon of April 15th, 1942, and the three hundred prisoners were escorted from the train on a quarter-mile walk along a country road through the woods to their new camp. Even with the low temperature and the snow, it felt good to be outside and to stretch their legs. There was desultory chatter about where they were, how bloody cold it was, and what the camp might be like. John was very quiet and thoughtful, silently taking in what was around him. Despite his burns, and having had minimal food and sleep for the week he had spent being methodically interrogated and beaten by the Gestapo, he was in surprisingly good spirits. New arrivals were brought to the German end of the compound where they had their pictures taken, followed by a three-minute hot shower, then a thorough body search. The German guards checked their identification, methodically ticking off names on their lists, and then shepherded them through the gates into their new home. Twelve-foot high barbed-wire fences defined the camp's perimeter, with guard towers at regular intervals making precious little of the compound that could not be shot at by the watchful soldiers manning them. Outside the fence, tall fir trees surrounded the compound. You could be forgiven for seeing similarities to a summer camp in Muskoka, apart from the machine guns. The camp did in fact bear an ironic resemblance to a Canadian POW camp in Gravenhurst, Ontario, whose previous incarnation had been the Minnewaska Summer Resort on beautiful Lake Muskoka. In 1942, it was used to imprison many of the most malevolent Nazi POWs.

Stalag Luft III was one of the largest German camps. At the end of the war, it spread over 60 acres, had a five-mile perimeter, and housed 10,000 airmen from every Allied country in four expansive compounds. When John arrived, however, it was only a month old. The camp's compound was filled with 21 rough, single-storey wooden huts, set well back from the fence to discourage tunnelling. Four additional huts were located at the south end of the camp to house the German guards and officers. Huts were constructed on brick footings that raised them off the ground, so any digging would be visible to the guards. There was a concrete block foundation in the centre of the hut that encased the rudimentary plumbing. Apart from the smell of fresh-hewn wood and the still-pristine mortar, the camp seemed very similar to others the men had seen.

The camp had been designed with a number of features intended to make escape difficult, if not impossible. To begin with, the barbed-wire fencing and guard towers that surrounded the camp's grounds would have to be breached. As the camp was located on the war's eastern front, escape would necessitate travelling hundreds of miles south through Czechoslovakia and Hungary, north through Poland and into Russia, or back west through Germany.

There were basically three ways of escaping the camp: over the fence; under it; or through it. Of these, tunneling was one of the most common – quiet, hidden, and not subject to pitchfork searches. But the Germans had anticipated this and had planned for it. Seismograph microphones had been buried in the ground surrounding the huts to detect any sounds of digging. The elevated huts provided easy access for special duty guards, called "ferrets," to watch for any tunnelling activity. At night, they would roam the camp, peering under the huts, and thrusting long steel probes into the earth to try and find hollows. English-speaking ferrets would crawl under the huts and eavesdrop on the prisoners' conversations, but the men soon learned not to discuss anything important when the compound fell quiet.

The most challenging obstacle was the ground itself. The camp had been constructed on earth that had vivid orange-yellow subsoil.

Tunnellers trying to dispose of the earth would have to haul it above ground, and then dispose of it on the dusty grey topsoil of the compound. It was impossible. Even traces of the subsoil, if found on the prisoners' clothing, would give them away. Not to mention its fetid, lingering odour. Worse still, while such loose sandy soil meant easy digging, it was impossible to avoid cave-ins. If anything, the digging conditions were worse than they had been back at Barth.

When he had first arrived at the camp, John was held in isolation in the Cooler. These cells, used to "cool down" new arrivals and to discipline troublemakers, have been portrayed in movies and novels as being bleak concrete chambers used to punish prisoners' transgressions with the torture of solitary confinement. In fact, they were warm, dry, restful rooms, admittedly bare, but refreshingly quiet and vermin-free in contrast to the crowded barracks. As spring and summer came on, these cells were eponymously cooler as well, making a week or two's stay with a couple of good books in hand a pleasant holiday from the maddening throng in camp.

Sergeant-Major Hermann Glemnitz, a veteran pilot from WW I known as "King of the Ferrets," was the senior non-commissioned officer responsible for escape prevention. He had been at Barth and knew many of the men now relocated to Stalag Luft III. He and Scruffy had come to know one another during those first weeks at Barth. In the evenings, he would often come through the barracks counting heads. He was alarmed to come upon John, sound asleep with his eyelid-less eyes wide open and staring. "Mr. Weir…? Mr. Weir! Are you dead?" – awakening John but reassuring Glemnitz. They developed a friendship out of basic consideration for one another. Glemnitz was married to a much younger woman, and the men in camp were always needling him, saying things like, "When we get out, we're gonna pay her a visit, Glemnitz!" that drove the poor man crazy. Scruffy reassured him that they were just horsing around, something Glemnitz appreciated and never forgot. He was a decent man, who hadn't joined the Party and was simply trying to sit out the war without getting killed. He was well liked and universally respected, but he was no one to trifle with. Some referred to him as "that bastard Glemnitz," for he was a dedicated discoverer of escape plots.

Unlike most of the guards, Hermann Glemnitz had an appealingly dry sense of humour. The POWs organized an impromptu game of rugby in the first month that Stalag Luft III was open. The ground was as hard as rock, but it didn't seem to interfere with the exuberance of the game and the men playing it. A burly Canadian, Ken Toft, captained one team. Glemnitz watched Toft and his side play with interest, as he had never seen the game before. Noticing this, Toft came over to Glemnitz, and said, "Look, Hermann, this rugby is a great way to burn off your frustrations and a hell of a lot of fun. What about getting up a team with the guards?" Glemnitz watched the men pummel one another, breaking noses and blackening eyes, then nodded said, "Yes, sure. But only if you let us keep our guns."[4]

Despite the camp's other comforts, the food served to prisoners in the cooler was largely limited to the classic bread and water. But during John's two weeks there, he did not go hungry. The day he arrived, Glemnitz came to John's cell and, forestalling pleasantries, put a finger to his lips and pointed at the ceiling. The butt-end of a microphone could be seen poking its head through the cement. John nodded, then smiled and shook his old friend's hand. Glemnitz handed John a small box. In it were some bread, cheese, and a bowl of soup. He smiled and left, returning each day with a similar gift. This earned Scruffy's enduring appreciation, and he made a point of never betraying Glemnitz's trust.

Once the men had completed the official German processing and entered the confines of the camp, the prisoners came under the command of the Senior British Officer (the SBO).[5] This individual supervised all prisoners' activities behind the wire. His subordinate officers were charged with vetting out each new arrival to get his measure. The officers challenged each with a battery of questions: the name of the squadron he had been attached to, the names of men in his squadron and on his crew, details of his squadron's operations, where he had enlisted and trained, and many specific questions about his hometown. This was a preliminary screening to collect general intelligence – not unlike the German operation at Dulag Luft in Frankfurt – and also to avoid the infiltration of German "stooges" – spies who spoke excellent English, had first-hand knowledge of life in England or North America, and would try to blend into the camp to collect information about RAF operations or of any escape planning within the camp. Several attempted to slip through, but none are known to have succeeded.

---

4    Courtesy of F/O Jack Lyon.
5    Such acronyms aren't jargon, but are the lingua franca of the military, expedient shorthand to communicate in an abrupt way of life.

Once these questions had been satisfactorily answered, the SBO had established a final safeguard: no man was allowed into the general population, let alone assigned sleeping quarters, until someone already established in camp had vouched for him. Simply knowing someone was not enough: you had to be vouched for by someone who had known you in the city or town of your upbringing, and your information had to jibe with facts already on record. Waiting to be acknowledged in the "reception" area – a common room in one of the Allied huts stringently policed by the British – could take hours or days, depending on whom you knew and vice versa.

When John's initial vetting was complete, he found himself unable to come up with the name of anyone who might know him from back in Canada. Being among the first wave of prisoners to arrive at Stalag Luft III meant there weren't many familiar faces apart from those on the train and from his previous camp. After many frustrating hours drawing a mental blank; sitting, stewing, and wishing he had developed a taste for cigarettes, if only to kill some time, it dawned on him that his old friend and squadron mate Wally Floody would have arrived on the train a couple of weeks ahead of him. And with Wally's confirmation, John became a part of the life of the camp.

But when he entered the compound, the British Intelligence Officer (IO) was waiting for him. He asked John to come for a chat. The safest place to talk was walking around the perimeter the fence, which was a low wooden marker (sometimes a wire) that was knee-high and located about 30 feet inside the barbed wire fences that surrounded the compound. This was the warning line or wire that defined the edge of No Man's Land: cross that and you would be shot on sight. But what this circuit also unwittingly created was a corridor of privacy. It was far enough from the tower guards, and the other men in the compound, to allow for a quiet conversation or to just be left alone with your thoughts. Walking circuits kept many men fit and sane during their years behind the wire, walking hours on end, sifting through worries, frustrations, and hopes. The IO knew John in passing from their previous POW camp at Barth, Stalag Luft I. As they walked, the IO told John that his room assignment would be in a hut with Wally Floody, his old friend who had vouched for him. Hank Birkland, Jens Müller, and Zbischek Gotowski, all of whom John had roomed with at Barth when he was first captured, would join them. It was like old home week, and John was pleasantly surprised at his good fortune.

The IO explained that the camp's SBO, Group Captain Harry "Wings" Day, had recommended rooming them together. Day was a decorated naval officer of the Fleet Air Arm, the air force division of the Royal Navy, and had been SBO at Stalag Luft I. "Wings" was a veteran of several escape attempts, and his irresistibly plucky nickname spoke well-deserved volumes of experience and courage that made him a natural leader and an astute judge of character. He too had been aware of John at Stalag I; and although he was unable to say exactly why, he thought that this Weir could be a valuable asset in continuing to wage the war from behind the wire. The IO had been charged with the responsibility of drawing John out to obtain a clearer picture of what he might be able to offer the X Committee. This was the camp's escape committee, which oversaw all escape attempts and provided intelligence and support. And there were hundreds of attempts, if not thousands, during the life of the camp.

With the IO's first questions, John sensed trouble. Too much curiosity. The IO was a Squadron Leader, senior in rank to John, so John politely answered his questions. He was asked about his friends and his family, where he'd travelled and what kinds of people he knew. John chose his words carefully, but was caught off guard when the IO said, "Weir, who are you?" He bristled a bit, then made it clear that he was just exactly what he appeared to be: nothing more and nothing less. The IO assured him that he wasn't a Gestapo plant; he was just interested. John encouraged the IO to ask Wally, or any of the others who knew him, and they wouldn't have anything more to offer than he did. The IO thanked him and went on his way.

John continued to walk, mulling over this conversation. It had really thrown him. Back at Barth, he had been surprised to be invited to a meeting of the escape committee. Newcomers were never included in those discussions. Someone must have been speculating that he had some kind of special connections or talents to bring to the table – but on what basis? He had never spoken to anyone, not even Hughie or Wally, about his special ops training or his work with Adrian. Now he was sure he was being watched. But by whom, for what purpose? It spooked him.

He continued walking the circuit by himself, remembering the admonitions of his "Dutch Uncle"[6] in England. Adrian had drilled

---

6    John often referred to Adrian as his "Dutch Uncle".

into him repeatedly that there was never any need or excuse to say anything to anyone that they couldn't figure out for themselves. If you did, you were asking to be made a target. "Never forget: you're the most dim-witted boy on the block. And since you know nothing, you've got bugger all to say. Keep your head down, your mouth shut, and be invisible." Of all the special intelligence training he had had over the years and the experience he had picked up in the operations he had undertaken, this advice had been the most instrumental in keeping him alive so far.

He would need to stand by it to survive what was yet to come.

# Chapter 15

# THE WAR BEHIND THE WIRE

Stalag Luft III, despite the Luftwaffe's ambition to create something singular, was nevertheless a bleak place. Lt. Colonel Albert "Bud" Clark arrived in camp in the summer of 1942 with the first large wave of American prisoners. He was the Senior American Officer, and was welcomed by Herbert Massey, then the Senior British Officer. Sixty years later, Clark described what he saw:

> ... I was unprepared for the scruffy appearance of so many of the officer prisoners. Some were heavily bearded, barefooted, and clad only in homemade, ragged shorts... Everything in camp was a dirty grey colour: the unpainted, prefabricated wooden huts, the bare sandy soil, the dense perimeter barbed wire, and the guard towers. Even the air that hung over the camp was always full of dust and smoke.[1]

A typical hut in Stalag Luft III held 140 men. It was equipped with a toilet, a washroom, a kitchen, and 14 rooms, four of them small, and intended for senior officers. Each room had three or four triple-decker bunks (one double-decker bunk in the senior officers' rooms). Cooking duties were shared among the men in the hut, but the food was lousy. In 1943, in Stalag Luft III, a typical daily ration for each man was:

- 2-3 slices of black bread
- 1-1½ pounds of potatoes
- 1 cup of soup (usually watery turnip or potato)
- An ounce of sugar

---

1    *33 Months as a POW in Stalag Luft III*, by Albert P. Clark, pp.40-41, Fulcrum Publishing, Colorado 2004

- An ounce of margarine
- Jam, meat paste, and dried fish sporadically, small quantities

The Food Ministry in Berlin dictated the ingredients to be used in the POWs' black bread. A directive dated May 1941 listed the following:

- 50% rye grain (cattle food)
- 20% sliced sugar beets
- 20% tree flour (sawdust)
- 10% minced leaves and straw

The Germans provided a diet of about 1,500 calories a day, about half of what a young active man requires. Food was therefore a primary concern in camp. The saving grace was Red Cross parcels. From the British, the typical parcel contained:

- ¼ lb packet of tea
- One tin of cocoa powder
- One bar of milk or plain chocolate
- One tinned pudding
- One tin of meat roll
- One tin of processed cheese
- One tin of condensed milk
- One tin of dried eggs
- One tin of sardines or herrings
- One tin of fruit preserve
- One tin of margarine
- One tin of sugar
- One tin of vegetables
- One tin of biscuits
- One bar of soap
- One tin of 50 cigarettes or tobacco (sent separately)

The Canadian Red Cross parcels contained:

- One tin Corned Beef (12 oz)
- One tin Spam (12 oz.)
- One tin salmon (7.75 oz.)
- One tin Klim (16 oz.)
- One tin jam (6 oz.)
- One tin butter (16 oz.)
- One tin sardines (3.75 oz.)
- One packet raisins (7 oz.)
- One packet prunes (6 oz.)
- One tin cheese (4 oz.)
- One tin tea or coffee (4 oz.)
- One box sugar (8 oz.)
- One box biscuits (12 oz.)
- One tin salt and pepper (1 oz.)
- One bar chocolate
- One bar soap

The small pleasures of Red Cross parcels were a godsend. Morale would go up when these arrived. In the early years of the war, they were sent at the rate of one parcel per man per week, although this could be inconsistent at best. And in the last year of the war, the parcels became more and more scarce – likely being pilfered by the Germans, who were as hard up for food as were the prisoners.[2] Parcels from home would also supplement these staples, and letters from family gave them hope that the life they left behind was still intact, and that they would be able to get the hell out of Germany before another ten years passed.

The problem was that folks back home rarely understood what life was like living on the border of Poland in a German prison camp. "I hope you're getting lots of potatoes, because the Germans made such grand gravy," John's mother wrote. In another letter, she reminded him to "...wash your hair with eggs. Remember how I told you to do it: only use the yolks and do what you like with the whites." Eggs were

---

2    Prisoners in Japanese camps rarely saw any of their parcels, as their captors would hoard all of the contents for themselves. Hundreds of such parcels were discovered at the war's end when those camps were liberated.

scarcer than women, and often an equal object of fantasy. John had a particular craving for doughnuts; one of those yearnings you develop when the object of your hunger is utterly beyond reach. When he was with the squadron in England, he would send telegrams back home, simply saying, "Dear Klan, everything okie dokie. Send doughnuts, John." So when he was settled in Stalag Luft III, his letters home would regularly end with, "Send more doughnuts!"[3]

Chocolate was a particularly valuable commodity in camp as currency, not to mention the ability to eat it when there was little in the way of food. Again, this was not a concept grasped by one POW's mother. "In your last three letters, you have asked me to send you chocolate. I assume you are kidding and have mailed you underwear. Love, Mother."

Letters from that other world of "Home," as baffling and alien as they could seem, did provide some smiles. Freda Weir's gravy and eggs letters were posted on the bulletin board and brought chuckles and some ragging on John from the guys. Other letters could seem as though they'd been specifically written to sweetly torment the stir-crazy men. Consider the vague implications of one man's love note from his sweetheart: "Darling; to think I was only nineteen when you were shot down! I feel so much more experienced now, but you will have to find that out for yourself when you come home...". Or the mind-numbing obtuseness that generated such thoughts as, "I'm so glad you were shot down before flying became dangerous." And, "I'm happy to hear you are with such a nice crowd of boys. I hope the Germans will keep you there." Which is comparatively less exasperating than, "Your letter from camp reads like one glorious holiday!" and the philosophical, "Remember – freedom is only a state of mind." This is true, of course, but the emotional detritus of long-distance relationships could put a damper on that freedom.

There were many puzzling comments in letters from loved ones, such as, "Darling, I hope you are staying true to me." Bunked in with 2,000 other men, the odds were in this girl's favour. Eye-opening home front updates included statements like, "Darling, I've just had a baby. But don't worry – the American officer said he'll send some money."

---

3    This appreciation never left him. Years later, back in Toronto, he still took great delight in driving a few miles north to his favourite Country Style doughnut shop on Wilson Avenue, where he would pick up a couple of dozen assorted, tucking into them on the drive back home.

But these questions of fidelity were usually more welcome than the dreaded "Dear John" letter, emotionally concussive and conclusive, such as this singular update from home: "Dear Jimmy: You were missing for over a month, so I got married." And it could be a family affair, as demonstrated by a postcard written to an airman from someone who used to be his fiancée – and undoubtedly read by hundreds of pairs of eyes as it made its way to its recipient interned in Stalag Luft III – breathtaking in its telegraphic ingenuousness. "Dear Bob: I've just got married to your father. Love, Mother."

---

As John remembered it, the Americans fought among themselves and the Poles fought among themselves. The British and Canadian were the most stable, he said. The discipline of the British spilled over to the Canadians; there was no question about that. He felt that the Canadians were unusual – exceptional in a way – because they were more adaptable to language; at least in Stalag Luft III they seemed to be. The Canadians understood the Americans' ways a lot better than the English did. A lot of the time, the Americans literally couldn't understand what the English were trying to say. And the English didn't understand the Americans at all. There were so many different cultures bumping up against one another, with all the accents and personalities – the New Zealanders, the Australians, the South Africans, the Polish, the English, and the Americans. John thought the Canadians just seemed to be natural middlemen. But in any case, you just tended to move within your own circle of acquaintances.

One of the greatest problems facing a prisoner was the tedium of doing nothing. These were young men who had enlisted for adventure and excitement, and had been flying combat missions before they were shot down and captured. They wanted to get back into action. But severely limited food rations, a day-to-day existence with only the most basic of amenities, and the seemingly never-ending war, could undermine the spirits of any man.

John worked off a lot of his energy and frustrations in vigorous exercise. He did high-bar gymnastic workouts, ran races, boxed, wrestled, did calisthenics, and played rugby, hockey, baseball, volleyball, basketball, and anything else they could swing. The men even organized Sports Days where they'd compete for rankings that were posted in camp. A great deal of the time, the guys didn't have the strength to do some of the more strenuous stuff, but keeping fit was something that was always promoted. If nothing else, John remembered that they were encouraged to do 30 circuits a day around the perimeter of the fence, walking and talking. Such activities were essential in helping to keep fit and to maintain morale.

Twice a day the Kriegies were lined up for "Appell" – roll call – where ID numbers were called out in sequence to ensure a correct head count. This typically took a half hour or so, but could stretch on for hours if the count was wrong. Personalkartes - ID cards with the Kriegie's photograph on it – would then have to be presented and compared against the actual Kriegie. Clothing could be a problem, as any civilian outer clothing was strictly forbidden. But most men took pains to maintain their uniforms, properly displaying their rank and flying badges.

The prisoners had a library that was continually growing,[4] and lectures and classes were given in everything from history to electricity to languages. In his book *Goon in the Block* (1961; self-published), Don Edy, described it this way:

> *They came from all walks of life. There were schoolteachers, ministers, barristers, and bankers. Some of the richest families in England were represented in the camp, there were several titled men, and one of them was even a close relative of Winston Churchill's. We had electricians and welders, farmers, philatelists, and technicians of all kinds. With all this knowledge in camp a system of classes and lectures was started so that, if you were interested, you could learn a great deal. Some of the men wanted to take, or continue, university degrees. This was made possible through the Red Cross. Lessons and lectures were received from England when the student wanted to sit for his exams, and they were supplied from home and a Senior Officer was appointed by the SBO to act as scrutineer.*

Scruffy took advantage of these opportunities, working on polishing up his German, and even trying to pick up some Hungarian, but without much success.

---

4    The POWs' library at Stalag Luft III eventually grew to 10,000 books.

Card games of all kinds were popular (bridge having the most avid participants), as were chess and checkers. As time went on, concerts and theatre became a part of the culture of the camp as well. Men who had been shot down with tickets for the latest West End hit in their wallets were reassured that as often as not, the same play was in rehearsal in the camp and they could catch it there. The Germans encouraged this, facilitating costume rental and acquisition of instruments, thinking it would keep the POWs' minds off trying to escape. The prisoners even requested a camera and film, to take photographs of the productions so they could send snapshots home. The Germans would develop those films – but not the covert films the men also took, to create forged travel documents and ID papers. The men developed those themselves, using chemical and papers obtained by bribing the goons.

The men "tamed"[5] the goons with chocolate, real coffee, and cigarettes to get news, papers, and pretty much anything else they wanted or needed. The Germans posted news updates on the prisoners' bulletin board, but these were always slanted from the German perspective. Bits of news would trickle in with new arrivals to camp, or in the heavily censored letters, but both sources were fragmentary at best. The most complete source of news came from BBC radio broadcasts received by the camp "Canary." This was a wireless set that had been pieced together over many months and was constantly on the move to keep the goons from finding it. They could detect its signal, but found it next to impossible to pinpoint where it was in camp. One of the reasons for this was Dick Bartlett, who had been charged with the responsibility of keeping the Canary hidden and on the move.

Dick had been inspired by advertisements in his parents' *London Weekly News*. In 1938, he left rural Saskatchewan for England, joining the Fleet Air Arm because he wanted to fly. Before the war started, he had earned his commission and had flown the iconic Swordfish biplane torpedo bomber off the British aircraft carrier HMS *Ark Royal* (the same ship Scruffy had flown cover for). He had been shot down and badly wounded over Norway after dive-bombing the German battleship *Scharnhorst*. By the time he was shipped to Stalag Luft III, Dick was a veteran of three POW camps and several escape attempts. He had an easygoing manner that served him well as he kept the Canary floating around camp. He frequently had to improvise like mad, carrying the

---

5    "Taming" meant bribing or blackmailing the goons.

radio around in a sack, back and forth across the compound. When guards would stop him and ask what he had in the bag, he'd guilelessly answer, "Just some earth for tomatoes," or "Dirty socks and shorts, if you want to have a look." His sweet nature never inspired them to bother checking.

The Canary was both a source of news from home, and a conduit for the communication of covert messages. Broadcasts would start with, "Before we begin, please listen to some personal messages." Then would follow a whimsical phrase, or occasionally a line from a poem. "The underwear is on the line," or "There was a fire at the insurance agency." These were communications to specific resistance groups or individuals who would tune in to the BBC at a given hour and listen for words meant for them.

During 1942, the men heard several such messages, which they found baffling. One of the men told the others that the only one who might know about this was Weir. Pressed for an explanation, Scruffy reluctantly explained that what they were hearing were Trojan words; colloquial stuff that described what needed to be done, or what had been done; always commonplace and banal, impossible to connect to anything. Scruffy explained that this particular message meant that London had received a message that had been sent. They wanted to know more about it, but he said that was all there was to know.

By August 1942, the camp's population had swelled to almost two thousand. Hearing shreds of news from the Allied front – the disaster of Dieppe, defeats in North Africa, ineffective scattergun RAF bombing raids – it stood to reason that with that many men penned up, someone was going to figure out a way to get out and find their way home and back into the fight. Escape was an ever-present undercurrent in all POW camps. The challenge and excitement of it, against the sheer boredom of a prisoner's life, fueled the men's imaginations and nerve. At Stalag Luft III, as with most Stalags, plans had to be sanctioned by the Escape Committee (known as the X Committee at this camp), which was overseen by the senior camp officers. The Committee vetted all plans, and provided information and advice where possible. But the Committee was never an impediment to any attempt that wasn't completely doomed from the start, and there was no shortage of invention or enterprise. "Speed tunnels" were one example, where one or two men would burrow a few feet down into the soft sand of the compound and then, digging frantically like prairie dogs, try to scoot under the wire. The problem was the air: you could only get about twelve feet underground before it started to become thin and stale.

Scruffy had heard of this technique, and didn't think it had much promise. But he was reading a book from the camp library, *The Sun is My Undoing*, a popular novel of the time about the 19th century slave trade. One section was about how the slave traders, when they wanted to get rid of some of the slaves, would bury them up to their necks in the sand, and then bowl cannon balls at their heads. Terrible, horrifying stuff. But it sparked an idea in his mind of the air problem in the tunnels. He talked to Jens Müller about it, because he couldn't quite make the idea come together in his mind, and they talked it through. They devised a scheme where the diggers would shove a metal rod up through the earth as they dug, poking little air holes every couple of feet. It worked beautifully, but as autumn came on and the temperature dropped, you could see your breath in the night air, and unfortunately the guards could also see little columns of steam rising from the tunnel below.

A couple of guys tried digging a speed tunnel in stages, coming up for fresh air after an hour or two. They dug at night, and having started close to the warning wire figured they only had a couple of dozen feet to reach outside the fence. One evening, as they were preparing to make another assault on the tunnel, the Honey Wagon – the wagon that hauled away the waste from the latrines – rolled into camp and drove over their tunnel. The wagon slowed on the unsteady ground, and with a *"whump"* sank down to its axles as the tunnel caved in.

The most interesting variation on speed tunnelling was the "Wooden Horse." Three men built a vaulting horse from the wooden Red Cross boxes, and used it for gymnastics in the yard. As the guys practiced their routines, three men – Eric Williams, Michael Codner, and Oliver Philpot – took turns hiding inside as the horse was carried out to the same spot in the yard, an open area near the warning wire. Once it was in place, the man inside opened a trap door, below which there was a corresponding soil-covered trap in the yard leading down to the tunnel they were digging. He would slip down and dig like mad while the men up top did their routines. Earth would be piled back into the base of the horse, and at the end of the day, the routine was reversed and the diggers and the horse were returned to the barracks. It took them almost four months, but at the end of October the three of them managed to make it under the wire and escaped to Sweden.

There were several men who tried scrambling out to the fence on their stomachs and cutting the wire, but got a hefty shock in the process. They could never be sure which wire had been electrified, as the "hot" one had been hidden in the tangle of barbed wire. Jens did some experimenting and figured out how to locate it and short it out without making it spark up like a fireworks display. But those who made it through the fence still had a long way to go to make it to the woods. The guards' spotlights sweeping across the open ground invariably picked them up: frantic rear ends, lit up like khaki pumpkins, crawling the 250 feet between fence and forest.

A wonderfully quirky RAF pilot, Tom Kirby-Green, who had arrived in camp shortly before Scruffy, was champing at the bit to escape. He was exceptionally tall, too tall to tunnel or to slip unseen under the wire, and talked to Scruffy about his frustration. Scruffy suggested he try slipping out with the bath parade. (There were special showers in the hospital compound outside the main grounds, which were used to delouse the men.) Tom smiled broadly, congratulated John on having a brain after all, and made his plans. A multi-talented Polish officer, Minskewich, dyed some RAF tunics to look like German uniforms and dressed four men up in these, Kirby-Green among them. They waited for the right moment, and then slipped in alongside the guards when they marched the prisoners destined for the bathhouse out of the main compound. When they'd all exited through the gate, the four ringers turned left instead of right and made a beeline for the woods. Luck was with them, as no one noticed. They kept time marching in step, looking every bit the part of a soldier's working party, and were home free until one of the camp's brighter officers, Hans Pieber, happened to come strolling out of the woods. Kirby-Green, being unavoidably tall, caught his eye immediately. Pieber asked, "Mr. Green! What are you doing out here?" Tom smiled, and then Pieber marched them back through the gate and into the cooler, to a chorus of hoots and hollers from the guys who'd been watching. (Pieber became quite popular with the POWs.)

Some escape plans were intended to fail, as a means of obtaining information, as exercises in misdirection from larger operations, or even just to help out a friend. There was a guard by the name of Paul who knew what war was all about. He had been on the Eastern Front, fighting the Russians for a couple of years. He had been wounded, and ended up as a prison guard at Stalag Luft III. He was an honest fellow, and some of the men were able to bribe him to bring in radio parts and other odds and ends that they wanted. It all seemed harmless enough, and he didn't mind as long as he continued to receive gifts of chocolate, cigarettes, and coffee. Two POWs, Gwyn Martin and Kingsley Brown, became very friendly with him; Gwyn could speak German and asked him about his family. Paul was very distressed as a major bombing raid had struck very close to his home village and he hadn't had any word of his wife and five children for weeks. They asked him when he last had leave. Almost three years, came the answer. What did he have to do to get leave? Basically, the guard told them, you have to be a hero. But he was no hero – just an old man with flat feet.

Martin and Brown acknowledged that at forty-six, he was indeed very old. Kingsley asked him if catching a prisoner escaping would carry any weight. Or two prisoners, added Martin. Then you would be a hero and get your leave. Paul smiled and said he certainly thought so. Together they devised an escape plan whereby they would hide in the washhouse until night once the prisoners were confined to their barracks. Then at an agreed upon signal, they would begin their escape; Paul would happen upon them and catch them *in flagrante*; then he would haul them off to the Kommandant and collect his reward. It all went according to plan, with Paul waving his pistol around and shouting so enthusiastically that Gwyn and Kingsley were afraid he was going to shoot one of them for good measure. The Kommandant praised Paul for his fine work and he was given a week's leave to visit his family. For the prisoners, an escape attempt meant an automatic two weeks in the cooler, which Brown and Martin were rather looking forward to as a restful break from the routine of camp life. But no such luck. The Kommandant was in good spirits, pleased with how cooperative the prisoners were being and how quiet things had been in camp. He cancelled their stay in the cooler and allowed them to return to their huts, thus depriving them of a much longed for vacation in those lovely, cool cells.

One brave soul tried slipping out in the honey wagon. He crawled in onto the dung and underneath the grass clippings that workmen had dumped on top to subdue the stench. Guards routinely jabbed pitchforks into this mess looking for escapees; but somehow they missed him. His tragically large feet, however, poked out of the dung heap and gave him away. The guards escorted him to the delousing showers to rinse him off, keeping their distance.

Another ambitious fellow had the idea of slinging half a dozen mattresses up against the fence when the guards were distracted, then using them as a kind of spongy ramp to run up and hop over. It nearly worked, too. Men in the compound started a fight at dusk, drawing the guards' attention. The mattress king and his sidekick seized the moment and made a run for the fence. The key man made it up and over, and was home free. His sidekick, however, reached the top and then tried to climb down the other side instead of jumping. The clanging and ringing wires made everyone, including the guards, turn around to see what the hell was making all the racket. John roared with laughter, telling me this story. "Even the goons started laughing when they saw what was going on."

Scruffy could see the potential for escape, but was also extremely sensitive to drawing unwanted attention to himself. The odds were against success, as he'd seen over the previous five months and dozens of attempts. The situation changed in October with the arrival of Squadron Leader Roger Bushell.

Bushell had been shot down in March 1940, and was the veteran of at least four POW camps, as well as two escape attempts that had been excruciatingly close to being successful. He was a South African who had studied Law at Cambridge. He stood about 5' 10", and was solidly built with a deep voice and piercing eyes. He had earned a reputation as a razor-sharp defense lawyer, especially in courts-martial cases in which he defended pilots charged with dangerous flying. He was a natural leader with the knack of making tough decisions very quickly. He was an avid sportsman, and the finest skier in Britain in the early 1930s. While competing in Canada, he narrowly missed cutting his eye with one of his skis during a run, the resultant scar giving him a dramatic droop to his left eyelid. Like so many of his generation, all he really wanted to do was fly. In 1932 he joined the 601 Auxiliary Air Force, also known as the "Millionaires' Mob," because of the number of wealthy young men who had joined the squadron and paid to learn how to fly on weekends.

When war broke out, he immediately went operational with 92 Squadron and by the end of 1939, he was not only Squadron Leader but had been given the responsibility for bringing the squadron up to strength. He arrived at Stalag Luft III from an exhaustive Gestapo interrogation in Berlin. He was suspected of being a participant in the assassination of SS-Obergruppenführer Reinhard Heydrich, "The Butcher of Prague." The respect Bushell had garnered from senior Luftwaffe officers probably saved his life; the Gestapo did not want to risk conflict with the more respectable German air force. But before being returned to the Luftwaffe's care, he had been warned that he would be shot should he once again be caught attempting to escape. While he never spoke of what he went through with the Gestapo, it clearly left a profound impact on him and an absolute hatred of everything that the Nazis stood for.

At Stalag Luft I in Barth, Bushell had served under Lt. Commander James Buckley (Fleet Air Arm), who had established the escape committee there and recognized Roger's potential, appointing him as his deputy. Buckley was now at Stalag Luft III, and as Roger's reputation was widely known, he was brought on board Buckley's escape committee. In November of 1942, Buckley and other suspected escape artists were moved to another camp to disrupt the many attempts. Bushell found himself in charge of the X Committee. He spent the winter months listening to what had happened so far, looking for weaknesses in the attempts, and considering what might be the best opportunities.

Bushell had a predilection for tunnels, as these provided the possibility of escape for more than two or three men. He determined that the full attentions of the men would henceforth be directed to a unified plan. Three tunnels would be dug simultaneously – Tom, Dick, and Harry – and should any one of them be discovered, the ferrets would be unlikely to suspect the existence of two other tunnels. The most aggressive component of his plan was to take out 200 men in a single night. All would wear civilian clothing or uniforms, and all would possess a complete set of forged papers to allow them to pass through train stations and check-points. He presented his plan to the X Committee with a conviction that fueled the entire operation. "Everyone here in this room is living on borrowed time. By rights we should all be dead! The only reason that God allowed us this extra ration of life is so we can make life hell for the Hun... In North Compound we are concentrating our efforts on completing and escaping through one master tunnel. No private-enterprise tunnels allowed. Three bloody deep, bloody long tunnels will be dug - Tom, Dick, and Harry. One will succeed."

He was not naïve enough to believe that everyone would make it. But he believed that the thousands of German forces that would be pulled away from war duty to track down runaway prisoners would create havoc in German high command. That alone was worth the effort.

Tunnelling began as the ground began to thaw. Bushell decreed that they would dig down ten or twelve feet, instead of three or four. But the sandy subsoil made it all but impossible to dig a tunnel of any length without it collapsing. He sent out word that he was looking for anyone in camp who had experience digging tunnels; he wanted their input. Wally, Hank Birkland, and Scruffy were mentioned, all three having worked in the mines in Northern Ontario. They were invited to an X Committee meeting. Wally and Hank did the talking, while Scruffy, being the youngest, held back.

Roger – Big X as he was known in his capacity as head of the X Committee – wanted to know what they could offer. With the scale of the operation, the X Committee realized that everyone stood to gain by a unified effort, which meant no one's input or talents were overlooked. Great ideas could come from anywhere, and there was going to be a vast mountain of problems that would need ingenious solutions. Wally explained that if they wanted to dig anything that would last, they would have to make some serious changes. They had seen the problems at Barth, and conditions weren't much better here. If you're really going to try to do this, then you should start doing it right, he said. Wally described some of the techniques he, Scruffy, and Hank had learned in the mines, and how a few basic ideas, applied with some ingenuity, could make all the difference. The X Committee needed to start thinking differently unless they wanted to see everything come to another dead end. Bushell said, "Right. Thanks." And they were dismissed.

Once they were gone, the committee members began to debate the ideas. Bushell sat quietly. After about fifteen minutes, he broke into the chatter. Abruptly, he announced that all tunnelling would be stopped immediately, and that structural techniques would henceforth be adapted to comply with the Canadians' recommendations. "All tunnelling will stop now. Mr. Floody is in charge of all tunnelling, and he can use who he wants. But I suggest he uses the three men who have the mining experience."

And that was it, the start of what came to be known as "The Great Escape", the largest escape of prisoners of war ever attempted.

## Chapter 16

# AUDACIOUS RESISTANCE

The escape became an extensive and well-organized operation – indeed, an industry – within the camp. In addition to the extensive tunneling taking place underground (an entity unto itself), 600 men worked secretly[1] in three main areas of activity: forging, making things such as maps, compasses, equipment; and in a full-scale tailor shop. These initiatives were made possible by the extraordinary range of skills – what John referred to as a "talent pool" – now present in the camp. Jimmy James, another POW who had also been at Stalag Luft I, said:

> Soon after our arrival a number of new faces appeared in the compound; they belonged to members of an RAF draft from the Army camp at Warburg, Westphalia. They were seasoned prisoners who brought with them a number of new skills developed in collaboration with their army officer comrades; these included the art of forging false documents, map making, finesse in tailoring, and dyeing. [In preparing for the escape] there were special sections for duplicating maps, using gelatin from food parcels, and for the production of forged identity papers, and travel documents, the latter known as the "Dean & Dawson Travel Bureau" under the artist flight officer Tim Walenn.[2]

Wally became the designated Master Tunneller, with Scruffy and Hank Birkland working closely alongside. He sketched out what the

---

1    There were in fact 10,000 men in the camp, with 2,500 of them in the North Compound, where the escape was centred. It is not clear how much the others knew of these plans, but it is astonishing that 600 men could accomplish as much as they did, largely in secret. Much of this activity, John told me, took place in small "cells" scattered around the camp, each operating without the knowledge of the others. Only Bushell and one or two others knew the full picture.

2    James (Jimmy) James. 2006. *Moonless Night: The Second World War Epic.* South Yorkshire: Pen & Sword.

new tunnelling strategy would be. First off, no more speed tunnels. There would be three tunnels, called Tom, Dick, and Harry. Tom, the shortest, was to run west from Hut 123 into the woods; Dick was also plotted to run west from hut 122, slightly south of Tom; and Harry, by far the longest, was to run north under the cooler, almost 400 feet to the woods. One of the Norwegian POWs had been a surveyor in civilian life, and he provided an approximate triangulation to calculate the necessary length for each tunnel to reach beyond the fence into the woods. A fourth tunnel, George, was started some months later from beneath the theatre located at the sound end of the compound, and was laid out to run underneath the east fence.

The tunnel entrances were dug through the concrete and brick foundation beneath the centres of the huts. The foundation was used for the small area containing the kitchen and washrooms above. Minskewich – neither Scruffy nor Wally could remember him ever mentioning his first name – was an engineer and had experience working with concrete, as was Zbischek Gotowski, Scruffy's roommate from Barth. They had easy access to cement, which was always lying around for the camp's non-stop repair and construction work. With this, they were able to precisely sculpt a tunnel throat with an inset ledge. The ledge supported a removable concrete trap that, when inserted, made the entrance all but undetectable. In Hut 104 and 123, the entrances were beneath the stoves, while in Hut 122, the entrance was concealed in a shower drain.

From now on, Wally determined that the entrance to the tunnels would be dug straight down thirty feet before levelling and moving forward horizontally. It was unlikely that digging at that depth would be detected up by the goons' seismic microphones; and it would be a more stable stratum of earth to burrow through. Second, the tunnels had to be shored up and braced, just like the mines in Northern Ontario, especially if they were of any length: top, bottom, and sides. While the lumber supply in camp was non-existent, the bed boards in the barracks' bunks were just the right size for framing the top, bottom and sides of the tunnel, giving them a dimension of about 2 feet square.[3] At first, the boards were nailed together, which was noisy and demanded a constant supply of scavenged nails. Then "Pappy" Plante, a POW who had been

3    The bunks were equipped with about five to six boards apiece, to support the mattresses. At first, the tunnellers used only one or two of the boards from each bunk, but as the tunnels grew longer, and the need grew, more of the boards were used, replaced with string zigzagged under the mattresses.

a farmer back in the real world and looked like he never had more than a couple of eggs in his basket, suggested that they join the boards the same way you would construct a chest of drawers: tongue and groove, no nails, and very strong.

Getting rid of the dirt from the digging was the big challenge. A cubic foot of compressed, hard-packed earth doubles in volume when you haul it out of the ground, and each three and a half feet of tunnel produced approximately one ton of sand. That meant figuring out a way to move the tons of earth they'd have to deal with, not to mention trying to find a place to hide it all. Because the excavated earth was yellow-orange, it couldn't be scattered on the compound's grey topsoil, and there were going to be hundreds of tons of the stinking stuff. Peter Fanshawe, a Fleet Air Arm pilot put in charge of dispersal, came up with an ingenious solution: two socks with the toes cut out were slung down the legs of a man's trousers with a pin holding the ends shut. These sock bags were filled with sand, and then as the men walked around the compound they'd pull a string to release the sand in a steady trickle. Whoever was walking behind them would scuffle it into the topsoil to blend the two together. Men were always walking the circuit for exercise, so this would fit right in with the pattern of the camp.

The Red Cross unwittingly facilitated the tunnelling. Included in their shipments were flower and vegetable seeds, sent in the hope that the prisoners would be able to plant gardens to supplement their meagre food supply and provide a welcome diversion. X Committee enthusiastically embraced gardening, both for the produce as well as for providing another place for the sand to be dug into the topsoil. The men who dispersed sand were known as "penguins" because of the way the sand-filled socks hanging down their trouser legs made them waddle slightly as they walked.

Although the goons never caught on to these tricks of sand dispersal, the process was a slow one given the tons that had to be moved. The earth was basically moist sand, so the digging was easy enough using scoops fashioned from KLIM tins. These were the tins in which the Red Cross sent powdered milk to the camps (KLIM = MILK.) In fact, KLIM tins were used for pretty much everything. John Colwell, an RCAF Navigator, came to be known as "The Tin Man" and "The Tin Basher," because he could make virtually anything out of the tins: clocks, tools, coffee pots, cups, kettles, pots, pans, water heaters, stoves, and even a kitchen sink. (The German officers recognized Colwell's talent too; when he offered to fashion an artificial tin leg for a fellow POW, they happily supplied him with tools and materials.[4])

Creating light to work in the tunnels was an early concern. Lamps were made using bits of fat and margarine skimmed from the food the men cooked in the huts, and then poured into KLIM tins using wicks made from string and shoelaces. But as the tunnels' depth and length increased, it became increasingly difficult to see with the small light thrown by the lamps. And the smoke and stench of burning fat increasingly made the already musty air more difficult to breathe, especially in the deepest recesses of the tunnel at its face. Wally talked about installing electric lamps along the length of the tunnel, but Scruffy discouraged this as he felt the wire would make it too easy for the ferrets to trace it back to the tunnels. So for the time being they stuck with lamps and candles. But the stale smoky air became a critical problem as the tunnels started to move forward toward the woods.

Scruffy approached Jens Müller, who had been an engineering student before the war, to tackle the air supply problem. He and Bob Nelson, a Yorkshireman, designed an air duct made of KLIM tins. A wooden trolley had been built on the tunnel to expedite the moving of men and earth back and forth to the face of the tunnel and the air duct was buried nine inches in the earth beneath the tracks. But the natural flow of air from up top was scanty at best, and they couldn't figure out how to generate a flow of air down through the ducts. After a couple of weeks of wrestling with the problem, Jens and Bob devised an air pump that could be constructed by the odds and ends available in camp. More importantly, one man could operate it. It was made from duffle bags and hockey sticks[5] and bed boards, and it functioned like a bellows. When it was compressed, it expelled two cubic yards of fresh air. As digging progressed, the men kept adding tins to the duct, ensuring the delivery of fresh air right up to the face of the tunnel. The tunnel grew, increasing the importance of the trolley. But as it was constructed of wood, wear and tear wore down the trolley wheels very quickly. Jens suggested wrapping tin around wheels, which gave them the resilience

---

4    John Colwell gave me a copy of his "scrapbook" of tin creations from the camp. It's remarkable.

5    Hockey sticks, skates, and similar gear were sent through the Swiss Red Cross but were also provided by the Germans in an effort to keep the prisoners occupied and their minds off escape.

they needed. But this made them noisy. So Jens suggesting putting water on the trolley rails, which cut the noise down to virtually nothing. Such ingenuity was relentlessly encouraged in all details of the escape plan.

To navigate the substantial length of Harry, the tunnel was dug on a downward slope for about a hundred feet, where it came to a leveling off point known as "Piccadilly Circus," a stope of sorts, where you changed trolleys. The tunnel continued on more or less level for about another hundred feet to "Leicester Square," the second change station, then started sloping uphill again to level out at what was calculated to be a thirty-foot depth. Determining the length of the tunnel, while allowing for the slopes and rises, was also a tricky calculation requiring at least three measurable points of reference, which they simply didn't have. This necessitated some educated guesses to try and ensure that Harry would be long enough to extend beyond the screen of the fir trees. Working with makeshift equipment and insufficient points of reference, there was a degree of error as much as six or seven per cent. They wouldn't know how accurate their calculations were until ground was broken at the tunnel's far end on the night of the escape.

---

Security had always been good in camp, but as the plan for the escape evolved, it became crucial. Within the compound, security was the responsibility of an extraordinary individual, George Harsh. He made a strong impression on Scruffy and everyone else who met him; and he became a lifelong friend of Wally's. White hair, cold blue eyes, and stoic, he was someone you did not challenge and who had an inner strength that exuded cold resolution. He came from an interesting and complex background, although no one in camp knew anything about him apart from Wally. George, an American born into a prominent family in Atlanta, was attending the University of Georgia in the 1920s and doing all the kinds of foolishness that college kids do when they first taste the freedom of the world. He and four of his friends, all from wealthy families, would get together of an evening with a supply of corn liquor – it was more fun to get drunk on the cheap stuff – and trade challenges and lies, exploring who they were and who they were going to become.

The fewer thoughts there are in a boy's head, the more inclined to have them filled with someone else's. These frequently drunk college freshmen got to talking about how much fun it would be to undertake a harmless, anonymous crime spree. They talked about how Leopold and Loeb[6] had been too arrogant and cold-blooded, while they would play it more sensibly. Find an isolated roadhouse or store, two go in, one with a gun, take a few dollars and disappear into the night. Even after they sobered up, the plan seemed sound. They continued talking about it, debating the pros and cons, how nobody was going to get hurt, and generally worked out and polished their plan. Someone produced a gun from their parents' home, and within a couple of days they had begun a minor crime wave that lasted for several weeks.

They became known, tellingly, as the "Polite Gang." It was never about the money for them, which was penny-ante at best: it was getting that unbeatable rush of free adrenaline. They would look for some isolated establishment, small enough to not have many people (or any at all), and large enough to have a bit of cash on hand and not feel the pinch of getting a bit of it stolen. They would draw straws, and whoever drew the short one had to hold the gun. Then the bunch of them would drive up to the place they had chosen shortly before closing, and with the motor running, the boy with the gun and one other would go in and demand some cash. Whoever had the gun was usually terrified and shaking with nerves, but the folks they were robbing were even worse. As they tore away down a dark country road outside with a couple of dollars as a trophy, a delirious feeling of excitement and relief washed through these 17 and 18 year old college boys.

George's first night handling the gun was at a rural grocery store, typically the safest of places to hit. He walked in with the gun drawn and told the storeowner to put his hands up. For whatever reason, the owner wasn't going to have any part of this nonsense from a couple of kids, and told them to get lost. George started to panic, and shouted at him to hand over the money. A store clerk emerged from the back of the store with a gun and opened fire. George reflexively turned around and shot back, killing the clerk. The clerk's shots missed George, but hit and killed the storeowner, and George and his friend got the hell out of there. Badly shaken, they threw the gun away and retreated with their tails between their legs to the safety of their parents' homes. It didn't

---

6    Leopold and Loeb were two wealthy University of Chicago students who in 1924 murdered a 14-year-old boy to demonstrate their superhuman ability to commit the perfect crime.

take long for the police to narrow the search. George had tossed his bloodstained clothing into the household laundry, and the family maid reported this. Within days, George and the other boy had been arrested and were put on trial. The District Attorney declared that self-defense was not a legal option as a defense, and after a short trial the jury took less than a half an hour to find them both guilty. George's friend was underage and hadn't held the gun, so he received a minor sentence of house arrest and probation. But George, who had been the shooter, was sentenced to death. Because of his family's wealth and influence, the death sentence was commuted to life imprisonment, which in 1927 Georgia meant spending the rest of his life on a chain gang.

The camp that eighteen year old George was sent to was one of a few remaining holdovers from a more primitive penal age – even in the Twenties it was considered unconscionably brutal. Known as a "cage camp," two hundred and forty inmates were locked into steel cages at night. These had originally been mounted on wheels and mule teams would haul them from one temporary location to another. Since this was no longer as necessary, the cages had been planted in a haphazard circle around some unpainted shacks that served as mess hall and kitchen, with a latrine and wooden trough for water alongside. A high barbed wire fence surrounded the cages, on a tract of treeless, grassless clay. A stock box and a sweat box were used for punishment, but not as enthusiastically as a lash, a four-foot long, three-inch wide leather strop used to beat men who committed any one of a thousand minor infractions.

Rehabilitation had no place in the Georgia penal system in those days. One of the first lessons you learned in that prison was that, in George's words, "…if you wanted to live, you had damned well better mind your own business." His tenacious will to survive helped him stay alive for twelve soul-deadening years, helped by a friendship or two. His intelligence and education helped him secure a position as trustee to the camp's doctor. He relished this modest elevation in his life – the smallest privilege or change in routine could give a man hope. He seized on the opportunity to keep his mind active and curious, and he studied any book available to him in the small clinic with the thirst of a man who knew he might never again see a book. His life was reduced to getting by, day to day, with no hope of any future; and in this way he made the most of each day that he had.

One weekend, while Dr. MacDonald, the prison's doctor, was away from camp, a guard had a severe attack of appendicitis. With no hospital or treatment nearby, the man was as good as dead without an immediate appendectomy. Having no one to tell him otherwise, George coerced another guard into helping him perform the surgery on the now-unconscious man. He had seen the procedure done, knew where the appendix was, and had read a lot physiology and surgery books. To ensure the guard stayed under, he anesthetized him with ether, and cut him open. The appendix was easy to locate, being so discoloured and distended. George carefully removed it, cauterized the incisions, and stitched the man's gut back up again. The guard survived, and within six weeks was back on the job.

The other guards talked about what he'd done and decided they wanted to show George their appreciation. One night they came to visit him in the clinic, offered their thanks, and handed him a pouch of pepper. George asked what it was for. One of the guards said that no one would be watching at four o'clock in the morning two days from now. So if he happened to go for a walk that night, chances are no one would see him. He should sprinkle the pepper on his tracks for the first couple of hundred yards; it would throw the dogs off his scent. They heard rain was coming, so if he made it to a road chances were he wouldn't have do anything more except keep moving. They gave him forty dollars they'd pooled together, shook his hand and said goodbye. George was embarrassed and flattered. In the clinic, he had hung a print on the wall and beneath it had printed the aphorism, "Be not wise in thine own eyes." He stared at it and found himself at a loss as to what to do.

Unbeknownst to him, in the days following his successful appendectomy, Dr. MacDonald and the warden had written the Governor of Georgia impassioned letters on behalf of George, pleading for clemency in his sentence. They argued that he had made a foolish mistake all those years before when he was barely out of his teens, while none of the other boys had served a day's time in jail. What's more, they felt he had a great deal to contribute to the world, and having him languish in prison was serving no useful purpose. Shortly after George had decided to act on the guards' offer of help in making a run for it, his sister received official notice that he had been granted a pardon based on his age, time served, and his humanitarian efforts in the prison. George was always a little vague about when and how he left the prison, but he never denied his guilt, which haunted him for the rest of his life.

George knew no one in Atlanta would have anything to do with an ex-convict and murderer. So in 1940, he made his way north of the border to Montreal, where after some preliminary obstacles and a couple of nights drinking beer with a bunch of Canadians who had just signed up, he enlisted in the RCAF as an air gunner. He was duly shipped off to operations in England in 1942, where he earned his commission. On his twentieth mission, he was shot down and shipped off to Stalag Luft III.

How he and Wally connected is anyone's guess. During those years, no one but Wally knew anything about this part of George's life. He had shared his story with Wally only because they had bonded so closely. George was ten years older, and had great composure and reserve. Despite his cold baleful stare, he was a sweet and gentle man who no longer had friends or family. There was something about Wally's sense of humour and dedication to the escape plan that drew them together in a way that bound them like brothers for the rest of their lives. Being a POW in Stalag Luft III must have seemed like a summer outing compared to his previous life on a Georgia chain gang, and his self-possessed calm must have been a great source of strength and confidence for Wally.

With Wally's endorsement, George was assigned to work with USAAF Lieutenant Colonel "Bub" Clark, who was 'Big S', head of ground security for the camp. This meant managing the signals when goons were roaming the compound. Any ferret entering the compound was logged in and tailed until they were logged out. Elaborate signals – hand gestures, opening and closing shutters, sounds – were employed to give a heads-up to men working on the vulnerable areas of the escape, which gave them time to shut down and conceal their work. It took the ferrets about ten minutes to reach Hut 104 from where Harry was being dug. From the time the spotters got a signal from lookouts that goons were on their way, the escape team could get up two diggers, two guys hauling sand, a "pumper" (the man working the air pump), and conceal the tunnel entrance in about eight minutes. When the Americans were moved out of the North Compound to the South Compound in September 1943, effectively removing them from the escape plans, George was left behind having served as a Canadian. Bushell immediately assigned him the role of Big S.

Bushell knew he would be watched by the Germans (and the Gestapo) and had to distance himself from any suspicion of participating in escape efforts. He went out of his way to be as inconspicuous as possible: taking part in rugby matches and other sports, joining language classes and cultural lectures, and once the theatre was completed in late 1943, as an actor. The Kriegies who swapped information with the goons spread the message in fragments and innuendo that Bushell was out of the escape business. By early 1943, the X Committee ordered Wally, Scruffy, and Birkland to go nowhere near Bushell. Glemnitz knew them too well, and if they were to be seen coming and going from Roger's hut or even talking in the compound, it would endanger the security of the operations on Tom, Dick and Harry. But this was no impediment: virtually all of their waking hours were spent underground.

Being modest of stature, strong, and indifferent to claustrophobia, Scruffy was well suited to the digging. Each morning he was to dig, he would put on his long underwear[7] – or sometimes not bother and just strip down to the buff – then climb down into the tunnel for his shift of digging, often shared with Wally. They worked on Harry, the tunnel that ran north from Hut 104. Wally was a good deal taller than Scruffy, but as thin as a rake and highly motivated. Scruffy was equally motivated, but was also glad to be out of the general circulation of the camp. After his unnerving welcome by the British IO and the questions about the Trojan words, he wanted to be as inconspicuous as possible. But his real inspiration was Wally. Scruffy felt his old friend from Sunday school had been, in John's own words, "ordained for this job". He knew mines, and he shared Bushell's determination not just to dig a tunnel, but to confound the Germans with escape on a scale that they wouldn't have dreamed possible. Wally had found his calling, and he put his heart and soul into the successful execution of the plan.

Down in the tunnel, the two-man team took turns. The front man would dig out the earth with his KLIM shovel – digging the sandy soil was easy – and then push the earth back behind him, where the second man would load a trolley to be hauled back and emptied. They could manage five feet of tunnel during each work shift, then the sand would have to be removed and the tunnel shored up. In Harry, because of the length, there were two-way stations where full trolleys would be sent back and empty ones returned to the front. There were some who wanted to tunnel but couldn't because they were claustrophobic. Tom

---

7    Sent by his mother from home.

Kirby-Green tried it but he was a big man and got stuck behind Scruffy, who had to crawl back over the taller man, and then drag him out by the legs. When Scruffy got Tom out, he was absolutely ashen. Scruffy asked him why he hadn't told anyone that he was claustrophobic. Tom caught his breath and stammered out, "I didn't know I was…"

Wally was well over six feet tall, but had no trouble with the digging. One day when they were working together, the tunnel collapsed. The guys who had been digging before them had forgotten to put the top board up, and the earth buried Wally. Scruffy heard a "wump", then felt a rush of wind, followed by muffled shouts from beneath a mound of earth. He dug Wally out, dragging him free by his feet. They had to rebuild the thing and fill in the hole in the ceiling where it had caved in. The two negligent tunnellers never went down the hole again, although they were there for Harry's daily opening as well as its closing at the day's end.

When Scruffy was digging, he had a habit of drifting left and downward from the correct trajectory as he inched forward in the semi-dark thirty feet underground. What saved him from digging back around in a circle was learning to follow the KLIM tin air duct underneath the tracks, which he said was as good a guide as having a dotted line to follow. (Engineers would also come down a couple of times a week with a spirit level to confirm the tunnel's trajectory.)

There were breaks in between, although you had to pee where you lay. Appell was held twice a day, at eight in the morning and again at five in the afternoon. If he had time, Scruffy would dash in and grab a shower first. After a few hours of underground digging, sweating like a galley slave, he could be pretty ripe. The other guys in his hut were never less than enthusiastic to hustle him into the showers to hose him down. At one Appell, Scruffy didn't have time to shower and came directly from the tunnel. Hauptmann Pieber, on seeing this airman covered in dirt and reeking of sweat and mud, said, "Mr. Weir, I believe you have been playing in the sand piles, yes?" "Just working on my garden, sir," Scruffy replied with a smile. Hans Pieber, a likeable, gentle soul who could be a good friend to the prisoners, would lend them his Leica, and even have their photographs developed. He was wise enough to be aware of changes in the winds of war, an instinct that served him well in coming through it alive.

Escape was something of a game between the Germans and the X

Committee. The Germans knew that the prisoners would always be trying to find a way out, and the men knew that the goons were always watching, listening, and prodding about, waiting to pounce. There were personal grudges as well. Certain Army personnel had treated the non-commissioned Glemnitz with little respect. When some unruliness broke out, Glemnitz would draw his pistol, shouting imprecations at the POWs in a manner befitting his sergeant-major rank, then tuck his pistol away again, saying, "How's that for acting, boys?" He was also heard to say to some POWs who had befriended him, "Those army Dummköpfes know nothing; so I tell you escape!" But neither side knew everything about when or where or what the other was up to. The ferrets would get wind that something was up, let the prisoners continue to work away as long as possible allowing them their delusions of freedom; then at the eleventh hour, swoop down and collapse the tunnel or the plan, and revel in the triumph of crushing the spirit of the escapees.

The X Committee was well aware of this gambit. As tunneling proceeded, Big X began to encourage all manner of escape attempts, knowing most if not all were doomed. They encouraged the goons' belief that they were always one step ahead of the prisoners' desperate and failing attempts, so as to keep the real plan alive. Keeping this Three-Card Monte game afloat was essential to minimize any awareness of Bushell's greater plan. One ferret in particular – Corporal Karl Griese, nicknamed "Rubberneck" – was a much-despised guard. He had no sense of humour, was aggressive, unpredictable, and everything that Glemnitz was not, and he sought out any excuse to impose his modest authority. Outwitting Rubberneck was always a particularly welcome part of the game for the prisoners.

As the camp became increasingly crowded, the Germans began adding compounds to handle the hundreds of new American prisoners arriving each week. By the summer of 1943, workmen began clearing the woods to the west of the compound where Scruffy and Wally and the rest were tunnelling. This new compound effectively rendered Tom and Dick unviable, as they led directly into the area where construction supplies and workmen were beginning to arrive. This did have one positive dividend, however. An RCAF pilot, "Red" Noble, spotted a coil of electrical wire left unattended by the German workmen. He liberated it,[8] and brought it to Hut 104 where Harry was wired for electric light. Jens had been experimenting with tapping the camp's electricity without the goons being able to trace it. The X Committee decided that if they sacrificed a tunnel, it could be used as a repository for some of the backlog of sand that was choking Harry's progress. The penguins dumped as much sand as would fit into Dick, and when the time was ripe, clues were left for the ferrets to "discover" it. There was a great commotion when they did, upsetting a lot of the men who thought it meant the big escape plan had been blown. The goons were exuberant in having uncovered such a large tunnel (albeit half the length of Harry). They felt it was the obvious focus of the POWs' escape plans, and were smug at having soundly beaten the prisoners at the escape game.

To ensure that the tunnel could never be resurrected, they brought in explosives to destroy the tunnel's entrance. As they packed the dynamite around the end of Hut 123 (from where Tom was being dug), Scruffy, Wally and Hank watched them with educated interest. Scruffy said, "You think they know to tamp the charge?" (Tamping is the process of packing the dynamite to direct the force of its explosion.) The three men looked at one another, and then back at the demolition team. Wally said he didn't believe that those German boys knew *anything* about what they were trying to do. Then he suggested they move the other POWs who were watching back a dozen yards or so.

As Scruffy and the boys fell back, the goons set off their charge. And as Wally had surmised, the Germans did not have *any* idea of what they were doing. The dynamite blew the back off the hut, splintering fragments that fluttered down all over the compound, causing the chimney and the hut itself to shift off kilter like a drunken sailor. Some of the POWs were distraught at having had a tunnel discovered. But it kept the guys who knew the real story chuckling about it for weeks afterwards.

---

8    John used terms such as "purloined" and "permanently borrowed" to describe how useful items were acquired.

Dulag Luft POW camp seen from the air, with the letters "POW" painted on the roofs to prevent bombing by the Allies.

Dulag Luft, the interrogation camp for Allied airmen outside of Frankfurt.

The main compound of Stalag Luft 1 in Barth, in northern Germany on the Baltic Sea.

Stalag Luft III guard
tower and fence.

A typical room in
Stalag Luft III.

*Photographs courtesy of the
US Air Force Academy Library.*

| 1 | 2 | 3 | 4 | 5 | 6 | 7 | 8 | 9 | 10 | 11 | 12 | 13 | 14 | 15 | 16 | 17 | 18 | 19 | 20 | 21 | 22 | 23 | 24 | 25 |
|---|---|---|---|---|---|---|---|---|----|----|----|----|----|----|----|----|----|----|----|----|----|----|----|----|

**Personalkarte I :** Personelle Angaben

Kriegsgefangenen-Stammlager : **Stalag Luft 3**

Beschriftung der Erkennungsmarke

Nr. 735

Lager : Stalag Luft 1, Barth

Name : Weir

Vorname : John, Gordon

Geburtstag und-ort: 7.19 Toronto

Religion Anglikaner

Vorname des Vaters : James

Familienname der Mutter : Taylor, Frieda

Staatsangehörigkeit : Canada

Dienstgrad : F/O

Truppenteil : R.A.F.    401 Fl.Squ    Komp. usw. :

Zivilberuf : Student    Berufs-Gr. :

Matrikel Nr. (Stammrolle des Heimatstaates) : C 1650

Gefangennahme (Ort und Datum) : Abbeville 8.11.41

Ob gesund, krank, verwundet eingeliefert : gesund

Lichtbild

Nähere Personalbeschreibung

| Grösse | Haarfarbe |
|--------|-----------|
| 1,72 | braun |

Besondere Kennzeichen :

Verbrennungen im Gesicht

Fingerabdruck des rechten Zeigefingers

Name und Anschrift der zu benachrichtigenden Person in der Heimat des Kriegsgefangenen

Eltern: 272 Forest Hill Road, Toronto
Ontario, Canada

WEIR, J.G.    Wenden !

John's "Kriegie" ID card from Stalag Luft III, April 1942.

Fran in uniform, 1942. She was working for Research Enterprises Limited (REL), located in Leaside, Toronto. REL created technologies for Canadian, British, and American military forces throughout the war, as well as for the BSC, SOE, OSS, ISI, Camp "X", and possibly MI5. Radar and Aztec were developed at this facility.

John in Barth (Stalag Luft I), shortly after he was released from hospital in February 1942. The burns around his eyes are clearly visible.

A group photograph of Canadian officers in Stalag Luft III. John is 2nd from left in the front row; Hank Birkland is to his right. Hank Sprague is at the far left in the second row, and Wally Floody is fourth from the left in the third row.

Hank Birkland, Hank Sprague, Zbischek Gotowski (a Polish pilot), and John playing cards in their room, January 1943. Gotowski officer did the portraits pinned to the wall behind them.

John and Hank Birkland in Stalag Luft III, May 1942.

John had this picture taken in the East Compound, Stalag Luft III, July 9, 1942 to send to Fran and his family. He very likely had the photo retouched in order to reassure them that his burns and scarring weren't serious.

Clockwise from upper left: Sam Sangster, Scruffy Weir, Hank Birkland, and Wally Floody. The photograph was taken inside one of the rooms at the height of digging "Harry."

Sports at Stalag Luft III. In the lower right is a hockey game during the winter of 1942/43. John is the player in the right foreground.

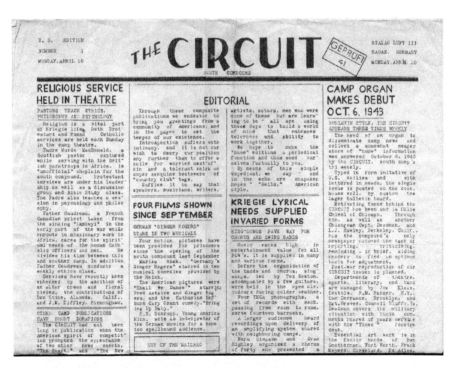

The Stalag Luft III camp newspaper, The Circuit, which the Germans would print for the Kriegies.

The theatre in the North Compound. George, a fourth tunnel, was dug from beneath one of the audience seats.

"Thark", a farce by Ben Travis, being performed at the Stalag Luft III theatre.

Sound effects for the plays were broadcast over the microphone/PA system in the theatre at Stalag Luft III.

A new lecture program was presented every three months in Stalag Luft III.

One of the guys playing a female role in a production at the Stalag Luft III theatre.

A tin can on the end of a stick was the washing machine in camp.

Art Crighton conducting one of the Stalag Luft III orchestras.

Wally Floody looks down from a top bunk in his room in Luft III.

Tom Kirby-Green, a good friend of John's, and one of the 50 executed by the Gestapo after the Escape.

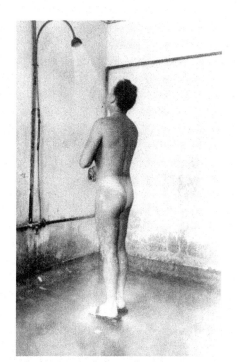

Hot showers were offered just twice a week.

Don Foster, Larry Barjaro, and John in Stalag Luft III, May 5th, 1944, the day John returned to camp following eye surgery.

Harry "Wings" Day, a long-time friend and mentor to John in Stalag Luft I and Stalag Luft III.

Roger Bushell (right), "Big X", with Bob Tuck, in Stalag Luft III, October 1943.

Photographs courtesy of the US Air Force Academy Library.

Hermann Glemnitz, the head guard at Stalag Luft I and Stalag Luft III, and a great friend to John. Glemnitz was flown over to Canada for a POW reunion at the POW's expense in the 1960s.

Hans Pieber, a well-liked hauptmann (a captain) at Stalag Luft III.

Standing L to R: F/Lt. Pengelly, P/O Mule, F/Lt. Sprague, P/O Anthony, F/O Noble, F/O Broderick, F/Lt. Jamieson, F/Lt. Weir, P/O McCague, P/O Wiley, P/O Avery, F/O McGill, F/O Armstrong. Sitting L-r: P/O Baker, F/O White, P/O Smith, P/O Sullivan, P/O Soper, F/O Monkhouse in Stalag Luft III in the summer of 1944.

L-R: Wally Floody (Toronto), Jens Muller (Norway), Hank Birkland (Calgary), Pop Collett (NZ), Hank Sprague (Hamilton), John Weir (Toronto), Barrie Mahon, DFC (Santa Barbara),Sam Sangster (Winnipeg), in Stalag Luft III, October 1943.

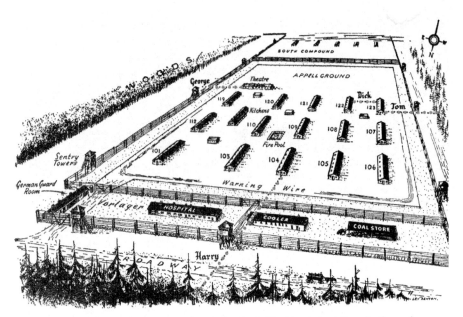

A plan view of the North Compound in Stalag Luft III. The dotted lines indicate the paths of the four tunnels. The tunnel code-named "Harry" is in the foreground leading to the woods.

*Drawings by Ley Kenyon.*

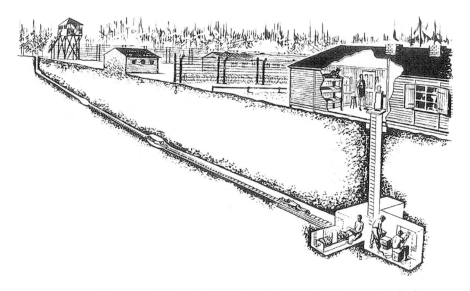

A section view of the tunnel "Harry", which began inside Hut 104, went straight down 30 feet, then ran 335 feet north underneath the Cooler, two fences, a guard tower, and a road, almost into the forest on the far side of the road.

## Chapter 17

# FOUR SHEETS TO THE WIND

By December 1943, the digging had hit a dead end. There was nowhere else to put the huge volumes of sand excavated from the tunnels. The abandoned tunnels had been filled, the space underneath the huts was packed with sand and earth, and with snow on the ground, blending it into the topsoil was all but impossible. The tunnellers were near the end of the tunnel and ready to make the final push, but everything had come to a standstill. Scruffy had slimmed down to about 130 pounds with the combination of hard work and scant rations. Like most of the guys, he had become considerably more interested in food than anything else like women or the war.

It was a frustrating time, to be just waiting. A work-in-progress celebration had been planned, largely centred on a special batch of booze. Liquor had always been brewed up in dribs and drabs using all kinds of ingredients, with various brands circulating the camp. A major moonshine effort was put into action for this party. Minskewich showed the guys in his hut how to make his own particular bathtub vodka – vodka being a loose term here – out of potatoes and raisins, with some spittle to help get things brewing. They mashed up this mush, spread cheesecloth over its top, and then left it to ferment in barrels buried underneath the huts to keep them cool (and to keep the goons from finding them). After about four or five weeks, the mixture was frothing and ripe. The barrels were tapped to run off the liquid into a metal pail, which was then heated a bit to condense the alcohol content. The final step was distilling the liquid in the shower room using a trombone as a distillation coil. At one end, the liquid would be brought to a boil and forced through a tube into the trombone. Cold water was run over the trombone's coils to make the mixture condense, and the distillate dripped out of the tail end of the horn. To evaluate the quality of the brew, Minskewich put a match to a teaspoon of it. If it burned yellow that meant it was deadly, so they'd keep the process going until the liquid burned blue, at which point it was relatively safe to drink and the liquor was collected a drop at a time.

Minskewich made several gallons of the stuff, and invited guys from the other huts to try it out. It was extremely potent. A sporting soul bet two squares of chocolate to anyone who could drink a small glass of the stuff and still be standing five minutes later. Everyone took the bet, Scruffy included, because how strong could it be? When his turn came, Scruffy took his small glass and knocked it back.

On the way down, it burned like the devil, which occasioned a bit of choking and such; but all in all it seemed pretty damned good for an amateur effort. Then something peculiar happened. A funny feeling descended over him like a rolling fog and he decided he'd best set his glass down. As he later told me, "I managed to miss the table – I wasn't entirely sure that there ever had been a table there – and the glass seemed to fall to the ground in slow motion, hitting the floor as gently as a feather, as though it had slipped the bonds of gravity. The glass broke as it hit, fragmenting into one shard at a time, each one drifting and floating through space in a most extraordinary way." Scruffy was trying to make sense of this when a curtain of blackness took him into a dreamless sleep. To the best of his knowledge, he came to several hours later, although for all he knew he could have been in a coma for a week.

When the party really got rolling, everyone got blind drunk, paralytic. George Harsh came out of one of the huts wearing a bed sheet as a toga and a crown of thorns on his head; with his mane of white hair and beard, he struck a very biblical image. The Germans were horrified at this; the Catholics were horrified; and the rest of the men were choking with the laughter of the truly drunk. George walked to the Fire Pool – a concrete water reservoir where the guys sailed model boats – and everyone swears George managed to walk three or four steps across the water before sinking like a rock. The only thing left of him was his crown of thorns, floating on the water's surface. When he popped up again, he said, "Right, boys. Now you can crucify me," and then slowly sank back down into the drink.

The next day, everyone was as sick as pigs. At Appell, the Germans were disgusted by the condition of the men who managed to stagger out; the huts were worse. There was vomit everywhere and comatose bodies on every surface. The guards were forced to haul in fire hoses and flush out all the rooms.

One wit posted a poem on one of the camp's bulletin boards the next morning, a timeless verse coined by American humourist George Ade:

> Last night at twelve I felt immense,
> Today I feel like thirty cents.
> My eyes are blurred, my coppers hot,
> I'll try to eat, but I cannot.
> It is no time for mirth and laughter,
> The cold, grey dawn of the morning after.

It was a party that none of the boys ever forgot.

# Chapter 18

# IN PLAIN SIGHT

Scruffy was the youngest in his small circle of friends, and was extremely fortunate that the other guys kept a protective eye on him. Wally was like an older brother to him, and was worried that Scruffy wasn't getting proper sleep because of his having no eyelids. He had seen how hard John was pushing himself digging in the tunnels, getting sand burns from digging in the buff, and how off-handed he was about the discomfort his eyes gave him. Wally requested a Red Cross doctor come to examine him, this being a regular service the Red Cross provided. The doctor who came a week or so later checked John over carefully, expressing even graver concerns than Wally had. He said that left untreated, John's eyes would become septic and he would eventually become blind. He recommended a German hospital outside of Frankfurt where a remarkable ophthalmologist might be able to rebuild some eyelids for Scruffy.

Scruffy was determined to stay and see Harry finished and to be a part of the escape. But Wally reminded him that the operation was shut down until they could figure out how and where to dispose of the backlog of earth from the tunnel. Tom and Dick had been filled with emergency supplies and sand. The Red Cross doctor had estimated that the surgery would take a couple of weeks, so Wally told Scruffy that he might as well go. Nothing was going to happen any time soon, Christmas was coming on, so why not have a holiday with some pretty nurses and get your eyes back in shape? This frustrated the hell out of Scruffy, because he was sure that as soon as he was gone, someone would figure out a way to get rid of the earth and he would miss the escape. But the snow was already starting to fall and it was getting cold in camp, and he didn't want to lose his eyes. So in early December, he reluctantly agreed to be sent to the hospital in Frankfurt-am-Main.

There were two other men who were also going to Frankfurt to have their eye problems dealt with. In consideration of receiving special medical treatment, all three swore oaths that they would not try to escape. They were all in need of help, and winter was upon them, so this was not a difficult prospect. That being said, for both the Allied airmen and the Luftwaffe officers, giving one's word was sacrosanct. This was a code of honour that stayed with most of the men throughout their lives.

Before entraining, the men had to be given inoculations for typhus. There had been an outbreak of that virulent and contagious disease in the region, and hundreds of thousands of prisoners in Nazi concentration camps – including Anne Frank – had succumbed to the disease. The inoculations were extremely painful. Scruffy dropped his trousers and took what was coming, with the other two following suit. The orderly was distracted by a phone call when giving the shot to a man suffering from an ulcer on his eyeball, which looked almost as foul as it must have felt. When the orderly returned, he had forgotten what he had done and gave the poor airman – already in agony – a second (and potentially) deadly injection. Halfway to Frankfurt, the man with the ulcer was in bad shape, shaking and sweating with a raging fever; but nothing could be done for him. By the time they reached the hospital, the man had fallen unconscious. The ophthalmologist met them and was alarmed to hear of the unfortunate double dose of the vaccine, which undoubtedly caused the fever and delirium that now consumed the man. The doctor covered the ulcerous eye with a patch and took him away to see what, if anything, could be done.

The hospital was located in a nunnery – St. Vincent's Marienheim – in Bad-Soden, a village immediately northwest of Frankfurt on the west bank of the Main River. It was high on a hill with a spectacular view of the city, and was run by an order of German nuns. The first nurse who visited John was nothing but loving and tenderness. "Ah, liebchen, liebchen. Rest. Just rest. I will take care of you." He rolled over like a puppy and let himself be coddled. She brought him a raw egg, which he wolfishly cracked and swallowed whole in one gulp. It was the first one he had tasted in years. The next morning on the ward, Scruffy woke and lay in his hospital bed, enjoying the sunshine through the windows and the calm of this corner of the hospital. Fresh sheets, clean clothes, and sweet and attentive nurses: he was in heaven. Then, lurching upright in bed from a dead sleep, the man with the ulcerous eyeball began to flail about, screaming, "I'm blind! I'm blind! I'm blind…!" Scruffy went over to him and forcibly pushed him back down in bed until he stopped struggling and his voice trailed off. Scruffy adjusted the man's eye compress, and said, "Your patch flipped over on the wrong eye. Now shut the hell up!" The ophthalmologist came to see what the racket was about. John told him, and the doctor said that the accidental double dose of vaccine back in Sagan probably saved the man's life. His temperature was almost 106, which burst the ulcer on his eye and allowed it to drain properly. Scruffy made a mental note to thank the orderly if he ever saw him again.

As it turned out, this doctor was someone very special. Major David L. Charters was a Scottish ophthalmologist who had been captured in Greece in 1941. When the Germans realized the extent of his expertise, they transferred him to this hospital at Bad Soden. They were in desperate need of his skills, which he agreed to provide as long as his services were offered to Allied POWs as well. In John's words, the Germans thought that Charters was "God Almighty when it came to eye surgery", and to show their appreciation they provided him with the latest Zeiss equipment. After several months of Charters working for them, the Germans offered to send him back to England – even allowing that he could take the new equipment with him – provided that he would send back another ophthalmologist who could work similar miracles. Charters declined, saying he would be of more use there in Bad Soden. He would prefer to stay put. From then on, in the Germans' minds, he could do no wrong, and he remained in Bad Soden until the end of the war.

What Charters lacked was practical experience in plastic surgery with eyes, although he had been trying to teach himself with the help of several medical texts. When he met John and examined him, he said, "You're going to be my guinea pig." This did not reassure John, who asked Charters what this meant. Charters said he felt he would be able to rebuild two new eyelids at least. And with a bit of ingenuity and luck, he might be able to rebuild all four. It would take some time, but they both had plenty of that. The one major drawback was that he had no anesthetic to help cope with the pain. There were small amounts of it in the hospital, but none was for use on POWs. Charters went on to explain that apart from the eyes, there was only one place more painful for a man to be "cut," which, ironically, was also the best place to get the appropriate skin for the grafting work he would have to do. John had already experienced the skin on his face and hands being peeled off with nothing but petroleum jelly to buffer the pain. Charters advised him that this eye surgery would be substantially more painful than that; this would be real pain and the procedure would take six to eight weeks. John would have to lie very still and not move his head or his eyes, not even a twitch, otherwise there would be a better than fair chance that Charters would blind John during the procedure. Above all, the doctor reminded John that as he had never done this kind of surgery before, they would have to trust each another completely.[1]

John listened attentively, trying to process this new and unsettling information. Charters explained that to manage the pain, John would have to learn self-hypnosis, which would take some time. They would start the next morning, and he would check on John every day to see how or if he was progressing. When John was capable of separating his mind from the pain, then he would be ready for surgery. But the odds were still slightly in favour of him losing his sight. John took this all into consideration, but knew that this was the only option worth taking. They started the next morning.

Charters had John lie down on an operating table and stare at the ceiling. He told him to think of the most beautiful place in the world that he had ever seen. He would have to be able to visualize it such that he would not only be able to see all the details in it, but would also be able to hear and smell everything as well: all the colours and sounds, the fragrance of the grass, the bees and trees and flowers and butterflies or whatever else might be there. Then he would describe what he saw in his mind's eye in as much detail as he possibly could. John thought of a Scottish glen that he remembered as being a most extraordinary place. Charters sat beside him, egging John on to give increasing detail, forcing him to dig into his memory for every fragment of information he could dredge up. John eventually lost track of time as he talked, and was only brought back to the present when Charters interrupted him and told him he had done fine; but added that he wasn't nearly ready. They went

---

1    John told another anecdote about Dr. Charters, unrelated to his eye surgery, and reflecting more on John himself than the doctor: "I was young, and pretty naïve back then. When I went to the hospital to be operated on by Charters at Bad Soden, he asked me, among other things, if there was any unusual sexual activity. And I didn't even know what the hell he was talking about. I said, "No, no. There's no girls there." I remember the look he gave me, and I thought, "Holy cats, what's he thinking?" Later I used to blush at how naïve I was. There was obviously some of that stuff going on in camp, but I was never any part of it."

through the same exercise each day for weeks: John visualizing the glen, constantly digging deeper and deeper into his memory. Each day as he re-told the story, he worked to expand the specifics of the scene he had so clearly in his mind. He would lose all sense of time during these sessions, with Dr. Charters sitting quietly beside him. Sometimes hours would pass without John realizing it, and in time he stopped waiting for the day when he might actually succeed in hypnotizing himself. How would he know when he had done it? It was like a Zen riddle: if he was aware of putting himself into some kind of a trance, then he wasn't really hypnotized.

This started to worry on him. One day, in the midst of a particularly detailed passage he started to that feel he had exhausted the subject. He broke his narrative to tell Charters he wasn't getting anywhere with this; all he was doing was saying the same things again and again. He didn't know how much longer he could do it before he would be ready. Charters told him that he had stuck a needle into John's hip thirty minutes earlier and John hadn't even flinched. They would begin in the morning.

The next day in the operating room, John's head was sandbagged on either side so he couldn't move it. Charters told John to tell the story again, with every bit of detail that he had been visualizing. But this time he would have to tell it to himself. He couldn't move any part of his lips or his face. He would have to be absolutely certain that he told the story thoroughly and didn't leave a thing out. There were two stages to the surgery. The first was harvesting skin for transplant. Charters had determined that the best skin to use for reconstructive surgery on the eyes would be a graft from the foreskin; but John had been circumcised, so that greatly limited their options. Charters settled for a wedge of skin from the soft flesh on the back of John's arms and legs. As John lay motionless on the operating table revisiting his vision of the Scottish glen, Charters gently sliced a piece of skin to be transplanted. He laid it in place on John's left upper eye socket, stitched it to the remnant of the upper eyelid, and then stitched the eye shut.

It took about a week for the skin to begin to heal and for them to see if the graft would take. When it was clear that the graft was successful, Charters repeated the procedure on John's right upper eyelid, again stitching the eye shut.

Now the problem was the lack of appropriate skin for the lower eyelid grafts. When he was confident that the two upper lids were beginning to heal, Charters had to find some appropriately fine skin for the reconstruction of John's lower lids. He took slices of skin from the soft tissue on Scruffy's underarm, and then grafted them on to his neck for future harvesting. The skin was too thick, but he had no other options. Charters hoped that the graft on the neck would heal and regenerate in a sufficiently pliable form to work on the lower lids, which would take a few weeks.[2]

Dr. Charters left John to heal in the ward and turned his attentions to a German officer who had come to the hospital for treatment. The rumour on the ward was that the general was the nephew of Field Marshall von Rundstedt, one of the most senior German officers. This nephew was a pilot ace who had been burned like John. The Perspex of his aircraft's canopy had shattered, showering tiny shards into his eyes and effectively blinding him. German High Command wanted to know if Charters could do anything for him. After an examination, he felt he might be able to restore sight to at least one of the General's eyes. The hospital staff was delighted and extended all the resources of the hospital to Charters, including whatever anesthetic he might need.

Charters agreed to undertake the work on the German pilot on the conditions he would receive no anesthetic. Since the POWs were denied it, the German pilot had to go without as well. That way he would know what the men had been going through. The work was going to be excruciatingly painful, but it was up to them, he said, if they wanted to tell the German pilot that in advance. In agony, he readily agreed. From then on, on Thursdays the German was laid on the operating table, his head sandbagged, and using tweezers Charters would pluck out a fragment or two of Perspex from the injured man's eyes. Usually he could only bear the removal of one fragment a day because he was unable to lie still, screaming blue murder in pain. The POW patients enjoyed hearing the German's suffering as much as they had suffered without anesthetic. It took several weeks to remove all the fragments, and in the fullness of time, the German pilot had full sight restored in one eye and about 50% in the other. Now it was time to return to John.

The grafted skin was ready to be re-harvested from John's neck and stitched into place on his lower lids. It was April 1944 before the grafting and surgeries were complete and John's eyes had healed. Learning to

---

2    John had four more corrective surgeries between the 1970s and the 1990s.

blink again with the new eyelids took some practice, but he managed. It was spring and the weather was warming up. Soon he was well enough to walk around the perimeter of the nunnery. After months of being bed-ridden and having to lie so still, he enjoyed being able to get out and stretch his muscles back into some kind of useful shape. Apart from a German dentist recommending that he could pull out all of John's teeth (although they were indeed in very bad shape, he declined this offer with thanks), his time in the hospital was a quiet respite from camp life and the war.

The atmosphere around the hospital changed abruptly one morning in the first week of April. One of the doctors took John aside and told him that there had been a mass escape from Stalag Luft III. There was still no confirmed information, but rumour had it that many of the escapees had been shot while resisting arrest. That was all he knew. John was shocked, anxious to know if any of his friends had been shot, and how things could have gone so badly wrong. He wandered around the grounds in a daze. Back inside, he asked Dr. Charters and everyone else he knew if they had any information. No one knew any more than he did. He stared out a hospital window that afternoon, trying to figure out how to get some news. As he stood there, a throbbing pulse seemed to be running through him; it was as though he could feel it more than hear it. He looked down at the tiled floor, trying to make sense of this strange sensation. Then the building began to resonate – *thromba-thromba-thromba* – a distinctive and vaguely familiar sound, but he couldn't figure out what was causing it. He looked out the window and saw what at first he thought was a flock of crows swaying gently back and forth in formation. A murder of crows, he thought; what a strange term. Then he realized that the swaying of the flock was evasive formation flying, and what he was looking at were a thousand RAF Lancaster and Halifax bombers on a raid headed directly toward the hospital.

A sky filled with that many large aircraft is a difficult sight to describe or even imagine. It transfixed John where he stood; he never gave thought to looking for shelter. He watched the endless waves of bombers as they passed over Bad Soden and the hospital and headed for the heart of Frankfurt on the far side of the river Main. He watched them cross the river and let their loads go, the five hundred pound bombs floating down like so many leaves fluttering off a tree in a gust of wind. Then he watched as the bombs erupted into puffs of smoke and flame.

Tens of thousands of tons of bombs were being dropped on the city, making smoke billow up 10,000 feet, obscuring the roofs of buildings and shooting ribbons of fire up through a haze of ash and dust.[3] The attack knocked out power and water in the city, effectively preventing a German counterattack. The aircraft slowly circled around to return to England, leaving a devastated city in their wake. Shortly afterward, the hospital's security officer came to warn John that it was no longer safe to venture outside. The citizens of Frankfurt were enraged because thousands of people had been killed during the raid, and if he were caught outside, even near the hospital, the mob would tear him apart. So he stayed in the safety of the hospital, watching from a window as the city burned.

Around three o'clock that afternoon, a less-familiar rumbling began to rattle the windows as another air raid came on. John knew from the sound that these weren't British aircraft. He crossed to the west side of the hospital and could see a beautiful formation of American B-17 bombers coming in to complete the mission. Since all communications had been destroyed in Frankfurt, little anti-aircraft defense was possible. John told me, "Not one German shot was fired" as the Americans crossed the Main River and dropped their bombs, completing the devastating attack on the city. That day over 30,000 people were killed in those two raids.

John felt no remorse. In his view, the raid on Frankfurt was payback for what the Nazis had been doing to millions of people over the past ten years. And knowing what had happened at Stalag Luft III, with the men shot while escaping, he revelled in the Allies' attack. He was now anxious to return to the camp as soon as possible to find out what had happened, why the escape had gone so terribly wrong, and who had been killed.

---

3  Bomber crews reported feeling the heat from these fires even at altitudes of 10,000 feet.

# Chapter 19

# THE RUSSIANS ARE COMING

Scruffy's instinct about the X Committee's ingenuity had been right. A few weeks after he had been sent to Bad Soden, they had solved the problem of disposing of the excavated earth from Harry. The Kriegies had built a theatre at the south end of the North Compound, with the Germans enthusiastically supplying materials and tools, seeing its construction and use as energy-consuming distractions for the prisoners from their relentless and irksome determination to escape. The theatre accommodated approximately 300 with seats constructed from the wood of the Red Cross parcels. The stage and audience were both "raked" – sloped – and this provided generous space beneath the floors for dumping excavated earth from the tunnel. The final tons of sand were dispersed under the seats and the stage, and a fourth tunnel, George, had been begun, heading toward the east fence. By January 1944, only six weeks after work had come to a halt, escape plans were back in full swing. The final drive to complete Harry was put into motion and the X Committee kept a close watch on the best possible conditions for a mass escape. Cycles of the moon, night time temperatures, potential inclement weather, and the impending invasion of Europe all played important parts in choosing the right night. And a moonless night was what they wanted, for obvious reasons.

The escapees would be heading for the town of Sagan, so a Friday night/Saturday morning would provide the advantage of quieter weekend railway traffic, and lackadaisical attention to security. Harry was complete in the early weeks of March, and the moonless night of Friday March 24th was chosen for the escape. Accordingly, all the forged documents were dated for the days around that weekend. Once the X Committee had committed to this date, there was no turning back. Principal contributors to the escape effort were offered the first places among the two hundred spots available. The rest were assigned by lottery. When the tunnellers broke through in the early hours of Saturday, March 25th, 1944, they found that the tunnel exit was just short of the tree line. Worse, there was snow on the ground that would show footprints as the men made their way out. Seventy-six men managed to escape during an air raid when the camp's lights were blacked out. As power was restored, a guard saw the 77th escaper scrambling out of the tunnel as the lights came back on, and the escape was over.

Luck played a great part in the fate of those involved in the escape. Had he not been in hospital, Scruffy would have been in the first wave of escapees.[1] In early March 1944, Wally, George Harsh, Peter Fanshawe, and several other notable escape artists were summarily rounded up. For some time, the Germans had suspected that a major escape activity was underway. These men, along with fifty or so other POWs who volunteered to be moved, were punished with a transfer to nearby Stalag VIIIC at Belaria, a former slave labour camp four miles away.

Back at Stalag Luft III, there had been last minute changes and substitutions in the escape order. Dick Bartlett, the "Canary" keeper, had been paired with a Norwegian, but in the days leading up to the escape it was agreed that two Norwegians were better suited to travel together, and Dick agreed to take a lower number in the order.

Ironically, Roger Bushell had not been one of the men singled out because of the very effective efforts to distance him from the X Committee's activities over the previous months. Rumours had been spread that the American, Lt. Col Albert "Bub" Clark, now in the South Compound and previously head of security, was the man to be watched, not Bushell. The Germans were persuaded that Roger's interests now lay primarily in sports and the theatre. To compound this ruse, in the weeks leading up to the escape, Bushell was busy rehearsing the role of Henry Higgins in a production of *Pygmalion*, which was to open on the 24th. (Bushell's understudy, who had been given a heads up, went on in his place.)

———————————

News of the escape of 76 RAF officers from Stalag Luft III had

———————————

1  John had been designated as Number 13 in the order of escape, but his place was assigned to another man once John had been transferred to the hospital at Bad Soden. It was his understanding that the replacement Number 13 escaper had been re-captured and subsequently shot.

reached Hitler within 24 hours. In a blind rage, he issued a *Grossfahndung* – a national manhunt alert – for the recapture of the men, ordering that all those recaptured would be shot. But D-Day, the invasion of Europe, was imminent and it was clear that the tide had turned against Germany. Hitler's most senior advisors, Himmler and Göring, tried to persuade him to be more reasonable in his demands. They had their eyes on Germany's relationship with neutral countries, especially how best to negotiate their own shelter from prosecution when the end finally came. As a result, there was a considerable debate and concern amongst these and other senior officers about obeying Hitler's orders to shoot the escaped men – somewhat ironic in light of their lack of concern for the millions of men, women, and children then dying in concentration camps across the continent. Ultimately, Himmler persuaded Hitler to reduce the number of executions to a list of fifty who would then be arrested and shot by Gestapo agents.

The German High Command removed Stalag Luft III's Kommandant Lindeiner in disgrace for having allowed such a massive escape from this supposedly escape-proof camp. A week later, the camp's SBO Group Captain Herbert Massey requested a meeting with the new Kommandant, Colonel Braune. He anticipated hearing bad news, and to ensure that he understood everything that was said he was accompanied by Squadron Leader Philip Murray to translate and produce an official transcript for both the Luftwaffe and the R.A.F. Kommandant Braune was clearly uneasy as he glanced at the communiqué that held the news he now had to convey.

"I am instructed by the German High Command to state that 41 of the escapees were shot while resisting arrest."

"*How* many were shot…?" asked Murray.

After a moment, Braune responded, "Forty-one."

Murray translated for Massey, who bristled and snapped, "Ask him how many men were wounded."

Murray complied, and Braune said, "I think none were wounded."

"How could forty-one men be shot in those circumstances and all killed?"

"I am only permitted to say by German High Command that 41 of your men were shot while resisting arrest," he said.

"Have you a list of their names?"

"I do not have that information."

Massey rose.

"I expect you to provide it as soon as possible."

Hans Pieber, the well-liked adjutant, escorted Massey and Murray out of the office, saying, "Please do not think that the Luftwaffe was involved in any way in this dreadful affair. It is terrible."

There was an awkward silence, Massey unable to muster any civil response.

In the wake of the escape, the Germans announced that no matter what excuse, if there were any further escape attempts, the men would be summarily shot; no court-martial, no second chances, no extenuating circumstances. The Germans posted a notice stating, "'To all Prisoners of War: The escape from prison camps is no longer a sport." It went on to detail the consequences should they try, rounding off with, "The chances of preserving your life are almost nil! All police and military guards have been given the most strict orders to shoot on sight all suspected persons."

---

When Scruffy was transferred back to Sagan in early June, the new IO was waiting for him. They went for a talk walking the circuit. The IO explained to John that they were no longer speaking to the Germans because of the murdered escapees. Life in camp had settled down to a new and bitter routine, with an icy tension between the Allies and their captors. To punctuate their boiling resentment, many of the defiant prisoners would walk up to a guard's face, stand about a half a foot away, and just stare at them. They would never touch them, because many of the guards would not have hesitated to retaliate quickly and brutally. At the daily Appells, the POWs would slouch in line, generally cultivating a surly disdain for the whole charade. No respect was shown the Germans, and they were infuriated.

Eventually the Germans stopped entering the compound unless absolutely necessary. There were exceptions. Auctions were held for the belongings of the murdered fifty[2], with the proceeds going to their families, and the bidding amongst the men was brisk. Glemnitz had returned to the North Compound and was present at the auction, egging the men on with shouts of, "Bid, gentlemen, bid! Bid!"

---

2    At first, the number of murdered escapees was thought to be 41. But after a week or so, as reports filtered into camp, the final number totalled 50.

Lectures, sports, and theatre productions continued, albeit with a more subdued, if determined, air. With escape no longer an easy option, there was less to keep one's spirits up, although by summer, the Allies invasion of France and the breakthrough in Normandy made the war itself their source of hope for the future. All Americans had been moved to a new compound to the west. With the Canary residing in the North Compound, news of the D-Day invasion was communicated across the wire by a Scottish padre to a Scottish-American POW. They both spoke Highland Gaelic, thus confounding the Germans who assumed it was some kind of new code that they were unable to break.

The rest of 1944 lacked the unified and exciting sense of purpose that Bushell's great escape plan had brought to the men. As fragments of good news and bad trickled into camp, spirits went up and down accordingly. In September, the men were treated to the sight of a Focke-Wulf 190 being chased by an RAF Mosquito fighter in the skies near the camp. The fast Focke-Wulf was diving to pick up speed, but the Mosquito could fly at least as fast. The Focke-Wulf disappeared with the Mosquito hot on its tail and exploded just out of sight. As the Mosquito flew off, there was a huge cheer from the men in the compound: they had the sense that the Allies were on the cusp of a final breakthrough. Perhaps the war would be over by Christmas after all.

By the autumn of 1944, the invasion of Europe and the increasing desperation of the German army had begun to choke off the much-needed supply of Red Cross parcels. The treasured packages appeared less and less frequently until there were none at all and the men started to experience real hardship. Fragments of war news continued to trickle in. The rank and file Germans in camp were visibly losing hope, but propaganda still was regularly posted on bulletin boards and in German radio broadcasts on loudspeakers in the compound. Films were shown, demonstrating some of the German doctors' inventive medical experiments, which they clearly felt were a contribution to the betterment of mankind. One film that several men remembered focussed on an attempt to graft the muscle and nerves from one man's legs to another's. Another showed an experiment with rabbits where they were trying to generate twin fetuses – in hopes of generating more German offspring to bolster the Reich – using a very fine hair to constrict a fertilized egg and divide it into two. Slave labourers, who had been seen working around camp for several years, disappeared. An atmosphere of doom seemed to be slowly taking over the men and their captors.

Scruffy's teeth were still in bad shape and he was sent to a dental clinic some distance from the camp. He had no idea where it was; only that it was about an hour's train ride away. When he and his escort arrived at an unmarked station and disembarked, Scruffy noticed ten cattle cars on a siding at the railway station. More particularly, he noticed a number of young women were standing by the tracks, wearing yellow stars on their clothing.[3] Some were quite beautiful, while others looked wan and forlorn. Scruffy assumed they were refugees being transferred from one camp to another, a common enough sight across Europe. He settled into the dentist's chair to wait for the work to begin. When the dentist had finished a couple of hours later, John asked him what the train cars and girls had been about. The man visibly paled and shook his head, then told John to say nothing about what he had seen. Then he was escorted back to the train.

> *When I was taken back [to the train], the train cars were still there but all the girls weren't. There wasn't a sound. The cars were mobile gas chambers. I was naïve, but I probably knew more than most people did about what was going on. The world was basically uninformed during the war, and after. They'd been told about Dachau, but didn't believe what they heard. There are guys still writing about it, saying that the Holocaust was a figment of the Jewish imagination. Yet even after all I'd seen first-hand, I still found it hard to believe that the Nazis would go as far as they did. What they did to the Poles and the Gypsies and the Jews: the experiments they did: they were proud of it! They used to show movies of some of the experiments in camp. Even though after the war people were always saying, "I wasn't a Nazi," or "I was Swiss."[4]*

As the war careened to an end, the Nazis diverted an increasingly large number of resources to expedite the killing of the enemies of the Reich. There was little that they were not prepared to do to eradicate traces of their ethnic cleansing, or avoid the subsequent accounting that would

---

3    Under the Nazi regime, Jews were required to wear a yellow star badge affixed to their clothing.

4    A short video of John talking about this was posted on the Internet a few years ago, and it elicited dozens of angry comments from anonymous critics who argued that such statements were simply propaganda of anti-German prejudice.

complicate their lives when the war was over. The German war machine was beginning to disintegrate and it was every man for himself.

---

Within the camp, the men had to piece together fragments of information about the war's progress. The increasing velocity of the advancing Russians and the crumbling of the Third Reich prompted talk about the chances of the POWs' imminent liberation, perhaps through an exchange of prisoners. There were also dark rumours of German High Command having issued orders to execute all prisoners should their negotiation attempts fail. SBO Massey had been repatriated because of ill health in late 1944. The new SBO, Group Captain D.E.L. Wilson, organized the men to create resistance units should the Gestapo come rolling in without warning. At the very least they would have the chance to go down fighting. And there was always George, the tunnel running from beneath the theatre, which was kept active as a storage space for emergency supplies and as a potential refuge.

The approach of the Russian army from the east was so swift that it displaced all other speculation. By Christmas 1944, the men were hoarding food and preparing for the likelihood of a forced march in the dead of winter west into the heart of Germany. Sleds were built and clothing revamped for inclement conditions. In Scruffy's hut, they made high calorie bars of chocolate, barley, and raisins, which could be tucked in a pocket and would keep a man going for twenty-four hours.

Scruffy tried building a sled but he didn't have the materials to finish it so, like the other men, he concentrated on winter clothing instead. In addition to wearing as many layers as possible, he wrapped a scarf around his midsection into which he tucked spare mitts and socks. The final touch was a turban of sorts that he fashioned out of another scarf. One of the men back at Barth had shown him how to do this, and it was extremely effective in protecting the head against the cold.

On Saturday January 27th, 1945, weeks before anyone expected them, the men in camp heard the Russian artillery rumbling in the distance. This meant the Russians were about a day away from reaching the camp. The Germans in camp were not about to consider surrender or even to defend themselves: the Russians had dealt ruthlessly with Nazis, seeking retribution for the millions of Soviets that had been slaughtered by the Germans. What was certain was that the prisoners were going to get caught in the middle, likely with a mass execution – unless they were able to move quickly.

That evening, the Germans issued orders that the prisoners were to collect their belongings and be ready to move in an hour's time. They announced they were going to march the men back into Germany for safekeeping from the Bolshevik rabble, although the reality was that they were hoping to use the POWs as hostages to bargain for their own safety. The camp became a flurry of activity as men scavenged as much as they could lay their hands on from the remains of Red Cross parcels. John and seven friends worked together and began packing everything that they wanted to carry into packs and sleds. But like everything else in the military, it was a case of "Hurry up and wait." John began writing in his Red Cross diary (all prisoners had been given one), and in short entries he kept track of the prisoners' forced march.

*January 27*
At 2.00 pm, roughly mid-way through the last act of the dress rehearsal of the camp production of The Wind and the Room[5], we were told to "...be packed and ready to move in an hour's time." We've all got kit bags, some concentrated food and extra food – but with 6 hours warning, we could have been much better equipped. Much has to be left behind – books, photos, journals, and the usual Kriegie "indispensable" junk. We have finished as well possible, and are standing by to leave.

*January 28 – Midnight*
After seven reprieves, we're still standing by. It's snowing and cold, and we aim to travel as a unit[6], and thus we're each carrying communal food as well.

*2:30 am.*
We're off! We've 75 miles to do in three stages of 25 kilometers in 3 days in a southwesterly direction. It's snowing

---

5    This is John being humorous; he's referring to the cold huts they were billeted in, and the winter storm that was raging outside.

6    Seven men from the same room set off together: Scruffy Weir, Lorne Chambers, Hank Sprague, Sam Sangster, Pop Collett, Kirby Martin, and Jody Wilson.

and cold – perhaps we should have built a sled after all. Each man has been issued a Red Cross parcel or more if he could carry it… many can only carry the chocolate, so the rest is discarded… what waste.

*1:15 pm.*
Freiwaldau – what a march – my back is sure sore from my pack. What bedlam – a thousand or more Kriegies milling about the market square, trading with the locals for bread, cheese, and wood. You can buy the town for a nub of "D" bar[7]. We've miles to go before we rest.

*6:15 pm.*
What a shambles! Really cold, snowing, blinding wind and dark as the grave. Everyone dead-tired trying to pass and get inside – so far no place to go into – goon discipline completely gone, strings of refugee carts passing add to confusion, spirits low, many are exhausted, frost bite. The sled has been our salvation – but we'd better be inside soon.

*7:30 pm.*
Inside at last in barn, hay, sleep… eat.

That was the end of their first day on the winter march.

The first leg of the journey was from the camp to Sagan, only half a mile away, and then on to Muskau, 35 miles to the west. The going quickly became rough as a storm swept in and the men found themselves trudging through six inches of snow. The temperature dropped to -20° C, which is cold at the best of times, but for these half-starved men, clad in rags and scraps, it was especially grim.

As they walked, they saw hundreds of odds and ends littering the side of the road, items that men had jettisoned once they realized there was only so much one could carry. As Scruffy and the other men moved along, they too discarded things they realized they wouldn't need and picked up bits and pieces that they might. Wally, George, and the rest at Stalag VIIIC were moved out on a similar march from Belaria to

---

7    An emergency chocolate energy ration bar.

the north two days later, but were headed to a different destination. From January to April, over eighty thousand Allied POWs were force-marched west across Poland and Germany in what came to be known as the Winter March.

The POWs marched 20 miles the first day, with the men finally crowding into shelter in several barns. They had been moving for sixteen hours with little rest and no organized meals. That night was one of the coldest of the year. The POWs' clothing and boots were wet from the snow, with some parts covered in ice. Cooking was impossible in those conditions, and there was little water to be had. The march resumed on Monday morning. Many prisoners began falling by the wayside through exhaustion, hunger, and cold. Some were fortunate enough to make it to a village, where many of the locals were surprisingly kind and helpful.

The main column of the POWs moved on again on Monday morning and reached Muskau by Monday evening. Here they found billets in a cinema, a glass factory, a riding school, a laundry, and a deserted French POW camp. There were no sanitary facilities or arrangements, and most of the men contracted dysentery.

*January 31*
Many fellows sick – either from overeating, the strain of the march, or change of water or a combination of all three. Sam and Hank aren't feeling too sure of their stomachs.

Scruffy had chosen to make the march with a group of men well suited to travelling and working together. It included an older vet, "Pop" Collett, from New Zealand. Pop was more mature, better informed about many things, and really knew how to organize the men. Pop told Sam Sangster, the cook in the group, that they were to drink nothing but boiled water. So they never touched any unless it had been thoroughly boiled. While Sam cooked, the others collected wood for a fire. Once they had found their billet, Scruffy slipped away from the crowd of men and into farmhouses around Muskau in search of food. Remembering Adrian's advice to be straightforward and fair when dealing with the enemy, Scruffy would knock at the front door, and was usually greeted with some caution. But when he made it clear that he was searching for bread and cheese, perhaps a bit of meat, and would exchange these for the coffee, chocolate, and cigarettes that the boys had plenty of, the reception warmed right up. In two instances, he was even invited to come back the next day to trade more of the same. Because of the pains they took to boil their water, Scruffy and his group managed to avoid the violent diarrhea that struck virtually everyone else. And with the cheese and bread Scruffy had scrounged from the locals, they were in pretty good shape.

After four days in Muskau, they were on the move again. They walked 18 miles to Spremberg and were mustered at the 8th Panzer Division's reserve depot. Soup and hot water were provided, but before they could get a chance to rest and eat, orders were given to march another 2 miles to a station, where the two thousand men and their German guards gathered in a train yard full of horse cars: "forty and eights", so called because they were designed to carry forty men standing or eight horses. The men were herded on to the cars – with as many as sixty packed men into each – in cramped and unsanitary conditions.

> *February 1*
> There are only five left of our original eight. The march has just about completely exhausted everyone. No one can say we've had a tougher struggle before. Hope to God it gets no worse. We've a week to look forward to travelling in cattle cars.

> *February 3*
> Dawn. Ruhland a junction on the Breslau-Magdeberg line. Being moved in trucks. What a night – room for only 20 to lie down to sleep at a time, while the other 20 sit up. We arranged it in 6-hour shifts. I'm on the 2nd shift to sleep. Fellows are beginning to feel very thirsty – no sign of water.

In the boxcar that housed Scruffy and his group, Pop Collett took charge. He told the men to do exactly what he said if they wanted to survive the trip in some reasonable health. First off, he said that a third of the men were to sit down now, another third were to lie down, and the final third were to stay standing. Everyone would stay that way for four hours, then rotate; each man had the same routine. For hygiene, he organized the cutting of a hole in the wooden floor of the car. If anyone was going to be sick or relieve themselves or do anything else that everyone would rather have outside, then it went down that hole. This would control the spread of any contagion. Although it was primitive, it was substantially more ordered and sanitary than the other cars.

Whenever the train stopped, Scruffy hopped out and ran up to the engine to get water. When he had been a child in Algonquin Park, there was a railway turntable near the family's cabin. Most of the trestles in Algonquin were too rotten to support the weight of the trains, so a turntable had been built to send the trains back on the return journey from that point. There he had the opportunity to climb all over the massive locomotives waiting to be turned around, and investigate the location of switches and levers, and – most usefully in the present circumstances – how to draw water from the engine's reserve tank. The men in the car behind Scruffy's were in really bad shape because they were so dehydrated, and he managed to get them several pots of water as well.

Corporal Griese, aka "Rubberneck," the hated ferret, spotted Scruffy's legs running back and forth and began to take pot shots at him. Rubberneck couldn't see who was doing the running with only legs to shoot at beneath the undercarriage, but Scruffy wasn't taking any chances and scrambled back on board. He knew that Rubberneck had been responsible for more than one POW's death and was proud of it.

By the time they arrived in Darmstadt, 16 miles northeast of Bremen, they had been travelling for two days with a ration of two-thirds of a loaf of bread per man and a few cans of water. Many men were in terrible shape and some had died, but no one in Scruffy's car had fallen ill. For most, it was the overpowering stench, thirst, and hunger that were the hardest to bear. Struggling through bitter winter conditions, with no food to be found, the men were desperately hungry and cold. The invading and liberating allied forces effectively created a blockade for supplies as they moved east towards victory. The column of 2,000 men cut a swath on either side of the roads they travelled hunting for anything to eat. Many simply dropped from exhaustion and died. Others, foraging for food, were shot by guards for attempting to escape. Disease became rampant. What meagre food supplies the Germans had been providing ceased to appear. The men were starving and hundreds died. So desperate was the will to live, some resorted to cannibalism.

On the trip, Pop Collett had developed intestinal bleeding and was sent to a hospital in Marlag-Milag for treatment. The rest were marched two and a half miles to Marlag-Milag Nord, a German POW camp that the Red Cross had already condemned as unfit and unsanitary. Apart from their unquestionable exhaustion, many of the men were suffering from frostbite, dysentery and malnutrition. More than seventy per cent of the camp's population suffered from gastritis, dysentery, colds, and influenza by end of the first week there.

> *February 5*
> After marching 55-60 miles, we reach Marlag–Milag Nord[8].
> It's not a very encouraging looking place.

The first night at Marlag-Milag Nord, it rained. Scruffy and his friends had stuck together on the ride there, and together they built a sod hut, which, while unglamorous, was warm and dry. It would be their home for the next forty-eight days. The camp was a ghastly place. It was little more than a field enclosed by barbed wire with no habitable huts. The Germans supplied no food, so for a month the men starved. Conditions were so bad that German civilians in the area brought food to the wire and threw it in. There was one sadistic ferret that signaled to three POWs to go to the wire and retrieve some food that had been thrown on the far side. As soon as the three stepped over the wire, the guard shot them dead.

> *February 11*
> We've been here a week – still no beds, blankets or utensils other than what we brought ourselves. Miserably cold and damp all the time – of 35 in this room, 33 have squitters[9]. Little or no fuel.

> *February 12*
> There are 35 of us in a room – 70' by 16', and all but six sleeping on the floor. We scrounged some wood – so by strict rationing this means lighting the fire at 5.30 pm and keeping it going until it burned out around 9 pm.

---

8    Marlag-Milag [*German for Marine Internment Camp*] had originally been a part of a concentration camp, then was used as a PoW camp for merchant marine seamen.
9    Diarrhea.

*February 19*
General opinion is the war has merely weeks to go – varying
from three to ten weeks – more like the latter. "Home by
June" is my motto.

The black market is and has been thriving – today a
communal system has been established. I hope it works – for
it will eliminate these bastards who bid against you and these
force prices up to where they are now (10 cigarettes per egg,
up to 20 cigarettes per loaf of bread).

*March 3*
We all have beds, 1 bowl per 2 men, 3 lights per 35 men, 3
tables, 5 benches, a cup per 2 men, 4 knife/fork/spoon/can
opener kits per 5 men. German rations are being reduced. The
main bones of contention are: (1) Lack of fuel; (2) No water;
(3) Lights, spasmodic if at all; (4) Showers only twice a month
– if you're lucky; (5) Crowded quarters; and (6) No cooking
facilities even if we had fuel. There are still no sheets and some
have no palliasse covers.

Scruffy and some others had been taming the goons with cigarettes and
chocolate, trying to find out what the hell they were doing in this ragged
camp. From a variety of sources, they discovered that the Russians were
closing in from the east, and that the Canadians and Brits were moving
quickly up the coast from the southwest. They were close enough to
the North Sea and England that they could receive BBC reports, and
it was clear that the Royal Navy was in complete command of those
waters. And with the Canadian and British armies moving up through
Holland towards them, the end of the war was at hand. But British radio
broadcasts warned the men not to try to escape. Conditions were very
dangerous, and they would be safer staying together until the liberating
Allied forces reached them. Everyone was on edge. Still, being so close
to freedom, some could not resist the urge to escape. But those who
broke out of the camp were never heard from again.

As pressures mounted from the encroaching Allied and Russian
offensives, the cornered Germans decided to move their hostages to
another camp near the Baltic port city of Lübeck. In that location, they

would have the Baltic Sea at their back, one less flank to defend in the event of attack. Scruffy realized the Germans were planning to march 2,000 men 150 miles with no food, water, or medical supplies. The men were already scraping by to survive, and the Germans continued to shoot stragglers and troublemakers.

Scruffy saw the march for what it was: a desperate final gambit for the Germans to save themselves. The more he thought about it, the more he became convinced that the POWs could not survive another march. The Germans were having trouble finding food for themselves, let alone for the POWs; and the desperate measures the men were beginning to take to feed themselves could unravel into brutality and chaos amongst the survivors. With the increasing desperation of the Germans, the lack of meaningful authority, and the unpredictability of the conditions they would be trying to survive in, Scruffy began to formulate a plan to get himself and his friends to safety.

# Chapter 20

# AT LARGE

The night before they were to start the forced march, Scruffy went looking for a goon that he thought might be receptive to a proposal. He found a burly, middle-aged guard who looked as unhappy about what was happening as the prisoners were. He offered him some cigarettes and led him to a quiet spot in the field. Scruffy explained he had a deal to offer: he and some friends were going to leave the camp that night and make their own way to Lübeck. He felt this final march would be a disaster. If the guard were willing to come with them and act as cover, they would work out some kind of amnesty agreement that would keep him out of prison after the war, which might even save his life. The man was wary and said nothing. Scruffy said he would write up a contract that night. He and the three friends he had picked to accompany him would all sign it, and then tear it in half. He would keep one half and the guard would keep the other. When the Allies came to liberate them in Lübeck, Scruffy and the others would explain how the guard had helped them. All he would have to do is to show his half of the contract as proof.

The guard wanted to know what would be expected of him. Scruffy said he would be responsible for finding a cart and horse, a driver, and some straw. He would stay in uniform and carry his rifle to make it appear as though he was escorting four POWs to a camp. But he would have to do whatever they asked of him without question, and they in turn would do what they had to. The guard considered this, weighing the dangers of being at large in the country against the possibility of his future freedom. He shook his head and said he would have to think about it; there was a lot of danger. Scruffy told him that there was no time to think about anything. They were going that night, so it was either a yes or a no. If he said no, then fair enough, they would find someone else. The guard said all right, he would let them know. Scruffy went back to the other three and reported what had happened. He was sure the guard would come through, but had his eye on a couple of other prospects just in case.

Around four o'clock in the morning, the guard kicked Scruffy in the foot and woke him up, and they had their escort. The guard had found a cart and a driver and left them waiting just outside the camp. Scruffy roused his group – Sam Sangster, Ed Bell, and Hank Sprague – and they hit the road. Scruffy had chosen this threesome for very specific reasons. They were all Canadians and he knew them pretty well. He felt confident that they would be more likely to work with him than against him. Sam was a good cook and could speak fluent German; he had been Scruffy's roommate in the last months at Sagan. Hank Sprague was a little older than the others and more mature and stable, which would be a good balancing factor, plus he had been on Scruffy's squadron back in England. Ed Bell was a terrifically good-looking guy, with typically Aryan features: pink cheeks, blue eyes, six feet tall, and a million watt smile. They could use him as a "goat" when they went foraging for eggs or produce. He would knock on the front door of a farmhouse and engage the hausfrau's dreamy-eyed attentions while Sam and Scruffy ducked around the side of the house or into the barn and grabbed whatever food there was to be found. Hank would stay on the road and keep watch with the guard in case any unwanted company showed up.

That first night, Scruffy decided they should keep moving through the night and all the following day. Travelling by cart and on foot he estimated that they could make three or four miles an hour. The two thousand men from Marlag-Milag with the guards escorting them would be lucky to make a quarter of that time; so with a head start, their foursome would be well out of sight and mind of the others.

At this point in time, mid-April 1945, the war was all but over, which brought out the best and the worst in people. Exhausted soldiers laid down their weapons. Fanatic Nazis dug in and vowed to fight to the death, charging blindly into murderous machine gun fire in service of the Fatherland. These were strange days where the bodies of dead German soldiers were booby-trapped with explosives by their comrades and left for Allied soldiers to discover when they went to bury the bodies. If you were on the loose and weren't obviously German, you didn't stand much of a chance. The country had been devastated by the war. Bombing raids had destroyed most of the major German cities, causing some infuriated civilians to lash out at POWs, shrieking, *"Terror Bombers…! Air Gangsters…! Baby Killers…!"* when they encountered one another passing through towns and villages. With the impending threat of the Russian and Allied offensives sweeping across the country, and all manner of displaced persons and forced labourers on the loose seeking revenge, the retreating German army was trapped. No one was safe.

Scruffy thought he knew what they might encounter on the trip. During that first day, he laid down his terms for what they would have to do if they were going to survive. Anyone was welcome to split off on their own at any time, but he would be calling the shots. He knew how to find his way across country, he understood the Germans, and he was aware of the dangers they were bound to encounter. The first hard fact was that if the Germans, the Russians, or possibly even the Allies caught them, they were dead. At night, one of them would always be awake, and they would sleep at least sixty feet apart from each other, fully dressed. If one of them were caught, he was to yell for all he was worth, which would give the others a chance to leg it. The guard and the cart driver would sleep well away from the four Canadians. If the German escorts were caught aiding and abetting prisoners, they would be dead too. During the day each of the four POWs would take a turn sleeping in the straw-filled cart for a few hours while the other three walked behind. The guard and the driver always rode. No more than two days would pass before the guard would find a new driver and a fresh horse in the villages they passed by, and they would send the previous driver on his way. No one but the four Canadians and the guard was ever to know anything about what they were up to. Any food they managed to scrounge would be split six ways: the guard and driver would get exactly the same as the prisoners. They were all living under the same conditions, so there would be no argument about it. If the guard or one of the drivers started to throw his weight around, then the four Canadians would have to decide if the problematic German was going to have an accident or not.

Scruffy told the group that he couldn't care less about "being in charge." But the simple fact was that he had lived rough before and knew some things that would help them. When they ran into problems – and Scruffy made it clear that they would – the others must never forget that the situation was kill or be killed.

---

The guard was uniformed and carried his gun at all times, acting his part as a prisoners' escort. Scruffy decided that they couldn't chance walking on the Autobahn, as convenient as it might be, for fear of being stopped. Instead, they would walk to the south of it on country roads, using the Autobahn as a directional guide but hanging back far enough to avoid any encounters. If they saw trouble coming, they would head south for a couple of days and continue travelling parallel to the Autobahn before slowly moving north again. By avoiding the main routes, they would also manage to avoid most villages and towns. More important, they would avoid any locals who would likely pass along the word about a dubious and tattered group wandering at large in the country. Still, Scruffy knew it was only a matter of time until trouble showed up.

The first encounter came early in the trip, two days after they had left Marlag-Milag. The group had been travelling close to the Autobahn while maintaining a safe distance. It was a hot, humid day. They came upon a bridge running over a country road, and Sam pointed to it and suggested that they could have a rest in the shade beneath it. Scruffy agreed, but never taking anything for granted, he went to make sure the coast was clear. He crawled up the embankment and peered over the far side of the bridge. There, almost a hundred German soldiers were stretched out on the far side enjoying the sun. Scruffy crawled back down to warn the others about what was waiting for them on the other side when they heard a sound that made them scramble for cover. It was a loud and distinctive, "throb-throb-throb-throb." Ed shouted, "Tiffies!"[1] They dove into a ditch as two British Typhoons swept down and raked the German troops with their machine guns and rockets. When they were finished, there wasn't anything left alive or moving.

When the smoke cleared, Scruffy said they had better get the hell out of there and head south. If anyone spotted them on the road, they would likely think this group of stragglers had called in the attack. He was extremely skittish now, constantly looking left and right, checking over his shoulder, knowing people would always be on the lookout for

---

1 Identifying sounds was an essential skill in staying alive during the war. Knowing the difference between a Sten gun and a Schmeisser, a Sherman and a Tiger tank, a Spitfire and a Messerschmitt: these things could keep you alive.

anything suspicious. He was especially twitchy about anyone walking in the same direction as the six of them. If anyone walked past them and did a double take, that meant trouble. And should they see that person again, Scruffy told the men it would be an "us or them" situation.

They stuck to back roads and passed few people. They tended to skirt around towns and villages, but occasionally went through them because it would look more suspicious if they were seen to be avoiding the main route. Scruffy never felt able to drop his guard. "That's the curse of having been trained in intelligence," he said to me. "Paranoids live longer." Whenever they encountered another person, he would search his memory to try to remember and if he had seen them before; and if so, where and when.

But apart from the pressure of being constantly on the watch, the trip was a decided improvement over the conditions they had been struggling through for the past ten weeks. They were free to scrounge for eggs, bread, and meat at isolated houses and farms. At one of the first they came across, they traded for two dozen eggs. Every man – the guard and driver too – popped a couple into their mouths and crunched them straight down, not pausing to remove the shells. The exercise and fresh air was also a welcome restorative after having lived for so many years behind the wire. The guard played his part without question or overt concern, regularly tracking down new cart drivers and horses so there was always a fresh ride. They settled into a comfortable routine with one man sleeping in the cart for a few hours with the guard and driver up front, and the other three walking behind or riding on the tailgate of the cart. The weather had turned warm and the winter march from Sagan to Muskau was a distant memory.

One particularly warm day, as they ambled along a quiet country road, Scruffy was enjoying his turn stretched out and dozing on the straw in the cart. Ed, Hank, and Sam sat sleepily on the tailgate, with only sound being that of the horse and cart on the gravel road. Then the guard muttered something under his breath, and Scruffy sat up, alert and anxious. He rubbed his eyes and looked down the road where a grey German officer's staff car, flags flying, was driving toward them, tossing up a tail of dust behind it. Scruffy snapped at the other three to hop off the cart and he rolled off the back to walk with them. He whispered not to look at anyone, but to shamble along behind the cart, stare at the ground, and look beaten and defeated. There was no time to say anything else.

The colour had drained from the guard's face as the car slowed down and pulled to a stop a few feet in front of the horse. The guard climbed down and saluted, perspiration pouring off him. In the car sat a colonel, two captains, and three sergeants. The colonel returned the guard's salute and asked him where the next village was. The guard pointed back in the direction they had come from and said he thought it was about four miles. The colonel stood up and looked at the four men skulking behind the cart, their heads hanging, their hair matted with sweat. The colonel asked the guard what they were doing travelling on that road. The guard explained he was escorting the prisoners to a Luftwaffe camp in Lübeck. Where had they come from? Marlag-Milag. The colonel looked at the cart filled with straw, and said, "A long way to travel like this, no?" The guard nodded and said that there was no other transportation for the likes of them. (In the last six months of the war, virtually the entire German army was reduced to the most basic of transportation, usually on foot.) The colonel smiled at the guard's response. He saluted and then told his driver to move on. If the day hadn't been so hot, the colonel might have had more reason to wonder at the sweat running down the guard's tunic.

That encounter was a sobering one, reminding them of how vulnerable they were out in the open. When they reached the next village, a new horse and driver were found. They moved away from the road they had been travelling on, half expecting to see a squad of Germans churning up the dust in pursuit. When no one appeared after a couple of days, Scruffy began to believe they had finally found some luck. But they were running low on food, so they had no choice but to chance approaching farms or villages to restock. Scruffy suggested that he and Hank break off and head through a forest to their south, and that Sam and Ed would go north towards the Autobahn with the guard, driver and cart to see if they could find some safe place to lie low for a day or two. With any luck they might turn up some meat, bread, or cheese. Food was what was on everyone's mind.

Hank and Scruffy headed into the woods. After walking for several hours, they came across a large, secluded pond, deep enough to have a reasonable stock of fish. They sat down and cooled their feet in the water and splashed some on their faces. But their hunger was insistent. Hank dug through his pockets and came up with a couple of safety pins and pieces of twine he had tucked away for just such an opportunity. Scruffy rolled over a rotten log and found a worm for each of them, and they tossed their lines in. It didn't take long before they had fish on their hooks; the first fresh fish they had seen in years. They collapsed on the bank, full of smiles and self-satisfaction, and talked about how surprised the other guys would be to see what they had caught. Hank chuckled and suggested that they could fry them up now and tell the others about it later.

Scruffy wasn't listening. He had spotted a swarm of Waffen-SS troopers who were emerging from the forest on the opposite bank and making themselves comfortable by the water's edge. They too were looking for a chance to cool their heels and maybe catch some food. Scruffy noticed some of them looking across the pond at the two of them and the thrashing fish on their lengths of string. They slowly set their catch down on the ground and kept their eyes focussed on the opposite bank. Under his breath, Scruffy said to Hank that they had made it that far and one of them had to survive. When he gave the word, he would run left and Hank should break right. Before Hank could answer, one of the troopers pulled out a potato masher – the familiar hand grenade of the German army – and lobbed it over the water. But he wasn't trying to hit the opposite shore: it dropped in near the middle of the pond and the explosion boiled up the water, sending dozens of fish bobbing to the surface. The Waffen-SS trooper pointed at Scruffy and Hank and their two fish, while a dozen Germans waded in and started scooping out as many fish as they could carry, grinning and waving at Scruffy and Hank. Following their lead, they also waded in and stuffed fish into their pockets and satchels. Despite the shared laughter, however, the two men didn't press their luck and wasted no time in getting the hell out of there.

Scruffy and Hank met up with Sam and Ed and the two Germans at the far side of the forest, carrying more fish than they knew what to do with. They crossed paths with two Belgians who were on the move in the opposite direction, and were able to trade some fish for a side of pork the Belgians were carrying and had had their fill of. To sweeten the trade, Scruffy had also been collecting snails, as he had learned to do in Algonquin. None of the Canadians would touch them, so to the delight of the Belgians, they were added to the exchange of goods.

It was now well into April. Coming out of one of the coldest

European winters of the century, this unusually warm spring was heaven on toast for four young men who had been underfed and locked up in damp, cold, and vermin-infested quarters for years. As they drew closer to Lübeck, towns and villages became more frequent, and the mundane traffic of everyday life gave a sense that the war was coming to an end. It was almost unimaginable that they had managed to make it through in one piece.

Whenever there were waterways, they would try to stay close to them; the water was plentiful and it was cooler on the shore. Following the streamflow would also lead them naturally toward the north coast and the sea, and in the direction of Lübeck. On one particularly hot day, they had followed a stream to the outskirts of a quiet town. Finding a stone bridge with an inviting pool of water underneath it and no one around, they stripped off and went for a swim, much to the distress of the guard. He was told to stay on the bridge and keep a careful watch. If anyone were to come along, he would keep his rifle trained on them while they were in the water and explain that he was letting his prisoners have a much-needed wash. Despite the guard's anxieties, the four men dove in. The water was fresh and cool and the air sweet with spring. Scruffy swam underwater for as long as his lungs would hold out, feeling like they finally had found freedom. When he came up for air, he was startled to see four giggling teenage girls standing on the bank and holding various pieces of the boys' clothing. One by one, the other three fell quiet as they saw that they had company.

In almost any other situation, this might have been the beginning of a memorable "boy meets girl" story. There was little doubt that the girls were keen to get to know the boys better, but this was disaster waiting to happen. If they were caught anywhere near a German woman in a situation like this, naked as they were, they would be gutted alive. Even if they had flirted a bit and went on their way, the girls would make it the talk of the village, and the four of them would be hunted down. It was a time when it was easy to disappear without a trace. Scruffy told Sam to get them to piss off; he tried, but they only giggled some more and playfully moved further away holding the clothing. The guard was watching this from the bridge, frozen with fear at what would happen if the girls didn't leave. Sam shouted at him to warn them they were damned serious. The guard nodded stiffly and shouted at the girls to leave, gesturing with his rifle to emphasize his point. They continued laughing, but dropped the clothes and left with a few flirtatious backward glances. Young men were something of a rare commodity in Germany by that point in the war.

After that encounter, the group moved away from the village as quickly as they could without drawing attention to themselves and found a new horse and driver. They were still four or five days walk from Lübeck when they started hearing big artillery guns in the distance and other sounds of approaching armies from the east. This compounded the dangers they would be facing. Scruffy decided it would be wiser to be back with a large group, so they headed towards the Autobahn to watch for other POWs they could join. There was the odd car or truck, but the highway was otherwise deserted. They had no choice but to continue on.

On their second last day on the road, May 1ˢᵗ, 1945, the group was walking alongside the Autobahn in the sloped depression off to the side, so that they were largely out of sight. There had been so little activity on the road that when a convoy of four German staff cars drove past, headed west with the soft-top open and flags flying, it caught their attention. The cars passed close enough that Scruffy was able to recognize one key man: Admiral Karl Dönitz, whom Hitler had appointed his successor for control of the Reich. Scruffy realized that this was probably a German delegation on its way to meet with Allied commanders to negotiate a peace. If so, the end was in sight, which meant that the Germans would be running for cover, the Russians would be looking for revenge, hundreds of thousands of POWs would be trying to find their way west, and millions of refugees would be adrift across the continent. Everyone would become a target. Scruffy knew that events would boil out of control within hours of an announcement of surrender. They had to find the other POWs they had left behind as soon as possible if they hoped to stay alive.

Their last day on the road, as they approached the outskirts of Lübeck, the guard and driver disappeared without a word. Scruffy, Ed, Hank, and Sam now had to find the camp on their own. As they walked into a scattering of houses on the western verge of Lübeck, they came across an old stone schoolhouse. It looked promising as a place to have a rest and figure out where to go next. A German man appeared in front of them, walking past the house, a newspaper tucked under his arm and oblivious to them. A shot cracked from the house, and he fell dead. All four of them dropped to the ground to wait for following fire. Through one of the windows, Hank could see a group of young, heavily armed Waffen-SS, most of them teenagers, moving around inside. They dropped back to find another way into the city, and came face to face with a British tank that was an advance reconnaissance patrol of the British 11th Armoured Division, spearheading the unit's advance on Lübeck. The Brits challenged them, but they were able to convince them who they were. They told the Brits about the isolated pocket of resistance in the schoolhouse, and the tank rolled on. Not ten minutes later they heard and felt the concussion of the tank's high explosive shells destroying the schoolhouse and the men inside.

Acting on directions provided by the tank crew, they soon located the POW camp. An hour later the four were reunited with the others, and able to rest easy for the first time in weeks.

---

When word spread that Scruffy, Hank, Sam, and Ed had showed up, Bill Jennings, the 2IC (Second in Command) of the camp — six and a half feet tall and feet the size of skis — tracked Scruffy down and asked him where the hell they had been. He had assumed they were all dead. Scruffy told him their story, more or less truthfully, which seemed to satisfy Bill. After three weeks on the road, the four of them were fat, healthy, and tanned. John had weighed 124 pounds when he had set out from Sagan, and 161 by the time he reached Lübeck. The POWs they had left behind at Marlag-Milag had been able to scrounge food on their march, but only enough to stave off starvation. Dozens had died. Jennings said he wished he had known what they were up to because he would have happily come with them instead.

The farm the POWs commandeered had formerly belonged to a German general, and while there were few buildings, at least it was free of the lice and bedbugs that had plagued them for four years. The Germans were too exhausted to do anything to control them; some had attempted to escape themselves and find their way home. As a result there were no guards; just "Do Not Escape" orders because local security was almost non-existent. Until the Allied forces caught up with them, it was extremely dangerous to be on one's own. Even though the men were sleeping rough in storage sheds and barns, the farm was a warm and safe haven.

Outside the camp, Scruffy said it was "the wild west". The Russians were sweeping in from the east, and civilians were fleeing before them, carrying everything they owned on their backs, and bringing horrific stories about the wrath of the Red Army. Compounding the confusion were the thousands of POWs of all nationalities, most ragged and starving, attempting to find their way to whatever their new life might be. Tens of thousands of concentration camp survivors, unimaginably emaciated and ill, were now "free," but had nowhere to go. At the same time, hundreds of thousands of German soldiers were returning on foot from the front, trying to find what might remain of their families and their homes. The more robust among the camp survivors often lashed out with furious vengeance against these debilitated German soldiers, sometimes physically tearing their former oppressors apart with their bare hands. For several uneasy weeks at the end of April, parts of Germany were considerably more dangerous than combat had ever been.

In Lübeck, as the war staggered to its end, a unit of vengeful Nazis sank two prison ships in the Harbour out of sheer cussedness. One ship was full of Poles, Gypsies, and other non-Aryans, and the other was full of Scandinavians. This was a tipping point for some prisoners. Hearing what had happened, a group of Scandinavians in Scruffy's camp got hold of some guns and headed into to town to even the score. Bursts of gunfire could be heard through the night, and if a German in uniform was spotted looking as though he was trying to escape, he would be shot dead no matter who he was or what he was doing.

German soldiers started being rounded up and moved into a holding camp of their own not far from the Allies' camp. They had to forage for their own food, and were allowed out of their compound to find what they could. They had to report in at 7:00 in the evening and could leave again at 7:00 in the morning. But they despised having the tables turned, and were not about to submit to the restrictions of the Allied armies. The senior British officers determined that they needed to make an example of one of the Krauts to impress upon them the need for some discipline. The men were asked to identify a guard they thought had behaved with egregious and inhuman brutality, and who would therefore make a good candidate for punishment. Everyone agreed that the universally hated ferret, "Rubberneck," was an obvious choice. No one knew what happened to him once he was identified and hustled off, but he was never seen again and there were no more problems from the Germans.

A question arose about one guard who had been taken into custody, and who had come forward with an unlikely story. Scruffy was approached and asked if he had signed some kind of agreement with a middle-aged man. Scruffy said he had, as had Hank, Ed, and Sam. He described how it had been signed in the presence of them all, then torn in half and the two halves shared. Scruffy produced his half, which matched the other half perfectly. Satisfied that the guard was who he said he was, Scruffy was asked what they should do with him. He looked over at a security cage and saw the man who had accompanied them from Marlag-Milag. He looked grey and beaten, and was clearly expecting the worst. Scruffy said to let him go; he had got them there in one piece. He had kept his eyes closed when he had to, and wide open when they needed him. He had played his part without complaint and had done them a great service. The agreement should be honoured, Scruffy said. The guard was released and then he was gone. They never knew his name or where he came from – but as far as Scruffy was concerned, the less he knew, the better.

By the 4th of May, the few remaining German soldiers in and around Lübeck who weren't being held had scuttled off as artillery confirmed the imminent arrival of the British Eighth Army. A new sense of security afforded the POWs an opportunity to stretch their legs and roam a bit beyond the fences encircling the farm, although Bill Jennings still encouraged everyone to stay close to the camp, as there was safety in numbers. Most POWs stayed put and restlessly waited for due process to repatriate them back to England, itchy with lice and the taste of real freedom. The civilians in Lübeck were warned that if they didn't surrender any and all weapons in their possession, retribution would be swift and harsh. Within days there was a mountain of arms in the city square, a storey and a half high: rifles, shotguns, swords, some dating back two hundred years. Four entrepreneurial POWs talked the guards monitoring this cache into letting them take a handful of them to pay for a road trip to Paris. They liberated a car that was sitting next to an abandoned house, its keys in the ignition, and scrounged a dozen Jerry cans of gas from the tank corps. This foursome piled into the car and headed out on the Autobahn for Paris. About a mile into their trip, they got the car up to fifty miles per hour and it exploded, having been booby-trapped. The doors blew off comically, like something from the Keystone Kops, and the four were thrown from the car, miraculously unscathed apart from some scrapes and bruises as they watched their transportation careen down the highway in flames. They limped back to the camp with their tails between their legs.

One POW broke into a jewelry shop in Lübeck and managed to buy his way south to France with his takings. Scruffy found a beautiful Mercedes convertible, but had to return it at Bill Jennings's insistence because it belonged to the local doctor. By and large, there was a tremendous sense of elation at being free. Just being able to move about without having to watch for unexpected visitors, or worry about being shot for looking at someone the wrong way, or accidentally stepping into No Man's Land, was positively heady.

Scruffy relished being able to explore the rural flotsam outside the city. In a copse of trees, he happened upon a Messerschmitt 262, the world's first operational jet fighter. It saw limited action in 1945 as a multi-role warplane for the Luftwaffe, and was dubbed der Schwalbe (the "Swallow") because the swallow, when in a dive, is one of the fastest birds known. He had just put his hand on the latch that would fold down the retractable step used to climb up into the cockpit when a thick Cornish accent stopped him, suggesting that he'd best not climb up. Scruffy protested that he didn't see what harm there was in just having a look. A short and sturdy Sergeant, the owner of the accent, explained that he was in charge of the bomb disarmament unit, that the Schwalbe had been booby-trapped, and that if Scruffy were to pull down the step that his fingers were holding on to at that moment, the charge would blow his hand clean off. And if he unlatched the canopy to climb in, there was another charge there that would blow his other hand off, too. If he decided to open the engine hood to have a look, the charge hidden in there would blow him up into little bits not worth keeping. Scruffy gently withdrew his hand from the step release catch and stepped back. The Sergeant explained that he had disarmed quite a few, and he invited him to come back in a day or two when he had finished cleaning this one up.

---

On May 7th, two civilians appeared at the camp asking to see if they could speak to "Scruffy". Bill Jennings found John sleeping in a barn and told him that there were a couple of civvies looking for him. John sat up and tried to make sense of this. It was like Thurso. Who would know who he was, know his name *and* his nickname, and know how to find him? All hell was breaking loose across Europe and two men show up wanting to have a word with him? Something wasn't right. Jennings added that they wanted to escort him to Bruges. That did it. Scruffy said "No. Not today, and not ever." Jennings said that they had papers and that they looked straight to him. John shook his head. No one was straight; at least not in this part of the world at this time. For all he knew, these men were coming after him with anything from a Gestapo execution order to a personal vendetta. He refused to meet with them.

Bill left to tell them, then returned a few minutes later, asking on what terms he would be willing to go with them. Scruffy had already thought about this. He said that if they were searched and had all their arms taken away from them, he might consider talking to them. He added that they should be searched for ankle pods, a little known deceit in the intelligence community. Sure enough, they had knives and guns in theirs. The men were stripped down to their underwear, and were pronounced unarmed. Only at that point did Scruffy come out to face them. Bill Jennings said, "So what now? Naked?"

Scruffy said that they would sit in the front seat of the car, and he would ride in the back with another guy. The two of them would be holding the strangers' guns. He added that maybe he would get shot, but then these two would get it too. One of the strangers protested, saying he was MI5. Bullshit, said Scruffy. "MI5 stick so close to the King's ass they wouldn't leave London for a seaside holiday. So try again. Tell me who you are, and I'll tell you if you're telling the truth or not." There was a long silence. The two strangers conferred with one another, and then one of them asked if the letters S-O-E meant anything to him. The SOE was unknown outside of government security circles during the war years, but Scruffy knew of the organization through Adrian. All right, Scruffy said; we're on. But you two are still riding in front.

They drove to a nearby airstrip, where a Lancaster bomber was waiting for them. John couldn't believe it, and still harboured suspicions. When they climbed on board, the pilot asked which one of them was Scruffy. He identified himself, and the pilot asked if he would like to have his spirits lifted by flying home via Cologne. John didn't know why, but said sure.

Cologne had been completely devastated by bombing in the past year. The city had had no water for three months, no electricity for five months, and was really nothing more than a shell, like Frankfurt. Flying over the ruins of Cologne eased some of the bitterness of the past four years. It had nothing to do with the people who had died there; what these shattered cities represented to him was the evisceration of the Nazis and the Third Reich.

# Chapter 21

# FAMILY REUNION

It seemed that the strangers had been on the level after all. Scruffy landed safely in Bruges and before he knew it, was back in England. He was driven to a hotel near Marble Arch for a security debriefing. All POWs and evaders (those who were shot down behind enemy lines but made it back without capture) were debriefed on their return to England, as a matter of course. In Scruffy's case, the questioning was something quite different. Much of what he was asked to talk about was confidential, so he was detained a great deal longer than was usual. His interrogators treated him with suspicion and hostility; they believed he knew more than he was willing to admit. Scruffy talked about his experiences on the squadron, being shot down and questioned by the Gestapo, and what he had seen in the various camps.

He went on to talk about what he believed to be the new threat from the Russians. His interrogators belittled his concerns, the exhilaration of the war's end still buoying everyone's spirits about the future. But Scruffy was firm about what he had seen and what he could see coming. He said that the Russians were vengeful after what the Germans had done to them. They wanted revenge and it didn't matter from whom. After listening to what he had to say, his interrogators told him he was going to be detained indefinitely for more questioning. He challenged them, saying they had no grounds and wouldn't follow through. One of the men said, "Because you think you have some hot shot connections. Is that it?" John repeated that they were bluffing, and that was all he need say.

The inexperienced interrogators hit a dead end trying to pry information out of him, and so he was moved under guard to another hotel off Trafalgar Square on the morning of May 8th. It was VE Day – Victory in Europe – and John could hear the cheering crowds outside celebrating, frustrating him even more. After an extensive harangue, he managed to persuade one of the guards to let him make one phone call. He had the operator connect him to Air Commodore Chamier at Adastral House, and when he came on the line Uncle Adrian's first words were the same as Bill Jennings' back in Lübeck: "Johnny, where the hell have you been? And where the hell are you?"

He explained he was being held in a hotel whose name he didn't know somewhere around Trafalgar Square, after having been flown in the previous day. Adrian said he was glad that John was able to get the connection through Bruges; John expressed his admiration for being able to locate him so quickly in Lübeck. He said that he had felt he was being watched and followed for the last few weeks on the road in Germany, and Adrian thought it likely as well. Then John asked why he was being held and questioned. Adrian told him to put the guard on the phone. The young intelligence officer picked up the receiver and listened wordlessly for a few minutes before saying, "Yes sir," and hanging up. Twenty minutes later a car arrived at the hotel, and took John to Adrian's flat.

Adrian wanted to hear exactly what had happened, from the day he had been shot down to the day that the SOE agents had come calling for him in Lübeck. Adrian already knew an astonishing amount: about his escape from the train; that the bartender at the fateful whorehouse in Stettin was part of Adrian's organization; and that Jens Müller, one of the three who had escaped from the camp and made it back to safety, was also part of Norwegian intelligence.

Adrian pressed John to talk in minute detail about his experiences through the war. Again and again, Adrian asked if John's cover had been compromised; had he done anything that might incite retribution; who had he killed, and more importantly how, and why, and when, and where. Finally the conversation stopped. It could perhaps have continued, but Adrian said that he had what he needed. He told John that there was much he had said that he could never speak of again. What he had been through had changed him, and talking about the things that had been the catalysts of that change would mean nothing to anyone else. He suggested that he go stay with his sister, Nancy, who had a flat a few blocks away. He told John that she had just returned from North Africa, where she had been working as a cipher clerk with the SOE. This was news to John. He wondered what else his family had been involved in that he was unaware of.[1] Adrian told him just to enjoy himself. Money would be no object, because his pay had been accumulating over the previous four years when he was in the camps. Adrian called a cab for him, and told him he would be in touch when he had to be.

During the weeks he stayed with Nancy, John did little but sleep (in a bathtub, as there weren't enough beds in the flat), take day trips, and generally lose himself in the city. Being on the loose in post-war London helped immeasurably with the transition back to civilian life. Everything was rationed, but there was more of everything than he had seen for years. His scars from the burns and surgery were settling down, and his eyes were beginning to feel normal again. Patty Boyer, a friend of his sister's, said, "You're an awfully nice guy, John, but you're no great hell to look at." He shrugged it off. He knew how others looked at him, but after his interview with Adrian he had resolved to keep his war to himself. The wrenching emotions that had marked the last weeks of his war seemed unreal now. His only thoughts were about getting home.

By the middle of June, he was back in Canada.

---

1    There was a great deal of which he was unaware, as he discovered in the decades after the war. Gordon and Adrian, of course, were deeply involved in intelligence work. Nancy was a FANY: a First Aid Nursing Yeomanry volunteer. This fiercely independent organization of women drove ambulances and set up troop canteens under appalling conditions and usually in great danger. But Nancy, like so many FANYs, used their organization as a cover for their real work in sabotage and espionage for the SOE (Special Operations Executive) behind enemy lines. Auntie Ted served with the SOE, and she more than likely recruited Nancy. Fran Weir was a driver for Research Enterprises Limited., which created technologies for Canadian, British and American military forces throughout the war. Also the BSC, SOE, OSS, ISI, Camp "X" and possibly MI5. Not least of which, Radar and Aztec were developed at this facility. John's cousin, Janet (Fitzgerald) Grubb was secretary to William Stephenson ("Intrepid") in the British Passport Office in New York. Her close friend Charm (Manchee) Vaughn was Mr. Stephenson's personal secretary and cypher in Toronto. As I went through a list of friends and family that John had given me, adding to notes about their war service, it became clear that many had been part of the intelligence community in one way or another. It is just that no one ever spoke about it, so no one knew. Note: During my interviews with these individuals they continued to be decidedly vague about their rolls and what they actually did all these years after the official secrets act had expired. Unfortunately, in a growing number of cases, this piece of history will remain untold.

# Chapter 22

# POSTSCRIPT

What makes a survivor? What skills or traits allow a person to survive conditions that take the lives of others?

Estimates of World War II casualties vary widely, and no one can be sure of the total number of combatants, or the proportion that were killed or wounded. Military personnel died in battle, but also in accidents, from disease, from starvation (often in POW camps), and from many other causes. But even the most conservative estimates suggest that more than 22 million soldiers, sailors, and airmen died in the war, 5 million of them as prisoners in concentration camps. Not to mention the deaths of millions of civilians who were collateral damage victims of the war.

Scruffy's story bears this out. Many of the friends that entered the war with him were dead by 1944. Pat Chamier, Auntie Ted and Uncle Adrian's youngest son, was an RAF pilot who was killed in South Africa; friends on 401 Squadron – Paul Henderson, Joe Reynolds, Freddy Watson, and Bruce Hanbury. Then there were the over-eager and impulsive sprog pilots like Dal Owen and others like him who pranged their aircraft in training. From Stalag Luft III there were several, but Hank Birkland in particular, John's friend and tunnelling cohort, who was executed by the Gestapo. John had been scheduled to go out ahead of Hank in the Escape, and who knows what might have happened had John not been away having new eyelids sewn on? Adrian's air cadets, like so many, caught in the crossfire of war. Still, there was that core group – Scruffy, Hughie Godefroy, Jeep Neal, Ian Ormston, Hank Sprague, Deane Nesbitt – who made it through the war and lived long and happy lives.

There is no question that some stayed safe by serving behind the lines: in administration, teaching new servicemen and servicewomen how to

fly and march and sail; and the thousands of other support roles essential
to the war effort. But this was certainly not the case with Scruffy and
his fellow flyers, cool-headed risk-takers. What makes Scruffy's story so
compelling is his ability to combine audacity with resourcefulness. In
part, that resourcefulness was taught and then became instinctive. We
have the sense that from earliest childhood his father and Adrian were
intentionally preparing him for the kinds of challenges he might one
day confront.

In the air force, there is a saying: "There are old pilots and bold
pilots, but there are no old bold pilots." George "Buzz" Beurling was
generally recognized as Canada's most famous pilot of the Second
World War. Beurling flew with Hughie Godefroy during the war, and
Hughie thought Buzz was, technically, the finest fighter pilot he had
ever known. "But unnerving to fly with," Hughie said later. "Too bold
and too reckless."[1]

Scruffy was never reckless. Years of training with his father, with
Fiji, and later with Uncle Adrian had taught him to analyze a situation
carefully before taking action. Over time, this analysis became second
nature, reflexive. When most men were still pondering whether this
action might be appropriate, or perhaps that one, Scruffy was already
moving to avert a crisis. This difference was perhaps most apparent
when he was leading a flight with inexperienced pilots who had had
only a few hours of operational flying. But his analytic sense remained
true through his months at Stalag Luft III and throughout the Winter
March of 1945. His ability to analyze, weigh options, and *decide* in an
instant set him apart.

But it is also clear that Scruffy's personality contributed a great deal
to his survival. He was a cheerful, optimistic man, traits that got him
through the bad times, but also allowed him to support others who were
losing hope. At a Stalag Luft III reunion in Toronto in the late 1960s,
several veterans spoke candidly about how John had saved many men
in camp, but not by planning escapes or digging tunnels. In the last
months of the war, when food was scarce and some of the boys were
sinking into black holes of depression, even becoming suicidal, Scruffy

---

1    During the war, Beurling wanted a newer model Spitfire, but his commanding officer
insisted he keep flying the one he'd been assigned. So Beurling flew his plane over the
Channel, then blithely climbed out and parachuted off the wing as the plane went down into
the ocean. He got his new Spitfire. He was killed by saboteurs while delivering an aircraft to
Israel in 1948.

would talk to them and help them find ways to get through the tough times. Suicide is for cowards, John always said. Do whatever you must to survive. Do what you have to do: just keep moving forward.

Just like Gordon before him, John seemed to have limitless patience for fellow veterans who continued to be challenged by life after the war. Late night phone calls from old war friends, looking for a sympathetic ear and liable to go on for hours, were always taken in the Weir household. John would say to me, "If you weren't concerned for others, you'll never be any good to yourself." There were limits, of course, when it came to such things as negative behaviour, opportunism, or the lack of common courtesy. But if someone fell by the wayside, John would always go out of his way to help them get back on their feet, just as his father had done.

Scruffy was intensely curious about other people. Over time, he developed an ability to read people accurately – to interpret subtle verbal and nonverbal cues in a way that most of us never learn. He was extremely good at this. Even trapped at the whorehouse bar with the Gestapo, Scruffy was sizing up the bartender. He recognized that the man was probably an Allied agent, embedded there in Stettin to collect information from the Germans who visited the place. His ability to intuit the professor's buried rage, and abort an ill-advised escape attempt on the train to Stalag Luft III probably saved his life.[2] And his affable manner often allowed him to talk himself (and others) out of sticky situations, such as when he persuaded the German guard to escort him, Sam, Ed, and Hank across the chaotic Germany of April 1945.

And of course he made lifelong friends – not *too* many, as Deane Nesbitt had cautioned him – but friends who were always a part of his life. Although he never said as much, his ability to understand the skills and attributes of these others helped him be a member of, and to build, tight and powerfully effective teams, whether in the mines of Northern Ontario, in the air, or digging Harry at Stalag Luft III.

Perhaps more than anything else, his father had taught John to think independently, to be self-reliant, and to stick, metaphorically speaking, to his guns. This independence of thought and self-reliance served him

2    John wasn't infallible, though. Out at a pub one evening with guys from the squadron, an attractive blonde came over to John, making obvious advances to him. Not only was he an innocent with girls, he had no interest in talking to this one. But he didn't know how to politely ask her to leave him alone. Jeep Neal rescued him, stepping in and telling him it was time for them to get back to their friends. As Jeep led him away, John said, "Thanks for saving me from that girl! She wouldn't take no for answer." Jeep said, "John, that wasn't a girl. That was a man. Now finish your drink and let's get out of here."

especially well, as for example when he made the decision to leave the Winter March with his three friends. While those that stayed behind struggled to survive, John and the others avoided the chaos that was growing.

And John had grit. In part, this was a family trait. Both Gordon and Freda were strong-willed and dynamic personalities and excelled in athletics: Freda in figure skating, Gordon in boxing and horsemanship, and both of them in skiing.[3] Even within their challenging marriage, they never failed to set an example for their children of the importance of stressing the positive and continuing to move forward.

But John's personal resilience and determination to succeed – to survive – were driving forces throughout his life, from camping in Algonquin Park to the horrific Winter March of 1945. From his earliest years, he'd been trained and disciplined with what, at times, was an almost paramilitary rigour. This is fundamental to John's story. And because of this, time and again when he was knocked down, he got up again, and went on – and survived.

When I asked John what made him a survivor, he thought for a moment and said, "Believe half of what you see and half of what you hear. But keep that to yourself. Looking unremarkable is a good place to start."

And then of course there was Fran, to whom John was married for almost 64 years. As John put it, "I did all right, because I had the right wife. I met her before going overseas. She and I could dance like a son of a gun. Maybe it was subconscious, but I thought if we can dance that well together, maybe we could work well together, too. And that's exactly how it worked out."

There's a lot to be said for a happy marriage, too.

---

John and Fran were married in October 1945. They had kept in contact the whole time he was overseas, with constant letters back and forth. Both she and their families knew about his injuries, but as Fran said to me in 2009, "I didn't care one bit about how bad he thought he looked. He was alive and that was all that mattered to me!"

The only real challenge arose when he was demobbed and returned

---

3    Auntie Ted was also a skier. She was a competitor on the Canadian Olympic ski team during "Hitler's Olympics" held at Garmisch-Partenkirchen in 1936.

to "Civvy Street."[4] He found it damned challenging trying to figure out what he was going to do and where. He'd had a lot of experience learning what he *didn't* want to do, so he decided he wasn't going to jump into anything too quickly. He knew the investment world well from living with Gordon all those years, but a job with McLeod Young Weir wasn't an option because of his father's nepotism policy. He applied to Wood Gundy, another investment firm, but there were no opportunities in the city. However there were some on the road. So he took up the challenge of selling bonds and securities out of the trunk of his car as he drove around Ontario. His good-natured personality and ability to strike up a conversation with pretty much anyone about anything served him well. He was sincerely interested in what other people had to say, without question. But he also had the common touch. And after a couple of years on the road he was more successful than the salesmen at head office, and was offered a position with Wood Gundy in Toronto, where he stayed until he retired – somewhat reluctantly – at the age of 80.

He wasn't much of a letter writer, and didn't stay in touch with most of the guys from the camp. There were exceptions, of course. Wally and George had made it back in one piece, and Wally became the advisor to the 1963 film *The Great Escape*. Brian Floody, Wally's son, remembers many laughter-filled evenings at the Floody household when Scruffy came by to see his old friend. George Harsh had a couple of failed marriages, and for the last years of his life lived in Toronto with Wally and his wife Betty. Scruffy loved George too, and when Harsh moved in with the Floodys, that friendship was renewed. Paul Phelan, John's pal from Camp Borden and Trenton, worked for his family's business, Cara Operations (of which John became a member of the board). Deane Nesbitt joined his father's investment firm, Ormie got a job in the chemical industry, and Jeep Neal went into business in Montreal.

Occasionally, John would go to a Stalag Luft III reunion, when Wally and some of the other guys who knew him got in touch and persuaded him to come. Glemnitz was invited to a gathering in Toronto in 1970, all his expenses paid. At that reunion, John learned that Pieber, another guard that John had liked and respected, had been a "mischling" – a person deemed to have both Aryan and Jewish heritage[5]. The Nazis

---

4    Discharged from the armed forces and back to civilian life.
5    In German, mischling has the general meaning of hybrid, or half-breed, and was the German term used during the Third Reich to denote persons deemed to have both Aryan and

apparently never discovered this, and Pieber was smart and managed to keep himself alive through that dark time. There was a bunch of ex-fighter pilots, just old friends really, who got together once a year for a weekend barbeque, often at Ian Ormston's place out in the country. There, they could relax and talk about the stuff that they didn't talk about with anyone else. But generally speaking, Scruffy wasn't too keen on reliving the old days. He was always happier looking forward and moving on.

Then of course there was Hughie.

Hughie not only survived the war, he retired from the service as a highly decorated Wing Commander and one of Canada's acknowledged "Aces." He studied medicine at McGill, and practiced as a doctor in various cities across Canada over the next forty years. He and John never lived in the same city again, but they always got together whenever possible. Driving back to Toronto from one of Ormie's barbeques in Kitchener, they got wrapped up telling stories and laughing at stuff they had done together over the years. Fran, who had been sleeping in the back seat, poked her head up and asked where they thought they were headed. Lost in conversation, they had driven 60 miles past Toronto and hadn't noticed a thing.

What kept John such a vibrant and vital man was his enthusiasm about what he was going to do today, and maybe tomorrow; he wanted to keep moving, never to sit back and reminisce. "Look back, but don't stay there," he would say to me. He was one of the four founding members of the Canadian Warplane Heritage Museum in Mount Hope (Hamilton), and was also one of the financiers in 1969 of African Lion Safari in Flamborough, Ontario, near where his father had been born and raised. And Women's College Hospital, whose board he first joined to simply lend a hand, became a significant focus of his energies and extensive community work for the rest of his life.[6]

Over the years, there were many people who were great influences on his life, helping him refine his skills and ability to see the world in a certain way that undoubtedly saved his skin more than once. Uncle Adrian was one of these, of course. Highly educated, versatile, and

Jewish ancestry. The word has essentially the same origin as the 17th-century English term *mestee*, or the French *métis*.

6    John and I talked about the importance of Women's College to him. I gave him my word that if there were any revenue generated for him from his story, I would ensure that it went to the Women's College Hospital Foundation.

always curious, he was a tremendous role model for the young John Weir. Deane Nesbitt, his CO of 401 Squadron, helped him understand the need to do his job and let the other pilots do theirs, and not get too emotionally tied up in the process. Gordon, his father, made sure John knew what survival meant; how to act on what you know, not merely on what you feel; and imparted the importance of a pragmatic attitude in making your way through life, and above all, the inestimable value of a life lived for others.

---

After the war, John described his relationship with Adrian's organization as being, "...unconnected, but on call. Once you're involved, you're involved. They tell you when you can leave." Although Adrian died in 1974, Adrian's network continued to maintain contact. And while John never met anyone else, the organization remained extremely well informed about John's activities and movements, and continued to make use of his skill and experience.

When they needed his services, he was contacted through a familiar routine. He would receive a telephone call at his office – never at home – and the voice on the other end would recite a string of numbers. John would make note of these (mentally eliminating the extraneous ones), and then leave the building to place a call from a neutral phone booth on the street. The anonymous contact that answered would then give John the specifics for his job, which was typically the gathering of information.

John travelled internationally quite frequently, for both business and pleasure. In Europe, and Austria in particular (where he went skiing every year), he could never escape the feeling that he was being watched and possibly followed. It was not uncommon for him to get a phone call a few days before leaving, with an assignment specific to the area he was travelling to.

One task in particular had personal significance for him. In 1979 he was travelling to Argentina on business. Two days before he left, he was contacted by the organization and asked to verify the status of two fugitives who had been spotted in Buenos Aires. It was explained that these two had been involved in the execution of the 50 escapees from Stalag Luft III in 1944, but had continued to elude capture and were still being tracked.

John protested that he was not an assassin, and could not carry out any action against them. He was assured that his only responsibility would be to locate these criminals if possible. He would be contacted on his return for his report.

During his weeks in Argentina, John was able to determine that both men were dead, apparently having been killed in a recent automobile accident. After he returned to Canada, he was contacted again and gave his report. The person on the other end of the line said the men must have "…regrettably met with an unfortunate accident", but that "exemplary justice" had been served.[7]

The last call he received was in 1991. John was 72 at the time, and still working full time as an investment advisor. He hadn't been contacted by the organization for some years, and he had come to assume that its operations had been wound down. However, the day before he was to leave on a trip to Switzerland for a friend's daughter's wedding, he got a call: his services were needed.

He was given details of a man who was thought to be hiding in plain sight in the city to which John was headed. During the war, this suspect, a senior German officer, had acquired a king's ransom of jewelry that belonged to a prominent Russian family, most likely after he had murdered them. After the war, he had disappeared with the jewels. Then several years later, the suspect, or someone very much like him, was seen in Switzerland, where he was now thought to be living. John's mission was to locate him and attempt to confirm his identity. John found him and tailed him over two days, gathering enough information to be convinced that this was the man. John was telephoned anonymously at his hotel in the usual manner. He found an outside phone, called and gave his report, and then put the whole business out of mind as Adrian had taught him. Some weeks later back in Canada, he came across a small news item in the paper concerning the man. He had been identified by the authorities, apprehended at his bank attempting to withdraw the contents of his safety deposit box, and arrested. No record of a trial could be or will be found.

John's work with Adrian's organization never officially ended, but then again he never knew anyone apart from Adrian, long deceased.

---

7    British Foreign Secretary Foreign Secretary Anthony Eden addressed English parliament in June 1944 conerning the Nazi executions of the recaptured escapees. He promised that exemplary justice would be served on those responsible for the murders.

Perhaps the organization's work continues; perhaps not. We will never know.

But holding so much inside for so long took its toll. Decades after the war, John's body began reliving experiences and feelings that he thought were long forgotten. This began most dramatically with nightmares from which he could not be roused. His body would be drenched in sweat when he awoke, although he had no memory of the dreams. Then fragments of the past slowly began to revisit him during his waking hours, and the past became a part of him again. During the war both he and Hughie had been extremely keyed up when they flew off into battle, but neither experienced any crippling fear in doing so, and they both served with distinction and bravery. John began to recall that after he had safely landed after a dogfight, his tunic and flight gear would be soaked through to the skin with sweat. Before changing, he would unbuckle his parachute then head to the Squadron Mess where he would hungrily down a quart of milk and a Mars bar or two before he began to feel like himself again. Combat veterans' bodies absorbed inconceivable levels of stress in the course of their frontline duty. They managed to do what had to be done by forcing the violence they encountered back into the darkest recesses of their minds. That, compounded with the loss of friends and comrades in arms, closer than brothers, forged memories that their minds and bodies are unable to forget.

Not long before I met him, John had been asked to give a Remembrance Day talk at the Albany Club in Toronto about some of his experiences in the war – what Stalag Luft III had been like, how it felt to fly a Spitfire, and other similar wartime reminiscences. Simple stuff. As he talked about some of the very funny things that he and the other daring young men had managed to get themselves into and tangled up in, he was suddenly overcome by a wave of crippling emotion, and found himself unable to continue. After that, he avoided such invitations. Then, some months later, he was shown a small model of a Messerschmitt similar to the one that had shot him down in 1941, had killed his wing man, and had very nearly killed him. He was struck by unexpected anxiety and panic, and had to ask that the plastic replica be taken away. His body was remembering what he had laboured for so long to leave behind.

When we reflect on what the men and women who served their country in wartime have endured, it would be wise for us to consider

241

everything with which their subconscious minds and bodies continue to struggle, and are forever trying to put to rest. John lived the remainder of his life keeping far too many soul-wrenching experiences buried deep within himself, choosing to live his life with the fullest possible grace, purpose, and appreciation of all that life had given him.

He's an inspiration to me still.

---

On a cloudless afternoon in late September 2009, several hundred people found their way out to one of the playing fields at Upper Canada College in Toronto. It would not have been unreasonable to assume that the people, who ranged in age from toddlers to those well into their nineties, had just left a commencement ceremony or perhaps had been the audience at some school entertainment.

What was most unusual was that this well-dressed crowd remained on the grassy field, making conversation with one another and behaving as though they had no particular or better place to be. They *were* where they wanted to be.

Around two o'clock, a throaty rumble came from the southwest, and slowly everyone's eyes turned skyward to watch the silhouette of an unfamiliar aircraft come into view, and then make a wide and lazy circle over the field of people below. It was a four-engine Lancaster bomber, quaint in comparison to the size of modern aircraft, but, in its active years during World War II, one of the largest planes in the air. One of the Lancaster's four engines had been feathered, an extraordinary posthumous salute to the man that the crowd gathered below had come to celebrate. Shutting down a bomber's engine in such a flypast is not a typical ceremony to acknowledge a fallen comrade. A more traditional salute for a fighter pilot, such as this man had been, would be a flypast of a squadron – a flight of planes flying in formation – with the fallen man's position in that formation left vacant. But the rare sight of this vintage aircraft acknowledging the passing of an extraordinary man was overwhelmingly powerful unto itself.

It was done in honour of John Gordon Weir – Scruffy – whose memorial service had just taken place in Upper Canada College. It was more of a friendly get-together, really, a service enlivened by fond remembrances, a shared sense of the loss of a great friend, and underscored by the song, "*I'm Getting Married in the Morning*", from *My Fair Lady*, one of John's favourite shows. There was nothing typical about any part of it, rather like the man himself. But each person there carried with them the memory of an extraordinary man: inquisitive, mischievous, steadfast, and brave.

And above all, a true survivor.

Jens Müller, a friend of John's, and one of the three POWs who successfully made it back safely to Allied territory after the Escape.

George Harsh in 1969. Tom Lane was a Lancaster pilot who knew George at Stalag Luft III, as well as at the satellite POW camp, Belaria. Tom remembers George's cold, steel-blue eyes. When Tom saw Peter O'Toole in the movie "Lawrence of Arabia," O'Toole as Lawrence vividly brought George to mind. "He seemed hard and ruthless," said Tom, "But he was actually a very warm and generous guy."

John sits on the ground on the front left, with Tom Kirby-Green kneeling behind him, Bishca Gotowski next to Tom, and "Doc" Lybey holding G2, a pet cat. In the upper left background, a German guard can be seen filling in the crater that was created by the Germans blowing up the tunnel that they "discovered." The guard was ordered to use effluent from the camp's sewage system to do so, which made John and Tom smirk.

Kate, the mother cat, with her two kittens, U2 and G2. Kate was a pet for the men. But the men were slowly starving to death. When the lack of food became desperate, they bred Kate for her kittens, who then became part of the food chain. Not an appealing thought, but not really any different than what Fiji had alluded to a decade earlier in Algonquin Park.

## THE ROBERT SIMPSON COMPANY LIMITED
### TORONTO, CANADA

SHOPPING
SERVICE

LR

April 18, 1944.

Dear Mrs. Weir:

Thank you very much for your recent order which was placed
by Mrs. C. W. Floody, and we wish to advise the following
was carefully prepared:

Records:

| | |
|---|---|
| Mairzy Doats...... I've Got Ten Bucks | .50 |
| Not So Quiet Please....I'll Take Tallulah | .75 |
| The Waiter and the Porter...Little Albert | 1.00 |
| Frenesi......Begin the Beguine | .75 |
| | |
| 10 Folders | .20 |
| 1 pkg Red Seal Needles | .25 |
| 1 pkg Ordinary Needles | .25 |

and forwarded on your behalf to:

Flt. Lt. John Weir,
Canadian Prisoner of War 715,
Stalag Luft 111,
Germany.

We are always glad to be of service, and assure you of our
continued personal interest in your wishes.

Yours very truly,
The Robert Simpson Company Limited.
Personal Shopper,

*Catharine Bell*
Catharine Bell.

Mrs. John Weir,
15 Clarendon Ave.,
Toronto, Ontario.

Charge 5172

**YOU'LL ENJOY SHOPPING AT** *Simpson's*

A letter to Freda Weir confirming supplies shipped to Scruffy at Stalag Luft III (ordered
by Wally Floody's mother). Freda was President of the Canadian Prisoners of War
Relatives Association of Ontario, and would have been able to facilitate the shipment
to Stalag Luft III. The letter was mailed four weeks after the escape, of which no one in
Canada was yet aware.

St. Vincent's Marienheim hospital at Bad Soden, Germany, where John had plastic surgery on his eyelids in 1944.

Major David Charters, the Scottish ophthalmic surgeon who reconstructed John's eyelids at St. Vincent's Marienheim hospital.

Lancaster bombers marshalled for a bombing raid on Frankfurt, 1944.

A devastated Frankfurt after being heavily bombed in the spring of 1944.

Looking down the entrance to "Harry" from inside Hut 104.

*Photographs courtesy of the US Air Force Academy Library.*

Ferret Karl Griese, more commonly known as Rubberneck, basking in presumptive glory of the discovery of the tunnel that Wally and John allowed to be found.

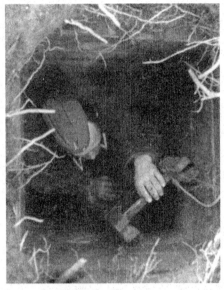

A ferret inspects the exit opening of "Harry" days after the escape.

Colonel Friedrich-Wilhelm von Lindeiner, Kommandant of Stalag Luft III at the time of the escape.

*Photographs courtesy of the US Air Force Academy Library.*

A letter from John to Fran, written just before Christmas 1944, about a month before the men were marched out of the camp and across Europe. The Censor's marks are clearly visible.

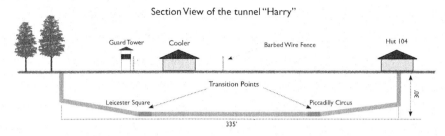

Section View of the tunnel "Harry"

Guard Tower    Cooler    Barbed Wire Fence    Hut 104

Transition Points

Leicester Square    Piccadilly Circus

30'

335'

A cross-section of "Harry" illustrating its key access, transfer, and exit points.

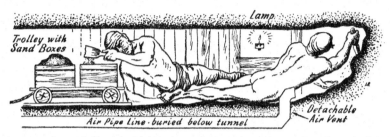

*Lamp.*

*Trolley with Sand Boxes*

*Detachable Air Vent*

*Air Pipe Line · buried below tunnel*

A section view of tunnel digging. This is the technique that John used, and at which he excelled, when he was digging "Harry." He much preferred using his gloved hands to scoop away the sandy earth as opposed to using the improvised tools made in camp.

*Drawing by Ley Kenyon.*

*Photograph courtesy of the US Air Force Academy Library.*

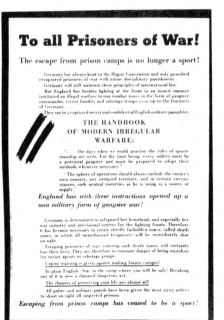

The warning that was posted in camp after the Escape.

A German ferret demonstrates the air pump used in "Harry."

The grueling Winter March across Europe from Stalag Luft III, January - April 1945.

Grand Admiral Karl Dönitz, Hitler's successor as Head of State at the end of the war. John and the others saw his motorcade pass on the Autobahn in early May 1945 in Northern Germany, presumably on Dönitz's way to surrender.

German soldiers returning home at the war's end by horse cart. This is similar to the cart that John travelled across Germany with on his cross-country trek.. There were few working motor vehicles and almost no gas in Germany by April 1945.

A German staff car like the one John, Hank, Sam, and Ed encountered on their trek across Northern Germany in the spring of 1945.

A Messerschmitt Me 262, the type of jet fighter John stumbled across in the last days of the war outside of Lubeck.

Red Army soldiers on the Reichstag, Berlin, raising the "Victory Banner" after the fall of Nazi Germany. May 2, 1945.

*Photograph by Yevgeny Khaldei.*

VE Day celebrations in London, May 8, 1945.

Hughie Godefroy, Squadron Leader, DSO, DFC & Bar, with his new daughter, Isabel, at the end of the war.

Fran Weir with Gordon Weir in the 1950s.

Steve McQueen with Angus Lennie and Wally Floody during the making of "The Great Escape" in 1962. Wally was the technical advisor on the film.

Wally Floody with Charles Bronson and director John Sturges during the making of the movie in 1962.

Hermann Glemnitz (left), the senior guard from Stalag Luft III, with Harry "Wings" Day, at a reunion in the 1960s.

Hugh Rowe (left), John Weir, and Harry "Wings" Day (right) at a British POW reunion in the 1960s.

Wing Commander Harry "Wings" Day at a British POW reunion in the 1960s.

John exiting Women's College Hospital, his favourite charitable organization.

John Weir at the time of our first meeting at the Royal Canadian Military Institute in Toronto, June 2001.

# ACKNOWLEDGEMENTS

The idea for this book began when I first met John in 2001, but took on substantially more weight in 2006 when John and I began our long collaboration. We worked together on the telling of his story until shortly before his death in 2009. Since then there have been many to whom I am indebted for their support and encouragement.

First and foremost is John aka Scruffy Weir. Without the unquestioning trust and generosity of spirit that he showed me throughout our partnership, this book would have been without its heart and soul. He is missed.

The Weir family— Fran (MacCormack) Weir, John and Fran's children, Suze, JS (John Scott Sr.), and Ian; and Mary (MacCormack) Bunnett, Fran Weir's sister.

Dr. Hugh Godefroy, Squadron Leader, DSO, DFC & Bar, who was every bit as delightful in later life as he must have been when he and John were stirring things up in their youth.

Douglas Bassett, Dr. Gail Regan and the Langar Foundation, Dr. Frederic Jackman and The Jackman Foundation, and the F.K. Morrow Foundation for their support of the ongoing Testaments Archive work.

Special thanks to Garfield Mitchell for his support and encouragement over the years, as well as his hours of work spent copyediting and providing insightful feedback my final drafts: I'm indebted to you.

Major-General Pierre Lalonde (retired) has been a tireless supporter of the Testaments of Honour project work for the past 11 years. Without his support, so much of the work of the Testaments of Honour project would have been impossible. And Barbara Duncan, who has been endlessly helpful in coordinating cross-country interviews.

Brian Floody (Wally's son) and Anne Dumonceaux (Dick Bartlett's daughter). Jamie Jordan (Jimmy Jordan's son), who helped chase down stray errors in the eBook draft.

Scott Richardson for his infusion of creative inspiration and generous friendship (and a terrific writer to boot). As well, Martha Kanya-Forstner, Suzanne Brandreth, and Janet Joy Wilson for their support in the early days; David Johnston for his enthusiasm and objectivity; and Rex, Thom, and Guy Grignon, big-hearted cousins and great friends always willing to bounce ideas back and forth; Rebekka Augustine, Brenda MacMillan, and Tom Prittie, who are always helpful and supportive. Rebecca Bartlett, a tremendous archivist and researcher who has shared enthusiasm for the telling of Scruffy's story for the past six years. And special thanks to Heidi Poapst of Library and Archives Canada for her guidance through a baffling process.

Just some of the many RCAF and RAF veterans who spoke with me and generously shared their experiences of these war years, including John Acheson, Tom Lane, Grant McRae, Dick Bartlett, Clem Pearce, Al Wallace, Dick Corbett, Tony Cowling, Jim Finnie, Harold (Red) Hayes, Jim Kenny, Tony Little, Lorne Shelter, John Colwell, Geoff Marlow, Jack Fleming, Don Cheney, Jack Gouinlock, John Dix, Bonnie Joan Graham, Jim Kelly, Art Kinnis, Ian Ormston, Art Sager, Cy Yarnell, Stocky Edwards, Don Lush, Don Morrison, Bill Paton, Gilles Lamontagne, and Bert Coles. Rob Davis and his detailed website on the Great Escape.

My two lovely daughters, Elizabeth and Maggie, who are always an inspiration. And Suzanne, for all her detailed work on the final edit of the manuscript.

And finally Isobel Heathcote. Although she is my big sister, she is also a first-class editor for both copy and content. Without her help and support, this book would not have seen the light of day. Any remaining errors are the author's alone.

Blake Heathcote
March 2014

# BIBLIOGRAPHY

Ash, William and Brendan Foley. *Under the Wire: The World War II Adventures of a Legendary Escape Artist and "Cooler King".* London: Bantam, 2005.

Bailey, Roderick. *Forgotten Voices of the Secret War: An Inside History of Special Operations in the Second World War.* London: Ebury, 2008.

Binney, Marcus. *Secret War Heroes: The Men of Special Operations Executive.* London: Hodder & Stoughton, 2005.

Borrie, John. *Despite Captivity: A Doctor's Life as Prisoner of War.* London: William Kimber, 1975.

Brickhill, Paul. *The Great Escape.* New York: W.W. Norton, 1950.

Brickhill, Paul. *Escape – or Die.* London: Pan Books, 1957.

Buckham, Robert. *Forced March to Freedom.* London: Sentinel, 1995.

Burgess, Alan. *The Longest Tunnel: The True Story of World War II's Great Escape.* New York: Grove, 1990.

Carroll, Tim. *The Great Escape From Stalag Luft III: The Full Story of How 76 Allied Officers Carried Out World War II's Most Remarkable Mass Escape.* New York: Pocket Books, 2004.

Chamier, J. A. *The Birth of the Royal Air Force.* London: Pitman, 1943.

Clark, Albert P. *33 Months as a POW in Stalag Luft III.* Golden, CO: Fulcrum Publishing, 2004.

Clutton-Brock, Oliver. *Footprints on the Sands of Time: RAF Bomber Command Prisoners of War in Germany 1939-45.* London: Grub Street, 2003

Copp, J. Terry and Richard Nielsen. *No Price Too High: Canadians and the Second World War.* Whitby, ON: McGraw-Hill Ryerson, 1996.

Edy, Don. *Goon in the Block.* n.p.: Don Edy, 1961.

Foot, Michael Richard Daniel. *SOE: An Outline History of the Special Operations Executive 1940-1946.* London: British Broadcasting Corporation, 1984.

Forrester, Larry. *Fly for Your Life: The Story of R.R. Stanford Tuck, DSO, DFC.* London: Mayflower, 1979.

Gill, Anton. *The Great Escape: The Full Dramatic Story With Contributions from Survivors and Their Families.* Philadelphia: Review, 2002.

Godefroy, Hugh. *Lucky 13.* Stittsville, ON: Canada's Wings, 1983.

Harsh, George. *Lonesome Road.* New York: Norton & Company, 1971.

Hinsley, Francis Harry. *British Intelligence in the Second World War.* Cambridge: Cambridge University Press, 1979.

James, Jimmy. *Moonless Night: The Second World War Epic*. South Yorkshire: Pen & Sword, 2006.

Macintyre, Ben. *Agent Zigzag: A True Story of Nazi Espionage, Love, and Betrayal*. New York: Broadway Books, 2008

Marks, Leo. *Between Silk and Cyanide: A Codemaker's War, 1941-1945*. London: HarperCollins, 1998.

McIntosh, Dave. *High Blue Battle*. Toronto: Stoddart, 1990.

Mignet, Henry. *The Flying Flea: How to Build and Fly it*. Translated by the Air League of the British Empire. London: Samson, Low, Marston, & Co., 1936.

Miller, Russell. *Behind the Lines: The Oral History of Special Operations in World War II*. New York: St. Martin's Press, 2002.

Pattinson, Juliette. *Behind Enemy Lines: Gender, Passing and the Special Operations Executive in the Second World War*. Manchester: Manchester University Press, 2007.

Perrin, Nigel. *Spirit of Resistance: The Life of SOE Agent Harry Peulevé DSO MC*. Barnsley: Pen and Sword, 2008.

Philpot, Oliver. *Stolen Journey*. London: Hodder and Stoughton, 1950.

Shores, Christopher and Clive Williams. *Aces High: A Tribute to the Most Notable Fighter Pilots of the British and Commonwealth Forces in WWII*. London: Grub Street, 1994.

Simmons, Kenneth W. *Kriegie*. New York: Thomas Nelson, 1960.

Smith, Sydney. *Wings Day*. London: Collins, 1968.

Soward, S. E. *One Man's War: Sub Lieutenant R.E. Bartlett, RN Fleet Air Arm Pilot*. Victoria, B.C.: Neptune Developments. Albuquerque: Neptune Development, 2005.

Vance, Jonathan F. *Objects of Concern: Canadian Prisoners of War Through the Twentieth Century*. Vancouver: UBC Press, 1994.

Wells, Mark K. *Courage and Air Warfare: The Allied Aircrew Experience in the Second World War*. London: Frank Cass, 1995.

Willatt, Geoffrey. *Bombs and Barbed Wire: My War in the RAF and Stalag Luft III*. Kent: Parapress, 1995.

CPSIA information can be obtained
at www.ICGtesting.com
Printed in the USA
LVOW04s1735241115

464029LV00019B/1364/P